Teaching & Learning IN College

A RESOURCE FOR EDUCATORS

· FOURTH EDITION ·

EDITED BY

Gary S. Wheeler
MIAMI UNIVERSITY

BOOK DESIGN AND TYPOGRAPHY BY

Susan G. Wheeler
UNIVERSITY OF CINCINNATI

ORDER INFORMATION:

 INFO-TEC
1005 Abbe Road North
Elyria, OH 44035
PH 800-995-5222 x4632
FAX 440-366-4636

Teaching and Learning in College
Gary Wheeler, ed.
@ 2002 Info-Tec
ISBN 0-940017-31-8

Credits
Jacket Design: Brian Sooy & Co.
Typography and Book Design: Susan G. Wheeler, University of Cincinnati

Printed in the United States of America

Teaching
& Learning
IN COLLEGE

A RESOURCE FOR EDUCATORS

· FOURTH EDITION ·

TABLE • of CONTENTS

•

TABLES

◆

PREFACE

◆

It is almost a cliché to note lists of key factors for excellence in teaching and learning. In an address to a conference on teaching and learning, Patricia Cross itemized several of these lists:

> For starters, there are the "three conditions of excellence," identified by a group of educational researchers in 1984 (Study Group on the Conditions of Excellence in American Higher Education 1984). Then there is the widely distributed and much talked about "seven principles of good practice in undergraduate education," set forth by a group of educational researchers in 1987 (Chickering and Gamson 1987). A study group in England has come up with "nine strategies" for enhancing student learning. (AAHE Bulletin 1993). There are the "twelve attributes of good practice," organized by researchers from the Education Commission of the States this year (1996), and "a teacher's dozen research-based principles for improving teaching" offered by my colleague Tom Angelo (1993).

There is also the widely disseminated list of three broad principles for good classroom practice—teachers should: (1) set high, but realistic, expectations, (2) promote and encourage active learning, and (3) provide prompt assessment and feedback. It would appear that the task of trying to understand the depth and breadth of the circumstances surrounding teaching and learning is so complex that we naturally try to find ways to simplify and to structure our understanding. Yet whatever we include in a list is like giving someone a hug: we create an inclusive sense of intimacy with some while excluding others.

As I began to think about the assignment I accepted in the summer of 2001 to rethink the content and structure of the widely used text, *Teaching in College: A Resource Handbook*, then in its third edition, I wondered which challenges should be highlighted, which interesting issues should be embraced. What would be the best way to present a collection of issues to a target audience of graduate students and relatively new higher education faculty? How does one begin to offer something useful for such an audience? The book's third edition felt outdated in many ways, superceded by information available through the many teaching and learning journals and Web sites. What would be my list of hot topics in higher education?

Certainly, since the previous edition of *Teaching in College* came out nearly a decade ago, the thinking about many well-established ideas has changed. Foremost among them might be the change of focus from the teacher as the essential agent and focal point in the classroom to a view that focuses on the interactions within the classroom between and among the teacher and students. The prior assumption was that good teaching (often defined as the delivery of clear information from a highly educated scholar) inexorably leads to student learning. And if learning did not occur as expected, the likely flaw in the process was the quality and effort of the student who failed to learn. Now, of course, we recognize no such simplistic formula. In any case, as I began to consider the structure of the new book edition, one of the first decisions was to alter slightly, albeit significantly, the book's title to include a reference to student learning.

The individuals involved in the higher education classroom appear different too. The dynamic changes in student and teacher demographics over the past decade suggest that the climate and environment for higher learning has changed. And in thinking about the environment for teaching and learning, it would be hard to ignore the impact of learning communities, service learning, the explosion of educational uses of technology and the institutionalization of expectations for assessing learning outcomes. Newly minted teaching scholars begin their careers at a wide variety of colleges and universities. My list of topics that called out for inclusion in a revised edition began to grow.

I knew I wanted to pull together coauthors who could speak authoritatively on their assigned topics, but who would also take the time to personalize the information. Narratives and stories can help the reader recognize themselves in the presented topics and the evident struggle in coming to terms with the day-by-day issues involved in becoming an effective teacher in today's diverse higher education environments.

Given the change in thinking about teaching and learning—that the more effective models are less individualistic and more community oriented—it was an easy decision to ask Milt Cox of Miami University to update his opening chapter to the third edition. His passion and creativity in thinking about learning communities begins the fourth edition and provides an initial flavor for the text. Increasing numbers of colleges and universities are examining the benefits of learning communities for rethinking the teaching and learning environment.

Those who attend our colleges reflect the growing diversity of the United States. Devorah Lieberman of Portland State University has been at the forefront of institutional responses to the diverse populations now attending colleges and universities. Her chapter speaks of the ways in which a variety of institutions have embraced the challenge and opportunity of diverse constituent groups.

I have had the distinct pleasure over the past several years of conversations with an extraordinarily thoughtful colleague, Peter Magolda. His chapter provides a richly examined narrative of what happened when he began to incorporate technology into a class. Rather than concluding that all technology is either inherently wonderful or disruptive, Peter and his coauthor, Mark Connolly, describe the logical consequences of instructor-led decision-making in the classroom and provides a useful discussion of the questions to ask and how to think about the impacts of technology on a class of learners.

Among the more exciting national programs is one whose aim is improving undergraduate and graduate education, the Preparing Future Faculty (PFF) initiative, (http://www.preparing-faculty.org/PFFWeb.History.htm). Begun in 1993 by the Association of American Colleges and Universities and the Council of Graduate Schools, PFF today includes almost 300 participating institutions including:

43	Research institutions
21	Doctoral institutions
86	Masters degree institutions
65	Baccalaureate institutions
61	Associates degree institutions
6	Specialized institutions

Laurie Richlin, director of the PFF initiatives at the Claremont Graduate University, involves four of her graduate students in writing a chapter about the types of teaching environments. By including data from their research and information about the history and missions of the various categories of higher education institutions, Laurie and her coauthors set a context for the reader who wants to understand the boundary elements of what it is like to teach in a variety of institutions.

The chapter by Marty Petrone is informed by her service as a communications faculty member with a wide array of experiences in conflict mediation, intercultural communication and the incorporation of personality assessment within the classroom. It is useful to note that among the legacies of change, including the many changes confronting the college teacher today—from diverse demographics to the integration of technology to the increased stresses of daily life—is the likelihood of conflict in classroom operations. Marty's thoughtful discussion of these issues provides a good beginning for the new teacher's exploration and discovery.

The American Association of Higher Education's Assessment Forum has provided an ongoing mechanism for examining the fundamentals of outcomes assessment and its practice in higher education. As a former director of the Assessment Forum and now director of an academic support center at Texas Christian University, Catherine Wehlburg knows how to make the confusing seem understandable. Her chapter provides a useable framework for seeing how creating a culture of evidence is possible.

Gary S. Wheeler
MIAMI UNIVERSITY

•

REFERENCES

Angelo, T. A. 1993. A "teacher's dozen": Fourteen general, research-based principles for improving higher learning in our classrooms. *AAHE Bulletin* (April): 3–7, 13.

Chickering, A. W., and Gamson, Z. F. 1987. Seven principles for good practice in undergraduate education. *AAHE Bulletin* (March).

Cross, P. 1996. Presentation to the conference, Teaching and Learning in the Next Century. In the National Teaching and Learning Forum on their Web site: http://www.ntlf.com/html/sf/teaching.htm.

Education Commission of the States. 1996. What research says about improving undergraduate education. *AAHE Bulletin* 48 (April): 5–8.

Oxford Centre for Staff Development. 1993. Deep learning, surface learning. *AAHE Bulletin* (April): 10–11. First published in *Improving student learning,* Oxford, England: Oxford Brookes University, 1992.

Study Group on the Conditions of Excellence in American Higher Education. 1984. *Involvement in learning: Realizing the potential of American higher education.* Washington, D.C.: National Institute of Education.

•1

The ROLE of COMMUNITY in Learning

*Making Connections
for Your Classroom and Campus,
Your Students and Colleagues*

Milton D. Cox

MIAMI UNIVERSITY

◆

What role does community play in teaching and learning? This chapter explores this question from many perspectives: inside and outside the classroom, online, in student learning communities, among early-career, midcareer and senior faculty, in academic departments, and in the college or university as a whole. In many of our disciplines we are rewarded for working alone, for being the sole discoverer and publisher of our research. We are trained that way, writing our dissertations, defending our theses, and professing as "sage on the stage." Many of us teach that way because our instructors did, and in our courses a wide range of student learning is summarized by a sole item: the grade earned by the individual student. Thus, for some, the notion of *community* may threaten us with a loss of autonomy, be a distraction hindering the coverage of content, or present a concept with which we are not familiar or comfortable in our teaching, department, or university culture. However, those willing to include community building in our roles in academe—incorporating cooperation into our academic lives

1

along with competition and providing a safe place for our students and colleagues to take risks and receive support—may find that learning and living outcomes are enhanced.

What is community? According to the *American Heritage Dictionary* (1982), one definition of community is "a group of people living in the same locality and under the same government." While political scientists may prefer this definition, as educators we can generalize and interpret *people* to be our students, *locality* to be our classrooms, and *the same government* to be our syllabi, with the instructor and students connected by some political and power structure in the course, the department, the discipline, and the university. Another definition in the *American Heritage Dictionary* states that community is "the district or locality in which such a group lives." In *How People Learn* (Bransford, Brown, and Cocking 2000), "community centered" refers to several locations of community: the classroom, the school, "and the degree to which students, teachers, and administrators feel connected to the larger community of homes, businesses, states, the nation, and even the world" (p. 98). Learning takes place in three intersecting environments: learner centered, knowledge centered, and assessment centered, and, as can be illustrated by a Venn diagram, these environments are encompassed by and connected to community. Calculating percentages using 180 school days each in year and 6.5 hours in each school day, Bransford, et al., (2000) report that students spend 14% of their time in school, 33% in sleep, and 53% in home and community. This underscores the importance of the connection between school and community.

This geographical and social interpretation does not tell the whole story, however. Our classroom locations and configurations may influence interaction and ambience in teaching and learning, but something is missing. Although the connections our students have to their experiences outside the classroom can be valuable in making meaning, what roles do openness, safety, and support play in making this possible?

The next definition of community, "a group or class having common interests," does encompass the students in our courses as they are connected by our common focus on a particular topic in our discipline. It also connects the learning enterprise to our students' experiences through families, neighbors, employers, and friends. In higher education, community is used in many contexts: We hear about "the community of scholars" in our discipline or the "university community." Hence the common interest can encompass a group of enormous size. As an example involving the university community, a call went out on the Professional and Organizational Development Network (POD) listserv asking the national community of faculty developers what important questions a teaching center should pose to a candidate for university president. One of three or four questions selected from those proposed by the listserv respondents was, "Describe what a 'community dedicated to teaching and learning' would look like. What community have you created and how did it function?" On the other hand, a much smaller group can also be considered a community. For example, a cohort of twenty students taking linked courses can be a student learning community, or a group of eight faculty working throughout the year to investigate and implement a process such as problem-based learning in their courses can be a faculty learning community.

The dynamic of community can change with the size of the group. And so it is time for the last definition of community we will consider: "common possession or participation." This begins to capture the dynamic meaning of community, as from the Latin *communitas* (fellowship) and *communicare* (to share). To enhance learning, we want to explore community as fellowship—the companionship of individuals in a congenial atmosphere, on equal terms, pursuing a common goal. As we investigate the role of community in teaching and learning, we include this last definition, the dynamic of community.

Consider the strength and fragility of community and the ways of expressing its value. In his visit to America in 1840 to determine the reasons for success of the fledgling democracy, Alexis de Tocqueville concluded:

> Americans of all ages, all stations in life, and all types of dispositions are forever forming associations. There are not only commercial and industrial associations in which they take part, but others of a thousand different types—religious, moral, serious, futile, very general and very limited, immensely large and very minute.... Nothing, in my view, deserves more attention than the intellectual and moral associations in America (Putnam 2000, 48).

Studying this phenomenon in *Bowling Alone: The Collapse and Revival of American Community* (2000), Robert Putnam notes with alarm the decline of membership in small communities during the last third of the twentieth century. For example, membership declined 42% in the League of Women Voters, 61% in the Red Cross, 58% for those attending club meetings, and 40% in bowling leagues. Putnam cautions that this loss of social capital—"the ways our lives are made more productive by social ties" (p. 19)—poses a threat to our way of life. Perhaps the tragedy of September 11, 2001, has begun to turn around this decline. Has 9-11 changed anything about your teaching? Has the nationwide decrease in community been mirrored in the way we teach, the way our students learn, the way our departments function, and the way the university exists as a community?

To answer this question with respect to your own teaching, please complete the following assignment at this point:

- Select a course you are teaching and list your learning objectives for the course.
- Describe community as an enabler of or a barrier to achieving each objective.
- State how you develop (or prevent) this community.
- Indicate how you assess the value of this community—what social capital (positive or negative) for learning does this community generate for you and your students?
- Has this gain or loss of social capital changed over the years?

Community Through Cooperative Learning

One of the learning objectives in my mathematics courses for non-majors is to overcome math anxiety, and by doing so enhance learning not only during the course, but long term. Before my second class meeting, I compose groups of four students and engage them in cooperative learning activities throughout the rest of the term. I do this no matter the size of the class. These small communities provide an opportunity for members of each group to be teachers *and* learners in a safe and supportive group of their peers. The cooperative groups also provide social support inside and outside the classroom, especially for first-year students.

What social capital do these communities generate, for my course, and how does this enhance learning? In the spirit of scholarly teaching, we first turn to the literature, where much has been written about cooperative learning. For example, in *Active Learning: Cooperation in the College Classroom*, Johnson, Johnson, and Smith (1998) report that:

Since 1898 there have been over 600 experimental and over 100 correlational studies of cooperative, competitive, and individualistic efforts.

These studies show that cooperation, compared with competitive and individualistic efforts, typically results in greater efforts to achieve, more positive relationships among students, and greater psychological health (pp. 1:15–1:16).

In these findings I see the potential of cooperative learning. If I carry out my cooperative efforts in my mathematics classes successfully, my students should become less anxious (enjoy greater psychological health), and they should be trying harder. This is the social capital earned by the cooperative groups.

To check on my effectiveness, I do a pre- and postsurvey to measure the amount of each student's math anxiety, then determine my success at decreasing anxiety and the reasons that students cited for the increase or decrease. I also read the beginning, middle, and final one-page papers that my students write for their learning portfolios about their past and present learning experiences in mathematics. Their stories and reflections often give me a qualitative measure of the sense of community of the class. And I do an end-of-class survey about the value of the group work in helping their learning. On a Likert scale, where 4 indicates excellent value, 3 good value, 2 fair, 1 poor, and 0 a waste of time, the means are between 3 and 3.5.

I did not adopt cooperative learning suddenly, but introduced it gradually over a period of three or four years. The reason I took this risk was because I was a member of a faculty learning community, a place where I found the nudge and support to investigate and initiate such a venture. I will say more about faculty learning communities later.

COMMUNITY ONLINE

IT SEEMS REASONABLE THAT AN INSTRUCTOR who chooses to do so can create a community-based sense of synergy in the face-to-face classroom, even in large classes. However, recalling that one of our definitions of community indicated that it is place-based, at first thought the task of establishing a community in the online distance classroom seems questionable and daunting. The aspect of shared interest and the communication process must be cultivated intensively to connect as community those in geographically scattered locations. In *Building Learning Communities in Cyberspace: Effective Strategies for the Online Classroom*, Palloff and Pratt (1999) discuss the aspects of electronic personalities and membership in virtual communities. Because some people may have difficulty communicating emotions in textual form, creating a mental picture of a partner in the electronic communication process, or developing an electronic presence online, they point out that "Entry into the virtual community and maintenance of membership in that community entails a very different process and may, in fact, be more difficult for some people to achieve" (p. 22).

Occasional face-to-face meetings, although helping to establish traditional trappings of community, do not seem to alter the dynamics of online community. The norms of community that are easily generated face-to-face require special planning and attention online, for example, cueing when to talk—sequencing and timing comments. Based on what they have found on the Internet and in discussions about online community in their seminars, Paloff and Pratt (1999) summarize basic steps for establishing a virtual community, which they claim fosters stronger connections than in face-to-face groups:

- Clearly define the purpose of the group.
- Create a distinctive gathering place for the group.
- Promote effective leadership from within.
- Define norms and a clear code of conduct.
- Allow for a range of member roles.
- Allow for and facilitate subgroups.
- Allow members to resolve their own disputes (p. 24).

I think that these are necessary steps for building community in *any* course. In my face-to-face classes, I apply these to the entire class and then to each cooperative learning group (my subgroups). My syllabus, leadership, modeling, and flexible approach enable this to happen. Online groups go through the stages of forming, storming, norming, performing, and adjourning (Tuckman 1965) just as face-to-face groups do. Some of the stages are more difficult to implement online, for example, achieving consensus or resolving conflict, due to difficulty in sensing others' feelings and a diminished sense of social constraint. However, conflict in the online classroom, when resolved by classmates or, if out of hand, by the instructor, seems to strengthen community and enhance learning outcomes, which is not usually the case for face-to-face classrooms (Palloff and Pratt 1999). Online instructors need to be comfortable with—even welcome—conflict, yet they must monitor it carefully, because unresolved conflict can discourage future dialogue. Online instructors also need to foster postings about personal issues and to allow discussions to wander off target more than in face-to-face classes.

Paloff and Pratt (1999) have identified six straightforward concepts that are critical to the success of distance learning. Without any one of them, a virtual learning community cannot function.

- **Honesty**—Community members must know that others are who they say they are and engage in open, honest postings. Posts must be received in an atmosphere of caring, support, and trust.
- **Responsiveness**—The instructor and students must respond quickly to each other in order to foster the continuous collaboration needed to achieve course learning objectives. The instructor needs to be available at all times to intervene in case of problems with technology, learning, and conflicts.
- **Relevance**—Students and instructor must be encouraged to share and relate their personal and learning experiences.
- **Respect**—Community members, including the instructor, must feel respected as people and equal as participants. Posts and feedback should be made and received in a constructive manner. Confidential and personal information must not be shared with people outside the community. The group should negotiate guidelines that include a code of ethics dealing with such issues.
- **Openness**—In an atmosphere of openness and safety, students and instructor can feel free to share their ideas, opinions, stories, and feelings without fear of retribution or ridicule. Openness builds the trust and support needed for those students in transition between stages of development.
- **Empowerment**—Students in online and traditional courses need to feel as though they are experts with respect to their own learning and have a sense of confidence in their ability to interact with knowledge. To accomplish this in any course is a worthy objective.

In traditional classrooms with face-to-face opportunities for simulations, visual confirmation of group activities, and other modes of active learning, community can be helpful, but not necessary for learning (remember those great lecturers). However, community is necessary for online courses. In the framework for distance learning, Palloff and Pratt (1999) include a meaningful figure (p. 30, fig. 2.1) that pictures five pieces of a jigsaw puzzle; the four outer pieces represent faculty guidance (teamwork, mutually negotiated guidelines), facilitation (collaborative learning), buy-in from everyone (focused outcomes, shared goals), and interaction and feedback (active creation of knowledge and meaning). The key center piece holding the other four together is simply labeled "community." For online learning, Palloff and Pratt speak eloquently (italics theirs):

> [For] the new paradigm for learning, which involves a more active, collaborative, constructivist approach, the link becomes clear and the missing piece of the puzzle falls into place. The principles involved in the delivery of distance education are basically those attributed to a more active, constructivist form of learning with one difference: *In distance education, attention needs to be paid to the developing sense of community within the group of participants in order for the learning process to be successful.* The learning community is the vehicle through which learning occurs online (pp. 28–9).

STUDENT LEARNING COMMUNITIES

IN THE 1920S AND 1930S JOHN DEWEY (1933) AND Alexander Meiklejohn (1932), concerned about the absence of active and student-centered learning and a coherent curriculum connecting disciplines, respectively, independently introduced the concept of cohorts of students taking courses in common across disciplines. This approach, after sputtering for fifty years—limited success at a few institutions followed by dissolution—finally caught hold at Evergreen (Jones 1981), then at other institutions in the state of Washington, and then across the nation.

Many institutions are currently incorporating variations of the five models indicated below that vary in complexity, faculty involvement, and residential components. The least complex model is linked courses, in which a cohort of twenty-five or so students enroll in two courses, for example, a content course such as history and a skills course such as composition. Other models may involve a cohort in the same residence hall in a themed set of two or three courses with an experienced student *peer learner* or faculty *master learner* attending classes with the cohort and conducting a seminar (proseminar) emphasizing the course connections. An excellent explanation of the five models, including the roles, challenges, and successes of faculty and students, is in Gabelnick, MacGregor, Matthews, and Smith (1990), *Learning Communities: Creating Connections Among Students, Faculty, and Disciplines.*

The community formed in the student cohorts plays a key role in achieving better student learning outcomes than those of students not in student learning communities. In *Assessment to Promote Deep Learning* (Suskie 2000), Macgregor, Tinto, and Linbald (2000) review a compilation of seventy assessment studies of student learning communities. They find promising results:

- The support of community aids retention. Students in learning communities, especially those at-risk, underrepresented, and making Cs and Ds, fare better academically, socially, and personally.
- Students' learning goes deeper, is more integrated, and is more complex. For example, student intellectual development takes place at a faster rate because students are exposed to ambiguity through opposite points of view in team-taught courses or in the proseminar.
- Learning communities can play an important role in faculty development: Those involved in student learning communities achieve significant gains in personal, social, and professional development.
- The integration of academic and social life connects faculty and students to enable the formation of community that includes both.
- Sensitivity to and respect for other points of view, other cultures, and other people are enhanced for both students and faculty.
- Civic contributions are higher, for example participation in student government and in service learning programs.

The Harry Potter series of books illustrates many features of a student learning community:

The Hogwart's House System is the mystical worlds equivalent of residential learning communities.... At Hogwarts, the simple premise is that students learn best in an environment that builds on their strengths and individual characteristics. However, Hogwarts also stresses learning from others and respect for difference" (Levine and Shapiro 2000, 10).

In answer to the question, Why learning communities, why now? K. Patricia Cross, David Pierpont Gardner professor of high education at Berkeley, gives three reasons: "*philosophical* (because learning communities fit into a changing philosophy of knowledge), *research based* (because learning communities fit what research tells us about learning), and *pragmatic* (because learning communities work)" (1998, 10).

As institutions explore moving from the instruction paradigm to the learning paradigm (Barr and Tagg 1995), student learning communities are an example of just how difficult the learning paradigm is to implement (Barr 1998). Tasks such as scheduling a cohort of students, rewarding team teaching, and teaching outside one's department are challenges that registrars, department chairs, and faculty find difficult: "When campuses begin to implement learning communities, whether they know it or not, they are embarking on a road that leads to a profound change in culture" (Shapiro and Levine 1999, front cover). Thus, building community in teaching and learning by way of student learning communities is rewarding, but challenging.

FACULTY LEARNING COMMUNITIES

WITH THE POSITIVE LEARNING OUTCOMES OF STUDENT learning communities in mind, is there a structure and process that can produce similar outcomes for faculty? Examples of these outcomes include increased retention, especially for at-risk faculty; deep learning rather than surface learning, a result of reflection and analysis with peers in the community; integrated learning beyond the perspective of one discipline; greater civic contributions to the common good of the university (and beyond); and faster intellectual development in the manner of the models by Perry (1970), Belenky, Clinchy, Goldberger, and Tarule (1986), or Magolda (1994). Investigating a definition of and approach to a *faculty* learning community requires an exploration of the following items: need, history, definition, necessary qualities, components, goals, outcomes, and recommendations for practice.

NEED

FIRST, LET US EXPLORE NEED. In higher education, early-career faculty are arguably our most important investment. The American Association for Higher Education (AAHE) working paper series, *Heeding New Voices: Academic Careers for a New Generation* (Rice, Sorcinelli, and Austin 2000), reported on results of structured interviews with newcomers to the academy. The newcomers included new faculty and graduate students preparing for faculty work. They came from a broad range of institutions, disciplines, races, ethnicities, genders, and geographical regions. Questions posed asked about their hopes, experiences, and what would make a faculty career more resilient and self-renewing. The findings echo the results of research done a decade ago (Boice 1992; Sorcinelli 1992). Things have not changed much. The study identifies a set of three core, consistent, and interwoven themes about what worries early-career faculty and graduate students as they observe the faculty with whom they work:

- Lack of a comprehensible tenure system
- Lack of community
- Lack of integration between their academic and personal lives

The researchers noted: "*Heeding New Voices* interviewees told us they want to pursue their work in communities where collaboration is respected and encouraged, where friendships develop between colleagues within and across departments, and where there is time and opportunity for interaction and talk about ideas, one's work, and the institution" (p. 13). However, as in our other looks at community in this chapter, barriers do exist—in this case being raised by the early-career faculty themselves as they envisioned their struggle to support community should the opportunity be offered. They cited, for example, the appeal of working from home as enabled by the Internet (and the easy access made available to it by their institutions), the responsibilities of two-career families, and the absence of other new faculty in their departments. I have noted that the cost of housing around their campuses has caused some new faculty to live at a distance, while institutions in small towns find many new faculty commuting to live in urban areas.

> Looking to an imagined future, one early-career woman in a research university concluded: 'My vision of the academy in the twenty-first century is one that breaks traditional department barriers, creates interaction among faculty across fields, conducts research around themes, gets rid of the huge gap between research and teaching, and incorporates students more so that the wall between students and professors comes down' (p. 16).

We must design a faculty learning community that will provide these opportunities for early-career faculty while decreasing the size of the barriers to it.

The AAHE report concludes with ten recommendations for good practice. The first four deal with establishing a more comprehensible tenure system; the next three call for one-on-one mentoring of graduate students and new faculty by senior faculty and department chairs; and the final three advocate support for teaching (provide model syllabi, encourage visitation to the teaching center), scholarly development, and a balance between professional and personal life. Remarkably, none of the recommendations speaks to forming community, another indication that higher education is not interested in or equipped to deal with the yearning expressed so eloquently by our early-career colleagues. The report itself says, "It's not that we don't know what to do, it's that we don't do what we know" (p. x). While the recommendations of the report are helpful in addressing some of the concerns, the concept of faculty learning community is informed more by the worries of our early-career faculty than the report recommendations.

Is there a need for community among senior and midcareer faculty? Reporting her study of midcareer faculty in a Canadian university, Karpiak (1997) found that some experienced a malaise that included burnout and a need for renewal, found teaching unrewarding, and blamed their frustrations on students' low quality and motivation. They felt isolated and on the periphery. Frustrated and angry, they turned to pursuits outside the academy. Others made meaning of their situation, were satisfied, and had a high interest in teaching, mentoring, and trying new approaches. They felt the administration and others were interested in and cared about them. The ten recommendations in this report, *University Professors at Mid-Life: Being a Part of... But Feeling Apart* (Karpiak 1997), included three that spoke directly to forming community:

- Promote among faculty a sense that they are involved in a joint enterprise, and that they are members of a team.
- Foster an environment in which colleagues stimulate each other's intellectual interests and help each other develop and grow.
- Develop support networks so that faculty know they are not alone—sponsored networks, wherein colleagues can offer support to others.

This report gives us additional goals and objectives that we must incorporate into our faculty learning community concept.

History

IN 1975 THE LILLY ENDOWMENT, recognizing that new faculty arrived at their posts with no teacher training in their past or in their future (and that not much had changed to address the concerns of Dewey and Meikeljohn in the 1930s), launched the Lilly Post-Doctoral Teaching Fellows Program (Austin 1992). Each year the endowment invited two research universities to join four others to develop an ongoing program to focus on the teaching enhancement of junior faculty. Although each institution received generous support during its three years in the program, Austin (1992) reported that all but a few of these efforts ended when an institution's three-year funding expired. Even though some vestiges of the effort contributed to the later development of teaching centers or orientation workshops, the structured junior faculty seminar series and events did not usually continue.

As of 1990, one of the few exceptions to this trend was Miami University, where in addition to the teaching enhancement component, the valuable aspect of community had been nurtured to become an essential part of the program. Started in 1979, the endowment's funding for Miami ended in 1982. The university president contributed $3,000 and the author, who has directed the program since 1980, contributed the balance to keep the program going for a fourth year. The university's Committee for the Improvement of Instruction and the University Senate strongly endorsed the program. For the fifth year, new provost C. K. (Bud) Williamson secured ongoing funding contributed by the Miami University alumni, and the program was named the Alumni Teaching Scholars Program.

Some senior and midcareer faculty who had not had the opportunity to be members of the junior faculty program pressed for a similar program for them. Williamson again secured funds, and in 1990 a similar program, the Senior Faculty Community for Teaching Excellence, funded by the alumni, was started for senior and midcareer faculty. As before, community was a key part of this program. The program was and is led by Muriel Blaisdell, a graduate of the junior faculty program. In 1994 the Alumni Teaching Scholars Program received the Theodore M. Hesburgh Award as the best faculty development program in the United States in the role of enhancing undergraduate education. Because of the recognition this endorsement brought, a similar program was designed to address diversity concerns that were arising on campus. The Faculty Program Using Difference to Enhance Teaching and Learning adapted the junior and senior faculty approaches, including the community component, to the topic of involving diversity inside and outside the classroom.

Suddenly, those involved with these programs at Miami University realized that our methods, structure, and outcomes were similar to those of student learning communities. From the outset of the program in 1979, junior faculty reported that the Alumni Teaching Scholars Program addressed the worrisome themes that were later identified in the *Heeding New Voices* study. Senior faculty reported that their community successfully addressed the concerns reported by Karpiak (1997). Members of the difference community modified methods and curricula to make their classrooms and courses more inclusive. After this, many other topics of faculty interest were raised, for example, problem-based learning and ethics across the curriculum, and we successfully applied our faculty learning community approach to them as well.

Before continuing, I should say a bit about Miami University. Founded in 1809, Miami is a state-assisted research-*intensive* institution (having nine doctoral programs as compared to research-*extensive* institutions, in which nearly every department has a PH.D. program), with 15,500 undergraduates, 1,500 graduate students, and 950 full-time faculty on the Oxford campus, plus two regional, urban, commuter campuses, each with 3,000 students and 70 faculty. Miami has a history and tradition of emphasis on undergraduate education. The faculty learning community program's objectives—emphasizing enhanced undergraduate learning, the ways that difference and international experiences can enhance teaching and learning, development of faculty in learning communities, and the scholarship of teaching—are consistent with the mission of the university.

Definitions

AT THIS POINT I WANT TO PROVIDE a definition of a faculty learning community and address how these communities work as the result of over twenty years of experience in developing, implementing, and leading them. First, I will discuss the definition based on the Miami model and those of institutions that have been adapting the Miami model at their institutions.

A *faculty learning community* is a cross-disciplinary faculty group of five or more members (eight to twelve is the recommended size) engaging in an active, collaborative, yearlong program with a curriculum about enhancing teaching and learning and with frequent seminars and activities that provide learning, development, interdisciplinarity, the scholarship of teaching and learning, and community building. A participant in a faculty learning community selects a focus course in which to try out innovations, assess resulting student learning, and prepare a course miniportfolio; engages in biweekly seminars; works with student associates; and presents project results to the campus and at national conferences. Evidence shows that FLCS increase faculty interest in teaching and learning and provide safety and support for faculty to investigate, attempt, assess, and adopt new (to them) methods. In the literature about student learning communities, the word *student* usually can be replaced by *faculty* and still make the same point; for example, "Learning community [faculty] generally fare better academically, socially, and personally than those in comparison groups."

There are two categories of faculty learning communities: *cohort-based* and *topic-based*. Cohort-based learning communities address the teaching, learning, and developmental needs of an important cohort of faculty that has been particularly affected by the isolation, fragmentation, stress, neglect, or chilly climate in the academy. The curriculum of such a yearlong community is shaped by the participants to include a broad range of teaching and learning areas and topics of interest to them. These communities will make a positive impact on the culture of the institution over the years if given multiyear support. Four examples of cohort-based communities at Miami University are the Alumni Teaching Scholars Community for junior faculty, the Senior Faculty Community for Teaching Excellence for midcareer and senior faculty, the Preparing Future Faculty Community for graduate students, and the Department Chairs Learning Community.

Each topic-based learning community is yearlong and has a curriculum designed to address a special campus teaching and learning need, issue, or opportunity. These communities offer membership to and provide opportunities for learning across all faculty ranks and cohorts, but with a focus on a particular theme. A particular topic-based faculty learning community ends when the campuswide teaching opportunity or issue of concern has been satisfactorily addressed. Examples of topics addressed by Miami University's topic-based faculty learning communities are team teaching, problem-based learning, diversity, teaching portfolio development, ethics across the honors curriculum, United States cultures course development, departmental assessment of general education, small-group learning, teaching writing-intensive courses, cooperative learning, and courses in common.

At Miami, the number of participants in a faculty learning community has varied from 8 to 14 participants, although at other institutions it has varied from 5 to 20. We recommend 8 to 12. The cost of each community at Miami varies from $20,000 to $30,000, and at other institutions the cost of each has ranged from $5,000 to $50,000. These are programming costs (books, food, travel, professional stipend or release time), not items such as support staff salary, space, or paper. The top expense items, if employed, are release time (or honorarium) and travel. However, providing first-class treatment for participants earns their generous time commitment, appreciation, and long-term support.

Over 5% of Miami's faculty participate voluntarily in a faculty learning community each year. Over one-third of the current faculty have participated in an FLC. Grants from the Ohio Board of Regents and the U.S. Department of Education Fund for the Improvement of Post-Secondary Education (FIPSE) now support Miami's mentoring of other institutions in the FLC approach.

Faculty learning communities are more structured and intensive than most approaches that gather together a collection of faculty to meet and work on teaching and learning issues, for example, teaching circles (Quinlan 1996) or a group coming together each week over "brown bag" lunches to read and discuss articles on teaching. Faculty learning communities are different from but in many ways like most action learning sets in that they both are "a continuous process of learning and reflection, supported by colleagues, with an intention of getting things done" (McGill and Beaty 2001, 11). Both faculty learning communities and action learning sets are more than just seminar series or formal committees, project teams, or support, self-development, or counseling groups. They have several aspects in common: Both meet for a period of at least six months; have voluntary membership; meet at a designated time and in an environment conducive to learning; treat individual projects in the same way; employ the Kolb (1986) experiential learning cycle; develop empathy among members; operate by consensus, not majority; develop their own culture, openness, and trust; engage complex problems; energize and empower participants; have the potential of transforming institutions into learning organizations; and are holistic in approach.

Faculty learning communities differ from action learning sets in that the communities are less formal; for example, they do not focus extensively on negotiated timing or other formal structures at meetings. Faculty learning communities concentrate less on the efficiency of getting things done and include more focus on the social aspects of building community: Off-campus retreats and conferences include times for fun, and a dinner or two during the year includes spouses or partners. Faculty learning communities include more emphasis on the team aspect (while still developing each individual's project) and on the ultimate beneficiaries of the program: the students in the participants' courses.

Necessary Qualities

THE FOLLOWING TEN QUALITIES guide the design and process of a faculty learning community, focusing on the important aspect of community.

1. **Safety and Trust**. In order for participants to connect with each other, there must be a sense of safety and trust. This is especially true as participants reveal weaknesses in their teaching or ignorance of teaching processes or literature.
2. **Openness**. In an atmosphere of openness, participants can feel free to share their thoughts and feelings without fear of retribution. For example, in the Community Using Difference, participants are able to discuss ways that other participants or colleagues may offend them.
3. **Respect**. In order to coalesce as a learning community, members need to feel as though they are valued and respected as people. It is important for the university to acknowledge their participation by financially supporting community projects and attendance at conferences.
4. **Responsiveness**. Members must respond to each other, and the leader(s) must respond quickly to the other participants. The coordinator should welcome concerns and preferences and share these with individuals and the community.
5. **Collaboration**. The importance of collaboration in consultation and group discussion on individual members' projects and on achieving program learning outcomes hinges on the group's ability to work with and respond to each other. In addition to individual projects, joint projects and presentations should be welcomed.
6. **Relevance**. Learning outcomes are enhanced by relating the subject matter to the participants' teaching, courses, scholarship,

and life experiences. All participants should be encouraged to seek out and share teaching and other real-life examples to illustrate them.

7. **Challenge**. Expectations for the quality of outcomes should be high, engendering a sense of progress, scholarship, and accomplishment. Sessions should include, for example, those in which individuals share syllabi and report on their individual projects.

8. **Enjoyment**. Activities must include social opportunities to lighten up, bond, and should take place in invigorating environments. For example, a retreat can take place off campus at a nearby country inn, state park, historic site, or the like.

9. **Esprit de Corps**. Sharing individual and community outcomes with colleagues in the academy should generate pride and loyalty. For example, when the community makes a campuswide presentation, participants strive to provide an excellent session.

10. **Empowerment**. A sense of empowerment is both a crucial element and a desired outcome of participation in a learning community. In the construction of a transformative learning environment, the participants gain a new view of themselves and a new sense of confidence in their abilities. Faculty leave their year of participation with better courses and clearer understanding of themselves and their students. Key outcomes include scholarly teaching and contributions to the scholarship of teaching.

COMPONENTS

AT THIS POINT IN FACULTY LEARNING community program development we have identified thirty key components of a faculty learning community. The degree of engagement in the components selected for a faculty learning community can vary and may differ by type of faculty learning community and institution. As an institution's experience with faculty learning communities increases, the degree of engagement with each component and the number of components involved will usually increase. When appropriate, the components should be considered both globally with respect to the overall faculty learning community program and locally for each particular community.

Mission and Purpose

1. Goals for the institution (What do you want the FLC program to accomplish?)

2. Objectives for each FLC (How do you plan to bring about the above goals through specific objectives for each FLC?)

Curriculum

3. What FLCs to offer (cohorts, topics)
4. What issues and topics to address within each FLC

Administration

5. Leadership (qualities and criteria) of FLC program and each FLC
6. Selection procedures and criteria for each FLC (striking a balance among disciplines, needs, gender, experience)
7. Public relations (advertising each FLC and recruiting applicants)
8. Financial support and budgets

Connections

9. Community (bonding within; support; safety)
10. Partnerships (bridging to and cosponsoring with other programs inside and outside the institution)
11. Engagement (serving the broader community: student and faculty organizations, K–12, statewide)

Affiliated Participants

12. Faculty or administrative partners (mentors, facilitators)
13. Student associates (undergraduate peer mentors, TAS, consultants)

Meetings and Activities

14. Seminars (length, frequency, topics)
15. Retreats (getting away, working and learning together)
16. Conferences (getting away, learning from others)
17. Social amenities and gatherings

Scholarly Process

18. The literature (articles and focus book)
19. The focus course (syllabus, project, TGI, CATS, SGID)
20. The individual teaching project
21. Presentations, both on campus and at conferences (by individual members of the FLC and/or the entire group)
22. Course miniportfolio (prepared by each FLC member for his or her focus course)
23. Publication (usually in a later year)
24. The scholarship of teaching and learning

Assessment

    25. Of faculty development

    26. Of FLC program components

    27. Of student learning in classes of FLC participants

Enablers/Rewards

    28. Reassigned (release) time for participants and the FLC leader

    29. Professional expenses for participants and the FLC leader

    30. Recognition by the provost, deans, department chairs, colleagues

GOALS

THE LONG-TERM GOALS OF a faculty learning community program for most institutions are similar to those of Miami University. These goals are to

- build university-wide community through teaching and learning,
- increase faculty interest in undergraduate teaching and learning,
- investigate and incorporate ways that difference can enhance teaching and learning,
- nourish the scholarship of teaching and its application to student learning,
- broaden the evaluation of teaching and the assessment of learning,
- increase faculty collaboration across disciplines,
- encourage reflection about general education and the coherence of learning across disciplines,
- increase the rewards for and prestige of excellent teaching,
- increase financial support for teaching and learning initiatives, and
- create an awareness of the complexity of teaching and learning.

OUTCOMES

WHAT ABOUT THE OUTCOMES we considered important in our discussion of the needs of early-career, senior, and midcareer faculty? Evidence of systemic change is discussed below for several of the communities.

The early-career faculty community provides a safe place for pretenure faculty in their second through fifth years to meet and work on teaching opportunities with peers from other disciplines. Most participants develop into "quick starters" (Boice 1992). The outcomes noted in table 1.1 indicate that they also become very interested in the teaching process and gain a perspective of teaching, learning, and higher education that extends beyond their disciplines. They become comfortable in the university community, overcoming the great stress often felt by junior faculty (Sorcinelli 1992). Evidence shows that the early-career faculty member's partner—an experienced faculty mentor—has a strong impact on their development (Cox 1997). At Miami, participants are tenured at a significantly higher rate than the junior faculty who elect not to participate in this community (Cox 1995), to some extent because the community discussion prepares them for the tenure system. It may also be because those who apply to be in the program tend to be quick starters. The key point is that their participation does not hurt them and may help.

The senior faculty community offers participants time, safety, funds, and colleagueship across different disciplines in order to reflect on past teaching and life experiences and to investigate and chart new directions. Evidence in table 1.2 indicates that this community values most of all the colleagueship—community—and learning from the other participants. Table 1.1 reports outcomes similar to those for junior faculty community members. The senior community fulfills Karpiak's (1997) recommendations for the involvement, stimulation, and networking that a university should provide for professors at midlife.

We created the Faculty Community Using Difference to Enhance Teaching and Learning in order to involve faculty in addressing perplexing diversity issues on campus. The strategy hinged on the belief that if faculty could connect diversity issues with ways to increase the learning of their students, instructors would get involved. The safety offered by this faculty learning community has been important in opening a constructive dialogue and fostering risk taking. According to Gabelnick, et al., "Learning communities have features that feminist literature suggests are important, such as cooperation and shared power, development of a personal connection to the material being studied, and emphasis on the affective aspects of learning" (1990, 79). Table 1.1 notes that members in this community have a level of "comfort in the university community" below those in other communities due to concerns raised by their investigations.

With respect to outcomes, the greatest impact across all communities is on the participants' interest in the teaching process. Research indicates that students learn more from enthusiastic, interested teachers. An outcome ranked fifth out of eleven across all communities is the participants' under-

TABLE 1.1
MIAMI UNIVERSITY
Faculty Learning Communities Assessment of FLC *Faculty Development Outcomes*

Results from the question: Estimate the impact of the community on you with respect to each of the following developmental outcomes. 1 indicates a very weak impact and 10 indicates a very strong impact.

Number in parentheses is the ranking of this outcome over the years the question has been asked. Number on second line is mean for that outcome over the years the question has been asked.

Outcomes (Number of years surveyed) Listed in order of impact across all communities	Junior Faculty Community (20 years)	Senior Faculty Community (10 years)	Difference Community (3 years)	Cooperative Learning Community (1 year)	Problem-Based Learning Community (1 year)	Team Teaching Community (1 year)	Technology Community (1 year)
1. Your interest in the teaching process	(1) 8.6	(1) 8.7	(1) 8.5	(3) 9.6	(2) 8.3	(1) 7.8	(1) 8.4
2. Your perspective of teaching, learning, and other aspects of higher education beyond the perspective of your discipline	(1) 8.6	(2) 8.4	(2) 8.4	(10) 7.7	(1) 8.6	(3) 7.6	(2) 8.0
3. Your comfort level as a member of the Miami University Community	(4) 8.0	(3) 8.1	(8) 7.5	(1) 9.7	(6) 7.3	(3) 7.6	(4) 7.6
4. Your view of teaching as an intellectual pursuit	(3) 8.2	(4) 8.0	(5) 7.8	(3) 9.6	(4) 7.6	(8) 6.6	(7) 7.3
5. Your understanding of and interest in the scholarship of teaching	(5) 7.9	(6) 7.7	(5) 7.8	(1) 9.7	(6) 7.3	(9) 6.4	(3) 7.7

6. Your awareness and understanding of how difference may influence and enhance teaching and learning	(10) 6.8	(8) 7.4	(3) 8.2	(5) 8.4	N/A	(1) 7.8	(9) 6.8
7. Your total effectiveness as a teacher	(6) 7.7	(6) 7.7	(9) 7.0	(9) 8.3	(6) 7.3	(6) 7.2	(4) 7.6
8. Your understanding of the role of a faculty member at Miami University	(8) 7.1	(4) 8.0	(7) 7.7	(11) 6.9	(9) 7.0	(7) 7.0	(8) 7.0
9. Your awareness of ways to integrate the teaching/research experience	(8) 7.1	(9) 7.2	(9) 7.0	(5) 8.7	(12) 4.7	(3) 7.6	(9) 6.8
10. Your research and scholarly interest with respect to your discipline	(11) 6.7	(11) 6.4	(4) 8.0	(7) 8.6	(5) 7.4	(9) 6.4	(9) 6.8
11. Your technical skill as a teacher	(7) 7.2	(10) 6.9	(11) 5.9	(8) 8.4	(10) 6.7	(11) 6.0	(6) 7.4
OVERALL MEAN FOR COHORT	7.6	7.7	7.6	8.7	7.2	7.1	7.4

Other items specific to a particular community were also rated and are available from the author.

standing of and interest in the scholarship of teaching. In almost every Miami department, a former faculty learning community member has published the scholarship of teaching.

Another measure of success is the support received from administrators. This is evident in that Miami's provosts have tripled funding over the last fifteen years to enable the initiation of new communities. Evidence that communities foster civic responsibility and contributions to the common good is found in faculty learning community participants' contributions to leadership of the university. Currently, one of Miami's six deans is a former participant, as well as nineteen of forty-six department chairs and almost half of the university senate faculty membership. Of the 142 faculty still at Miami who have served as mentors in the early-career staff community, over one-third (55/142) are former faculty learning community participants.

Evidence that student learning is enhanced is found in the analysis of student learning that appears in the participants' course miniportfolios, the results of teaching projects, and final reports. Evidence documenting improvement in undergraduate learning outcomes is given in the results of surveys of past faculty learning community participants who report (a) how and the degree to which student learning in their courses changed as a result of faculty learning community participation, (b) how they knew it changed, (c) what processes/approaches resulted in increased learning, (d) the categories of their faculty learning community teaching projects and the degree to which learning changed as a result of that project, and (e) the degree of change in student learning due to a change in faculty attitude as a result of faculty learning community participation. The learning objectives were categorized using the Angelo and Cross (1993) Teaching Goals Inventory. The degree to which student learning changed was rated using the following scale: 0 (students learned less), 1 (no change), 2 (learned more to a small degree), 3 (learned more to a medium degree), 4 (learned more to a great degree).

Some highlights of the results follow:

- Ninety-four percent of the respondents reported an increase in students' "ability to apply principles and generalizations already learned to new problems and solutions" (degree of change: 3.0). The same results were reported for students' "ability to ask good questions" and their "ability to develop an openness to new ideas;" 96% reported an increase in students' ability "to work productively with others" (3.2); 92% reported an increase in students' "capacity to think for oneself" (3.0); 98% reported an increase in the "ability to synthesize and integrate information and ideas" (3.1).

- Faculty were aware that student learning increased because of successful achievement of existing (62%) or new/more (58%) learning objectives; better class discussion/engagement (84%); greater student interest (64%); better classroom atmosphere/engagement (68%); more positive student evaluation comments (54%); and better papers or other writing assignments (52%).
- Some approaches that resulted in increased learning (and their degree of change) included cooperative or collaborative learning (92%; 3.0), active learning (92%; 3.1), discussion (88%; 3.1), student-centered learning (84%; 3.0), writing (82%; 2.7), and technology (74%; 2.6).
- The overall rating for the degree to which student learning increased as a result of the participants' faculty learning community teaching project was 2.9.
- The percentage of faculty respondents indicating a change (and the degree of change) in student learning due to a change in faculty attitude were as follows: your general enthusiasm about teaching and learning (98%, 3.3); your scholarly teaching and the scholarship of teaching (92%, 3.2); your being more reflective (94%, 3.2); your being more comfortable (88%, 2.9); your being more confident (90%, 2.8); your being revitalized (90%, 2.7).

Evidence that the faculty learning community program has an impact on the academic community is provided by its emulation and adaptation by others. Miami has received a three-year, $324,000 FIPSE grant to mentor the development of faculty learning communities at the Claremont Graduate University and colleges, Kent State University, Indiana University–Purdue University Indianapolis, Ohio State University, and the University of Notre Dame. This grant and the resulting faculty learning communities at each institution (two at each in 2001/02, four in 2002/03, and six in 2003/04) will provide interesting comparisons to the outcomes of the Action Learning Project at seven institutions in Hong Kong (Kember 2000). The Ohio Board of Regents awarded Miami a grant to establish the early-career faculty learning communities statewide. Miami has led adaptations that are enthusiastically

TABLE 1.2

MIAMI UNIVERSITY

Faculty Learning Communities Evaluation of FLC Program Components

Results from the question: Estimate the impact of the community on you with respect to each of the following program components. 1 indicates a very weak impact and 10 indicates a very strong impact.

Includes reports from those who engaged in a particular component and rated it.
Number in parentheses is the ranking of this component over the years the question has been asked.
Number on second line is mean for that component over the years the question has been asked.

Outcomes (Number of years surveyed) Listed in order of impact across all communities	Junior Faculty Community (20 years)	Senior Faculty Community (10 years)	Difference Community (3 years)	Cooperative Learning Community (1 year)	Problem-Based Learning Community (1 year)	Team Teaching Community (1 year)	Technology Community (1 year)
1. The colleagueship and learning from other participants	(1) 8.9	(2) 8.7	(3) 8.2	(1) 9.9	(3) 7.1	(1) 9.4	(3) 7.4
2. The retreats and conferences	(2) 8.3	(3) 7.8	(2) 8.3	(2) 8.9	(1) 7.5	(6) 7.2	(5) 6.9
3. Release time (junior, senior) or substantial funds for professional expenses (difference, cooperative, etc.)	(3) 8.1	(1) 8.8	(6) 7.7	(5) 7.7	(4) 6.9	(4) 8.3	(1) 8.3
4. The teaching project	(6) 8.0	(5) 7.7	(4) 7.7	(4) 8.1	(2) 7.4	(2) 8.8	(3) 7.6

5. Seminars	(4) 7.7	(6) 7.5	(4) 7.7	(3) 8.5	(5) 6.2	(5) 7.5	(2) 7.7
6. Student associates	(7) 5.8	(3) 7.8	(1) 8.6	(6) 7.6	N/A	N/A	(6) 5.1
7. A one-to-one faculty partnership (junior: senior faculty mentor; senior: faculty partners in learning)	(5) 7.9	(8) 5.9	N/A	N/A	N/A	(3) 8.4	N/A
8. Observation of a faculty partner's and others' classes	(8) 6.8	(7) 6.2	N/A	(7) 3.0	N/A	(7) 6.3	N/A
OVERALL MEAN FOR COHORT	7.7	7.6	8.0	7.7	7.0	8.0	7.2

Other items specific to a particular community were also rated and are available from the author.

underway at Bowling Green State University, Kent State University, Ohio State University, Ohio University, Sinclair Community College, Shawnee State University, and University of Cincinnati—Raymond Walters College.

RECOMMENDATIONS FOR PRACTICE

I ENCOURAGE YOU and your institution to join the consortium of colleges and universities that are initiating faculty learning communities on their campuses. We welcome you to a learning community of initiators who are trying to enhance the role of community in higher education. You can contact us at the Web site: www.muohio.edu/flc/.

As you contemplate the initiation of faculty learning communities on your campus, we recommend the following practices for ensuring that such communities are effective. An institution's culture and key players affect the manner in which these suggestions should be employed. Detailed recommendations for initiating and continuing faculty learning communities can be found in Cox (1995, 1997, 1999).

Initial Planning Overview. The campus teaching center and/or faculty development office should develop one or two faculty learning communities at a time. The type of initial cohort-based or topic-based community should be determined by a needs analysis. Administrators often are willing to invest funds in junior faculty and faculty involvement with technology or diversity, so these may be good starting points. Faculty and administrators must be convinced that a faculty learning community provides excellent learning, development, and community. To provide convincing evidence, campuses that already have student learning communities can cite evidence that the outcomes for faculty are similar to outcomes for students: increased collaboration across disciplines, increased retention, a more coherent curriculum, more active learning, more civic contributions to the common good, and, over time, a campus community built around teaching and learning. View the initial year as pilot testing.

Initial Planning Items. Engage these items as you begin:

- Obtain broad administrative and faculty support, including:
    1. president, academic vice president, and deans
    2. critical mass of department chairs
    3. respected senior and junior faculty (control stays here)

    4. respected advisory committee, part of university governance

    5. university senate.

- Survey faculty for needs, concerns.
- Emphasize outcomes about increased faculty and student learning, interest in teaching and learning, and so forth.
- Cite the literature and research to build support.
- Select a committed, conscientious, respected director/leader, such as a senior administrator; leader of faculty development or teaching center; experienced faculty member with the capacity to influence budget allocations, provide expertise about teaching and learning, have knowledge of useful resource people—both local and national—to attract positive recognition across campus; and be a community builder.
- Select your "best" faculty to establish the initial FLC as prestigious, not remedial. Include a balance of "needy" faculty in later years.
- Give the faculty participants a strong hand in designing the year's agenda.
- Design activities, accommodations, and recognitions to make participants feel valued and respected by the college or university.

Application. The application for membership in a community must include a section asking about the applicant's specific teaching needs and what experience or expertise he or she can bring to the community. These form a basis for early group interaction. The application must also have questions that elicit an applicant's openness to new ideas. The applicant's department chair must approve and sign off on the application.

Selection. Choose community members to create a balance across disciplines, interests, experiences, and needs; this will ensure a group with a broad and diverse background, one that can bring multiple perspectives to issues and opportunities.

Prestige. Advertise the community as an opportunity for faculty to engage in learning through projects, reflections, and conversation—a place for scholarly exploration, innovation, and change. Membership should be considered an honor. The community should be not viewed as a place for remedial activities for "broken" faculty.

Trust and Safety. Discussion may involve sharing members' concerns and frailties with the learning community. Hence, the elements of trust and safety in the community are very important. At the first meeting (and in application information), it is essential to make clear that all discussions are confidential and conducted with respect and openness.

Legacy. For a program in its second and later years, provide an opportunity each year for the new members to meet with the graduating members to share various aspects of the program, for example, what they learned, changes they made in their teaching, improvements in student learning, how they selected and worked with faculty partners and student associates, and so forth. The closeness, spirit, and scholarliness of those in the graduating community set a positive tone for the new group.

Activities. Let each new group select seminar topics, projects, and activities to meet their needs, which may be different from those of former groups, yet provide a scaffolding upon which they can build. Provide a focus book for each member, and select an opening seminar topic that interests the new group and that has been well received in past years. Encourage collaborative efforts that give pairs or small groups within a community the opportunity to consult about and present joint seminars or projects.

Scholarship of Teaching. Nurture the scholarship of teaching by incorporating a sequence of developmental events, for example, starting the year with discussion based on the focus book or reading; developing individual teaching projects with clearly stated learning objectives, literature reviews, and assessment plans for student learning; and providing access to relevant books and journals on postsecondary teaching and learning. Members should present the results of their projects at a campuswide seminar or teaching retreat, followed by a presentation at a national teaching conference.

Assessment. Provide a means for assessing the effectiveness of the objectives of the community, both short- and long-term. A midyear and final evaluation and report in addition to evaluations of each seminar provide evidence of success and ways to improve various aspects of the community. Collect pre- and postcommunity syllabi to illustrate changes inspired by participation. Have each participant select a focus course in which to incorporate his or her project and innovations. Participants should prepare a course mini-portfolio for their focus course.

Sharing. Near the end of the year, provide an opportunity for the community members to become peer consultants to the campus, for example, by presenting a university-wide seminar. Prepare and advertise a faculty resource list of members willing to consult with others on specified areas of teaching and learning.

Leadership. The director or coordinator of a faculty learning community should be a well-respected teacher-scholar, be well acquainted with the literature on teaching and learning in higher education, have good consulting abilities, and be a community builder. One of the leaders of a departmental community in the teaching portfolio project at Miami says it well:

> Stay flexible! Nothing happens as fast you think it will. Be willing to pause, take valuable side trips dictated by the ebb and flow of the group. Don't push too hard, and listen a lot more than you talk. Good things will happen, but it takes time and will not follow the road map drawn on day one. Also, be sure everyone is having fun and enjoying the process. Do fun things. Eat well. Build a culture of trust and mutual respect. Learn from the diversity and creativity of the individuals in the group.

The Role of Faculty Developer. Faculty developers or teaching center staff play a key role in managing the operations of faculty learning communities. At Miami, the director of teaching effectiveness programs coordinates the junior faculty community and oversees the others. This consists of working closely with each faculty coordinator. The teaching effectiveness programs office handles room scheduling, meals, travel, publicity, and budget items for all of the communities.

As developers, within our institutions "we need to promote an understanding of the process of faculty development over time, leading to a full integration of the fragments of academic work" (Kreber and Cranton 1999, 225). Providing a variety of faculty learning communities over the years enables faculty to concentrate on specific issues or developmental needs at various times during their careers. FLCs provide deep learning rather than surface learning.

Compensation and Rewards. Participation in a faculty learning community takes a lot of time and work: attendance at weekend retreats, national conferences, and biweekly seminars; interaction with a student associate and a faculty partner; reading the new literature of the scholarship of teaching; development of and work on a teaching project; and preparation of a seminar presentation for the campus and, perhaps, a national conference.

At Miami, we have two ways of compensating faculty participants. First, and best, is to provide release time from one course for one semester. This is done at the rate for adjuncts. If a department chair can create the release time in another manner, then the department receives the funds and usually allocates them to the faculty member, for example, to purchase technology or international travel. Also, each member receives funds to enable his or her learning plan or teaching project. Junior faculty participants each have $200 available, and senior faculty have $500.

Unfortunately, Miami does not have the budget to provide release time for members of many communities. In that case, each participant receives an honorarium of $1,000 to $1,500 to use for professional expenses. In the teaching portfolio project, each participating department received $5000. However, some of the adapting institutions have had success even with support at $250 per person. The desire for community participation can motivate well.

Each community coordinator receives one-course release time for both semesters plus the honorarium available for his or her particular community. Service as a coordinator must be approved by his or her department chair.

Overcoming Obstacles. Some obstacles must be addressed in order to start and continue faculty learning communities. One obstacle is the length of time needed for an institution to show a cultural change as a result of the community approach—at least five years. Other obstacles include cost, participants' time commitment, and the isolated nature of faculty life—the group structure of the community experience is not for everyone. These obstacles are similar to some of those that challenge student learning communities, as Barr (1998) observes: "Faculty experimenting with [student] learning communities are finding themselves hard-pressed to keep them going" (p. 22).

Communities do not appeal to everyone. For example, an excellent teacher, who had served successfully as a mentor in our junior faculty community and also followed a colleague's participation in the senior faculty community, approached me with an enthusiastic suggestion: Perhaps just one meeting of a community at the start of the year would suffice, enabling full concentration on one's individual teaching project the rest of the year. Another faculty member suggested that we bring in an expert at the start and avoid the "amateurish" discussions of the group. With this in mind, developers initiating communities should continue other support for individuals: grants, one-to-one consultations, and "one-time-only" campus seminars.

Nevertheless, once one successful faculty learning community is up and running, the positive outcomes for participants and the institution should convince administrators to continue and expand funding. Enthusiastic participants can convince reticent colleagues to join. The long-term rewards of community, collaboration, and better student learning are well worth the effort.

The Role of Community in Becoming a Learning Organization

Senge (1990) describes a learning organization as one that connects its members closely to the mission, goals, and challenges of the organization. These close connections are necessary for the organization to meet the demands of rapid change. While faculty often have such connections within their departments and disciplinary organizations, faculty usually do not have the broad interests of their institutions at heart. There are few rewards for doing so—most are department- and discipline-based. Rarely has a turf battle in a university senate meeting (when a quorum could be mustered) been resolved by the opponents offering to consult and consider the university's and students' best interests. As a result, faculty remain isolated from colleagues in other disciplines, and the curriculum remains fragmented. Thus, both faculty and students miss out on connections across disciplines. Campuswide action on issues (except, perhaps, parking and salaries) flounders from lack of interest, involvement, and support.

Senge (1990) describes the five components of a learning organization, components that foster close connections among the people within an institution. Patrick and Fletcher (1998) translate these components into behavior for the academy. Table 1.3 describes both perspectives and shows how faculty learning communities foster the reflection, learning, and action needed to establish these components in our colleges and universities.

Although effective faculty leaning communities alone will not transform an institution into a learning organization, over time they can produce a critical mass of key individuals and leaders plus the network necessary to connect campus units. Harper (1996) contends that "Creating such opportunities for conversation and community among faculty is imperative, not only to the personal and professional growth and reflection of individual faculty, but also for the growth of the higher education community at large" (p. 265). Learning communities, both faculty and student, can provide individuals, colleges, and universities with a means for achieving success in a rapidly changing world.

TABLE 1.3

*Senge's Five Components of a Learning Organization
and Ways that Faculty Learning Communities Enable Them*

GENERAL DESCRIPTION Senge (1990)	TRANSFORMING COLLEGES AND UNIVERSITIES INTO LEARNING ORGANIZATIONS Patrick and Fletcher (1998)	WAYS THAT FACULTY LEARNING COMMUNITIES ENABLE SENGE'S FIVE COMPONENTS OF A LEARNING ORGANIZATION
SYSTEMS THINKING View of the system as a whole, a conceptual framework providing connections between units and members; the shared process of reflection, reevaluation, action, and reward	Creation and recovery of a common language and processes across departments and divisions; setting and honoring institutional missions, goals, actions, and rewards	Time, funding, safety, teams, and rewards to enable multidisciplinary participants to discover, reflect on, and assess pedagogical and institutional systems; members' discovery and appreciation of the synergy of connected campus units
PERSONAL MASTERY Support for individuals to achieve their maximum potential as experts in their fields and to address opportunities and problems in new and creative ways	Support for faculty to continue as experts in their disciplines, yet broaden their scholarship beyond discovery to include integration, application, and teaching, particularly multidisciplinary perspectives	Development of individual teaching projects to address opportunities or shortcomings in one's teaching and learning; a developmental introduction to and practice of the scholarship of teaching with multidisciplinary perspectives; becoming an expert teacher inside and outside one's discipline

Building a Shared Vision	Collaborative creation of organizational goals, identity, visions, and actions shared by members; outcomes a result of teamwork, with each individual's contribution an integral part	Sharing of departmental and disciplinary visions across disciplines; identifying joint approaches to issues such as implementing student learning communities, improving student learning, integration of technology; creation of an intellectual community	Development of pedagogical goals and joint approaches in each community and sharing these with the campus, e.g., using technology in teaching, inclusiveness of classroom and curriculum, active learning, assessment of learning; discussion of campuswide issues; taking positions and action
Team Learning	Creation of opportunities for individuals to work and learn together in a community where it is safe to innovate, learn, and try anew	Colleges and universities with "learning communities for teaching and research with colleagues and students" (p. 162)	Team learning—the heart and purpose of a faculty learning community

Journey's End

OUR QUEST FOR COMMUNITY IN HIGHER EDUCATION has taken us from school to college or university, from face-to face to virtual, from home and neighborhood to classroom, and from early-career to senior colleagues. A disequilibrium in our lives may cause us to seek community: a personal loss, the desire to break an addiction, or a national tragedy. As teachers, it may be our need for survival in the academy, the inquisitiveness to try something new, the surprise of facing different students, or the challenge of teaching a new course. Parker Palmer (1998) writes, "The growth of any craft depends on shared practice and honest dialogue among the people who do it. We grow by private trial and error to be sure—but our willingness to try and fail, as individuals, is severely limited when we are not supported by a community that encourages such risks" (p. 144). Gabelnick, et al., (1990) implore us "to create programs that bring us together structurally in some cases, intellectually and emotionally in others. Learning communities are one way that we may build the commonalties and connections so essential to our education and our society" (p. 92). Why is this so hard to do? Why are there barriers to earning and investing the social capital that community can bring to life and learning? I encourage you to include building and involving community in your classrooms, your departments, your institution, and your life. Your loved ones, colleagues, and students will be the beneficiaries.

●

Milton D. Cox is the university director for teaching effectiveness, Miami University, Oxford, Ohio.

References

Angelo, T.A., and Cross, K. P. 1993. *Classroom assessment techniques: A handbook for college teachers.* 2d ed. San Francisco: Jossey-Bass.

Austin, A. E. 1992. Supporting junior faculty through a teaching fellow program. In M.D. Sorcinelli & A.E. Austin (Eds.), *Developing new and junior faculty* (pp. 73-86) New Directions for Teaching and Learning, No. 50. San Francisco: Jossey-Bass.

Barr, R. B. 1998. Obstacles to implementing the learning paradigm. *About Campus 3* (4): 18–25 (September/October).

Barr, R. B., and Tagg, J. 1995. From teaching to learning—A new paradigm for undergraduate education. *Change* 27 (6): 13–25 (November/December).

Boice, R. 1992. *The new faculty member: Supporting and fostering professional development.* San Francisco: Jossey-Bass.

Bransford, J. D., Brown, A. L., and Cocking, R. R., eds. 2000. *How people learn: Brain, mind, experience, and school.* Washington, D.C.: National Academy Press.

Cox, M. D. 1995. The development of new and junior faculty. In *Teaching improvement practices: Successful strategies for higher education,* eds. W. A. Wright and Associates, 283–310. Bolton, MA: Anker.

——. 1997. Long-term patterns in a mentoring program for junior faculty: Recommendations for practice. *To Improve the Academy* 16:225–68.

——. 2001a. Faculty learning communities: Change agents for transforming institutions into learning in organizations. *To Improve the Academy* 19:69–93.

——., ed. 2001b. *Teaching communities, grants, resources, and events: 2001-02.* Oxford, OH: Miami University.

Cross, K. P. 1998. Why learning communities? Why now? *About Campus* (July/August): 4–11.

Dewey, J. 1933. *How we think.* Lexington, MA: Heath.

Fulton, C., and Licklider, B. L. 1998. Supporting faculty development in an era of change. *To Improve the Academy* 19:51–66.

Gabelnick, F., MacGregor, J., Matthews, R. S., and Smith, B. L. 1990. *Learning communities: Creating connections among students, faculty, and disciplines.* New Directions for Teaching and Learning, no. 41. San Francisco: Jossey-Bass.

Gillespie, K. H., Hilsen, L. R., and Wadsworth, E. C., eds. 2002. *A guide to faculty development: Practical advice, examples, and resources.* Bolton, MA: Anker.

Harper, V. 1996. Establishing a community of conversation: Creating a context for self-reflection among teacher-scholars. *To Improve the Academy* 15:251–66.

Johnson, D. W., Johnson, R. T., and Smith, K. A. 1998. *Active learning: Cooperation in the college classroom.* Edina, MN: Interaction.

Jones, R. 1981. *Experiment at evergreen.* Cambridge, MA: Shenkman.

Karpiak, I. E. 1997. University professors at mid-life: Being a part of … but feeling apart. *To Improve the Academy* 16:21–40.

Kember, D. 2000. *Action learning and action research.* Sterling, VA: Stylus.

Kurfiss, J., and Boice, R. 1990. Current and desired faculty development practices among POD members. *To Improve the Academy* 9:73–82.

Levine, J. H., and Shapiro, N. E. 2000. Hogwarts—The learning community. *About Campus* 5 (4): 8–13 (September/October).

MacGregor, J., Tinto, V., and Lindbald, J. H. 2000. Assessment of innovative efforts: Lessons from the learning community movement. In *Assessment to promote deep learning: Insight from AAHE's 2000 and 1999 assessment conferences,* ed. L. Suskie, 41-8. Washington, D.C.: AAHE.

McGill, I., and Beaty, L. 2001. *Action learning.* 2d ed. Sterling, VA: Stylus.

Meiklejohn, A. 1932. *The experimental college.* New York: HarperCollins.

Palloff, R. M., and Pratt, K. 1999. *Building learning communities in cyberspace.* San Francisco: Jossey-Bass.

Patrick, S. K., and Fletcher, J. J. 1998. Faculty developers as change agents: Transforming colleges and universities into learning organizations. *To Improve the Academy* 17:155-70.

Putnam, R. D. 2000. *Bowling alone: The collapse and revival of American community.* New York: Simon and Schuster.

Quinlan, K. M. 1996. Involving peers in the evaluation and improvement of teaching: A menu of strategies. *Innovative Higher Education* 20 (4): 299-307.

Rice, R. E., Sorcinelli, M. D., and Austin, A. E. 2000. *Heeding new voices: Academic careers for a new generation.* New Pathways: Faculty Careers and Employment for the Twenty-first Century Series, inquiry no. 7. Washington, D.C.: AAHE.

Senge, P. M. 1990. *The fifth discipline.* New York: Doubleday.

———. 2000. The academy as learning community: Contradiction in terms or realizable future? In *Leading academic change: Essential roles for department chairs,* eds. A. F. Lucas and Associates, 275-300. San Francisco: Jossey-Bass.

Shapiro, N. S., and Levine, J. H. 1999. *Creating learning communities: A practical guide to winning support, organizing for change, and implementing programs.* San Francisco: Jossey-Bass.

Sorcinelli, M. D. 1992. New and junior faculty stress: Research and responses. In *Developing new and junior faculty,* New Directions for Teaching and Learning, no. 50, eds. M. D. Sorcinelli and A. E. Austin, 27-37. San Francisco: Jossey-Bass.

Suskie, L., ed. 2000. *Assessment to promote deep learning: Insight from AAHE's 2000 and 1999 assessment conferences.* Washington, D.C.: AAHE.

Taylor, P. G. 1997. Creating environments which nurture development: Messages from research into academics' experiences. *The International Journal for Academic Development* 2 (2): 42-9.

Tinto, V. 1995. Learning communities, collaborative learning, and the pedagogy of educational citizenship. *AAHE Bulletin* 47 (7): 11-3 (March).

Tuckman, B. W. 1965. Development sequence in small groups. *Psychological Bulletin* (June): 384-99.

Wright, W. A., and O'Neil, M. C. 1995. Teaching improvement practices: International perspectives. In *Teaching improvement practices: Successful strategies for higher education,* eds. W. A. Wright and Associates, 1-57. Bolton, MA: Anker.

2

DIVERSITY
and NEW
ROLES
for Faculty Developers

Devorah Lieberman
PORTLAND STATE UNIVERSITY

Alan E. Guskin
ANTIOCH UNIVERSITY

●

*O*ne *of the most important pressures for reform* facing higher education today is a direct result of the demographic changes that have been occurring in the United States for some time. Confronted with sharp increases in domestic, international and immigrant peoples of color, as well as older adult learners, and a growing expectation that nearly everyone should go to college, colleges and universities have had to face the reality that their academic and nonacademic programs need to undergo significant changes. These reforms need to respond to new educational needs and be appropriate for both majority as well as minority students.

At the same time that colleges and universities are responding to the needs of a more diverse student population, they also are facing great financial pressures and the need to undertake significant changes in how technology is used in all aspects of college life. These forces for reform will create new and powerful demands on the nature of the curriculum and faculty work. Success in these reform efforts will depend on members of the academic community, students, and community stakeholders. Faculty developers have a critical role in helping to shape and deliver the support needed for reform.

Diversity Data and Higher Education

The growth and changes in American society and its commitment to higher education for all qualified students has meant tremendous increases in the number of colleges and university students. For example, student enrollment in higher education increased from 156,756 in 1880, to 597,880 in 1920, to 3,639,847 in 1960, and to 14,304,803 in 1994 (Snyder 1997). As enrollment increased, so did student diversity. The following data illustrate this. As of 2001, higher education was 28% nonwhite, 55% female, and 43% over the age of twenty-five. The increase in African American students (40.2%) between 1976 and 1994 was greater than that of Caucasian students (14.8%) (Nettles and Perna 1997). Latino enrollment has increased by 39.6% since 1990. Carter and Wilson (1997) claim that the 4.6% increase in Latino enrollment in 1995 was the largest one-year gain among the four major ethnic groups. The Asian American student enrollment has doubled since 1980, with the largest growth at the four-year institutions (Carter and Wilson 1997). In 1992, the Asian American enrollment accounted for nearly 5% of the total enrollment at colleges and universities (U.S. Department of Education 1995). Finally, international student enrollment in 1996/97 was a record high with 457,984 students (Desruisseaux 1997).

At no other time in the history of the United States has higher education been as diverse as it is today. Yet, the response of higher education to these changes in the ethnicity, culture and socioeconomic backgrounds of these students has been fairly slow and usually piecemeal. The result is that while the statistics have shown an increasing balance among the students from different backgrounds, the gap between minority and majority representation is still wide. The results demonstrate that there have been, for some time, growing concerns about this gap and its impact on students and the colleges and universities they attend. Examples of these concerns are:

1. Feelings of marginality among diverse students (i.e., students from nonmajority backgrounds) in the higher education environment
2. The lack of coursework dealing with the backgrounds of these diverse students across the higher education curriculum

3. The exclusion of content or inaccurate historical representation within the curriculum content dealing with the social and cultural backgrounds of diverse students
4. The greater disparity in minority representation among student populations between undergraduate and graduate schools
5. Traditional hiring practices of content specialists within the discipline, without consideration for the diversity that candidates bring to a department or the demographics of students enrolled in departmental offerings
6. Ineffective retention methods for supporting junior minority faculty as they proceed through the promotion and tenure process, given the special demands placed on them by students, the institution and sometimes the communities in which they must live while working at the university

National Models for Campuswide Diversity Initiatives

As pressures from the need to maintain enrollment and the changing nature of the societal demographics on institutions intensify, diversity is an issue that is being taken ever more seriously. The following examples spotlight some institutions that are focusing financial and human resources on diversity recruitment and retention within their student bodies, their faculties, and their staffs.

Arizona State University
(www.asu.edu/provost/intergroup)

President Lattie Coor publicly proclaimed that cultural diversity would be central to the university's core mission and goals. In particular, in 1997, ASU formed an Intergroup Relations Center (IRC) that focused on positive relations among students, staff, faculty and administrators. The IRC assumed that diversity is an asset for campus climate and sought to provide activities that promoted this philosophy among all levels of the campus. The IRC had three basic goals: (1) intergroup education and training for the campus community; (2) a clearing house for information and intergroup relations at ASU; (3) support provided for research on the impact of programs activities on intergroup relations as well as information that faculty can use to revise and develop course curricula (Hurtado, Milem, Clayton-Pedersen, and Allen 1999).

University of California at Los Angeles
http://www.orientation.ucla.edu/guidepages/56.htm

UCLA CREATED A DIVERSITY COUNCIL that addressed diversity across the campus, in particular the racial demographics and conflict. In response to their assessment, a Conflict Mediation Program was designed. This program supports forty-five students, staff and faculty each year who design campus-based activities to reduce racial tensions and enhance improved intercultural and interethnic communication. This is tied to a credit-bearing course for students entitled, "Diversity, Conflict and Conflict Resolution." The program is an effort to increase educational opportunities for previously excluded groups. They also created the Center for the Study and Resolution of Interracial/Interethnic Conflict. The center supports faculty research that addresses issues of diversity, intercultural communication and culturally based conflict management (Hurtado et al. 1999).

The University of Michigan
http://www.bannisterdesign.com/diversity

THE UNIVERSITY OF MICHIGAN CREATED a Dialogues on Diversity forum to address diversity issues. Dialogues on Diversity is a campuswide initiative providing opportunities for the open exchange of views about the value of diversity. Their objective is to enrich campus discussion and facilitate honest dialogue concerning the broad range of topics relating to diversity. The Dialogues on Diversity partners with the Resident Education and the Program on Intergroup relations to provide two programming resources for residence staff: Pizza Dinner Discussions and Movie Nights. The Pizza Dinner Discussions take place in the residence halls among friends and hallmates. The Pizza Dinner Discussion Program creates a forum for residents to communicate their opinions on and experiences with diversity. Pizza Dinner Discussions topics have included:

- Examining multiple identities to introduce residents and analyze the effects of social categorization
- Affirmative action lawsuits against the University of Michigan
- Self-segregation observed in the dining halls and within student organizations
- Sexual orientation and religion
- Gender role expectations

Movie Nights is a partnership with Michigan Cable Network and Swank Motion Pictures' Residence Life Cinema and Dialogues on Diversity. The Movie Night program comprises a full-length screening of a box office hit, refreshments, and a facilitated discussion. The movies are selected because they contain issues of diversity that will lead to viewer discussion focused on deepening diversity awareness and raising cultural competencies.

Vanderbilt University
http://www.prometheus.vanderbilt.edu/odc/training

Vanderbilt university developed the Diversity Opportunity Tool (dot), which is an electronic program designed to address conflict management and interracial/intercultural communication strategies. This tool, grounded in theory, research and application, is designed so that when students are in interracial/intercultural interactions that need particular communication tools, the dot will provide them with strategic appropriate communication options. Individual students, trained by advisors, and also used within the classroom setting, use the dot. It is accompanied by a facilitator's manual (Hurtado et al. 1999).

Ohio State University, University of North Carolina and University of Washington Law School

These three institutions created the Diversity Discussion Workbook, which is embedded in and used extensively across the curricula. The workbook contains vignettes that are fairly typical of interracial/intercultural experiences that many students report experiencing on college campuses. The vignettes describe interracial/intercultural situations, with each situation ending without closure or resolution. This "open-ending" is followed by the phrase, "What is going on here?" The intent is for students to think about their interpretation of the vignette interactions and/or for a group of individuals to discuss their own perceptions of what occurred in the vignette.

The University of Wisconsin State System
http://www.wisc.edu

The state system designed a ten-year statewide plan, entitled the Design for Diversity, to increase underrepresented groups on all system campuses. The plan, a very ambitious program, states:

The problems associated with minority education and serving the needs of the economically disadvantaged cannot be short-term concerns. Similarly, this design for diversity should not be interpreted as a quick fix to a specific problem but rather as a series of long-term efforts designed to break the cycle of growing under-representation of minorities and economically disadvantaged people and to provide increased multicultural understanding and greater diversity throughout the system. Finally, this ambitious program cannot be successful without the cooperation and strong commitment from others—the elementary and secondary schools, state government, business and industry, community leadership, and young people and those who influence them. The uw System accepts and stands ready to fulfill its responsibilities and to work with others in this very important area.

The plan's goal is to have a statewide system adopt a multicultural teaching and learning environment focused on preparing students to live and contribute to a multicultural society. This plan is specific in pursuing goals for significant increases in diverse student enrollment, diverse faculty and staff hiring, and relationships with other institutions to increase the "pipeline" of students of color going on to college.

UNIVERSITY OF MARYLAND, COLLEGE PARK
http://www.diversityweb.org/manual

THE UNIVERSITY OF MARYLAND, COLLEGE PARK is an institution that has demonstrated much success with its diversity initiative. The university 's commitment to diversity has been expansive. The UMCP president, in 1984, publicly declared the diversity initiative a priority across the campus. This has resulted in organized efforts to provide resources for diversity hiring among faculty and administrators and resources allocated for recruiting diverse students (Diversity Blueprint 1998). The percentage of minority faculty, administrators and staff has increased 38%. Diversity among the student population has increased significantly. Students of color comprise 28% and international students comprise 8%. The DiversityWeb Web site, supported by the university, receives thousands of hits each day. The degree of diversity resources on this Web site exceed any other Web site of this type. The Web site is a joint effort of the University of Maryland and the Association of American Colleges and Universities. It offers diversity information that ranges from good practices, useful resources and diversity initiatives from across higher education. Within the DiversityWeb is the Diversity Newsroom, a database of resource materials for the media offering articles reports, surveys, news stories, and other materials highlighting the value of diversity on campus (http://diversityweb.org).

PORTLAND STATE UNIVERSITY
http://www.president.pdx.edu/initiativehome.phtml

IN 1997, PRESIDENT BERNSTINE, the new Portland State University president, identified a group of faculty, staff and students to become the presidentially appointed Commission on Campus Climate and Life. The president charged this group with assessing the climate for student learning at PSU and to make recommendations for its improvement. Over an eighteen-month period, they collected data and created a document citing thirty-eight points that could holistically enhance the campus climate for all students, staff, administrators and faculty. Diversity issues were a dominant theme throughout this final report which led the president to identify *diversity* as one of three campuswide Presidential Initiatives. He appointed a faculty member/administrator known on campus, as vice provost and special assistant to the president, to lead all presidential initiatives. This appointment communicated to the campus community the importance for the entire campus to participate in this initiative and to support its outcomes. The president's goal was that Portland State University would be a campus where majority and minority students choose to attend, where majority and minority faculty choose to teach and conduct research, and where majority and minority staff choose to work. A Diversity Action Council was formed. They developed a Diversity Action Plan that focuses on four goals that serve as recommendations for university direction and resource decisions as well as a five-year plan for the president's Diversity Initiative:

1. Create an institutional environment, curricula and scholarship that enhance learning about diversity and respect for diversity and equality.
2. Increase the number of students from underrepresented groups who apply, are accepted, enroll and graduate such that, at a minimum, they are represented proportionally to regional (for in-state students) and national (for out-of-state students) populations.

3. Increase the number of persons from underrepresented groups in the faculty, staff, and administration so that they are represented in proportion to their current availability in relevant job pools and/or their representation in the region.
4. Increase the number of sustained and mutually beneficial connections with diverse communities.

In addition to the Diversity Action Plan, the Diversity Action Council initiated the following activities:

- Meeting with departments who are hiring tenure-track positions to assist with designing a process that attracts the broadest pool of qualified candidates.
- Providing mini-grants to assist faculty with professional scholarship that address issues of diversity and to student groups to collaborate on a project that furthers diversity awareness across campus.
- Providing mini-grants to student groups who wish to collaboratively provide campuswide events that raise the visibility of diversity issues and diversity training.
- Providing term-long workshop series for faculty to redesign an existing course curriculum to include diversity issues that may otherwise have not been part of the curriculum.
- Providing a quarterly event designed for all diverse faculty, administrators and staff in order to create a "safe space" to meet and assist one another with sensitive issues.
- Providing an annual event designed for diverse undergraduate students to learn about graduate programs at PSU. At this event undergraduate students meet with diverse graduate students representing each college or school at PSU to talk about their experiences as graduate students at the university.
- Providing a monthly Focus on Diversity series open to all faculty, staff and students addressing issues of diversity related to curriculum design, classroom management and intercultural communication.
- Creating a rotating part-time faculty position (The Faculty in Residence for Diversity) in the Center for Academic Excellence that

focuses on coordinating a diversity newsletter, the diversity series, and a Diversity Institute.

THE FACULTY DEVELOPMENT PROFESSIONAL, DIVERSITY, AND HIGHER EDUCATION

THOUGH STUDENTS OF COLOR CONTINUE TO BE underrepresented in higher education relative to their representation in the college-age population, it is essential that the changes in the mosaic of the higher education population be considered when addressing campus climate, curriculum, faculty support and student support needs.

Morey and Kitano (1997, 16) sum up the types of changes needed:

1. Diversity should permeate the total campus environment. A comprehensive approach requires organizational management and change directed at diversity-focused hiring and faculty development and specific attention to the informal, hidden curriculum.
2. Content and materials should reflect the cultural characteristics and experiences of the students, critically examine social realities and conflict in United States and world societies, include the study of various cultural groups and historical experiences, and present and analyze diverse perspectives.
3. Instructional strategies should communicate high expectations for achievement, capitalize on students' experiences and learning strengths, and include opportunities for personal participation and growth.
4. Objectives should include fostering of skills important to informed citizenship, such as critical thinking decision-making, social participation, and intergroup interaction.
5. Assessment procedures should include methods that accommodate students' strongest strategies for expression of accumulated knowledge and skills.
6. Evaluation should be ongoing and systematic with relationship to multicultural-education goals and objectives.

Research indicates that when these types of programs have been implemented there is positive academic and personal impact on the students involved in these diversity initiatives. Daryl Smith (Diversity Digest 1998) writes:

> Indeed, it is clear that a focus on diversity often raises issues, which have needed attention for some time. Student success in the form of graduation rates, the significance of mentors, the campus climate for many students, issues of community, intergroup and intra-group relations, links between class and out of class learning have been concerns for many years in higher education. Recent diversity efforts, taken serious from an institutional point of view, can prompt fundamental improvements in these areas.

Smith, one of the major scholars on diversity issues, continues:

> Evidence in the literature suggests that comprehensive institutional change in teaching methods, curriculum, campus climate, and institutional definition provides educational benefits for both minority and majority students. Comprehensive diversity initiatives, beyond their capacity to improve access and retention for underrepresented groups, are related to satisfaction, academic success, and cognitive development of students (www.diversityweb.org/Digest/Sp98/complexity.html).

Smith's message, in effect, is that significant institutional change is needed in how colleges and universities educate students, whether minority or majority. Within this context, faculty development should take on new functions in order to support faculty members and administrators to develop the kind of institutional changes necessary to create new ways of educating minority and majority students in the first decade of the twenty-first century. These new roles break with the common expectations for faculty developers. For example, scholars of multicultural education tend to think about the importance of faculty development in terms of what can be offered in classroom and faculty support (Banks 1988; Suzuki 1984). Marchesani and Adams (1992) refer to faculty development support in terms of four dimensions: (1) understanding how students from diverse backgrounds experience the classroom; (2) faculty understanding of the diversity they personally bring to the classroom environment; (3) integrating diverse perspectives into the course curriculum; and (4) expanding teaching styles to encompass diverse learning styles.

As institutional demographics, missions, goals, and expectations change and institutions strive to deal with them, significant reforms will be needed in how faculty teach and students learn. To fulfill these needs it will be important for faculty development professionals to be recognized as important resources in these efforts. Table 2.1 begins to address some current responsibilities of faculty developers and new roles they will need to perform in order to support the institutional reforms necessary to educate minority and majority students in the beginning of the twenty-first century (Lieberman and Guskin, in press).

The following discussion elaborates on the role of faculty developers in supporting reforms in educating minority and majority students, especially as they relate to issues of diversity and multicultural education.

TABLE 2.1
Changing Responsibilities and Roles

Current Responsibilities	New Roles
Developing effective classroom techniques that meet student needs	Supporting faculty to effectively mentor students and to lead intensive discussion/workshop-type sessions
Increasing effectiveness of classroom evaluation systems	Creating assessment instruments to measure student learning
Creating new courses and syllabi that meet student needs	Creating standards for student learning outcomes to be measured by assessment tools independent of faculty teaching students Creating alternatives to present calendar for offering student learning experience, e.g., accelerated learning formats Creating new courses to address learning needs of diverse students, e.g., School of Ethnic Studies
Making problem-based learning relevant to current students	Creating community-based learning experiences that are problem-based where faculty members act as lead consultants working with diverse community partners

Continued on next page

TABLE 2.1—*Continued*

Current Responsibilities	New Roles
Utilizing technology to meet student learning needs	Developing content software/adaptation of "off the shelf" software to provide options beyond traditional classroom environment Developing online learning environments
Supporting students to do library research	Working in partnership with librarians to provide individualized learning environments for students; partnering with librarians who serve as the primary guide to information resources
Supporting interdisciplinary partnerships	Developing learning communities that integrate a number of different learning environments (i.e., community engagements, individualized and peers learning formats, integration of technology) and assess student learning outcomes in ways other than traditional grades and credit hours.
Supporting faculty to integrate their research interests and their teaching	Encouraging and supporting faculty to expand their conceptions of scholarship to include the scholarship of teaching and learning, the scholarship of community engagement, and scholarship that has a diversity focus
Faculty support of promotion and tenure materials	Aligning faculty reward structures so that they reflect commitment to diversity initiatives in higher education

Mentoring Student Discussion Leaders

As education becomes more student-centered, it will be necessary to change how faculty teach and work. Faculty no longer will be expected to stand in front of the classroom, lecture as the expert and the knowledge disseminator, and then assess and grade the student on how much of this knowledge they retained. Faculty will become facilitators of and mentors for student learning, creating learning environments that encourage the student to learn more independently. Examples of student-centered learning in these environments might include more group work, more classroom discussion, student-to-student interaction in a virtual environment, or community-based learning projects. As these new learning-centered environments are developed, it will be necessary to consider student diversity, whether it is diversity of learning styles, of gender, of ethnicity, religion, or of sexual preference. Light (2001) points out that students report the diversity student-centered classrooms are an aide to learning, "Student after student asserts that when the campus atmosphere encourages such assumptions, the diversity [in the classroom] leads to several kinds of learning from those who are ethnically or racially different" (p. 133).

Faculty developers will be a much needed resource to faculty as they shift from the "teacher-centered classroom" to deal with "learner-centered environments, especially as they are focused on issues of diversity." Faculty developers will be able to offer assistance through several avenues. First, there should be a resource library available to all faculty that includes literature on:

- adapting the multicultural learning environment to the student-centered learning environment
- encouraging problem-based learning
- creating student project groups that are inclusive and assist student learning
- fostering community-based learning
- enhancing inclusiveness in the classroom
- increasing ethnicity in the classroom
- providing effective learning in the virtual environment
- facilitating group discussion

Second, faculty developers should be available for one-on-one assistance to faculty as they design course curricula and as they strive to create a classroom environment that is welcoming and encouraging to traditional content-based topics as well as "hot, sensitive, or emotionally charged topics." Faculty development professionals should provide workshops and institutes that address diversity of student composition across the curricula and within the classroom environment.

Creating Assessment Instruments to Measure Student Learning

INSTITUTIONS OF HIGHER EDUCATION ARE INCREASINGLY including phrases in their mission statements or general education student learning outcomes such as "appreciation of diversity" or "ability to communicate with diverse individuals." If such issues of diversity are part of the expectations for student learning, then this learning must be demonstrated and assessed. Faculty are comfortable assessing student learning content that is related to discipline-based content. While most faculty might agree that diversity outcomes are an important part of the student experience, they generally do not feel comfortable designing assessment tools to measure them.

It is highly likely that faculty will welcome assistance from faculty developers in the creation of assessment tools that address the student learning outcomes that are not part of their traditional discipline content. A few of these assessment instruments might include student demonstration of their ability to communicate and interact in intercultural settings (Suzuki, Ponterotto and Mellers 2001).

Creating Courses for Diverse Students

CURRICULUM DESIGN AND COURSE CONTENT IN higher education is dynamic. As institutions increasingly address diversity content within the curriculum, faculty will need support to create courses and areas of study that address specific "diverse" areas of study. If diversity issues are woven throughout the curriculum it will challenge faculty teaching traditional courses to ask questions about the historical accuracy of what the students are studying as well as broaden student thinking in the traditional curriculum. If courses are devoted entirely to areas of diversity, students will be provided an academic environment in which to study these areas in depth.

Irrespective of whether diversity is integrated throughout the curriculum or whether courses and areas of study are tagged as "diversity" content courses, faculty developers have a significant role in curriculum transformation. Faculty developers can provide welcome assistance in (1) helping to define diversity for the teaching faculty, (2) helping to identify appropriate diversity student learning outcomes for the course curriculum, (3) helping to assist with virtual, face-to-face, or community-based activities that should lead to the diversity student learning outcomes, (4) serving as liaisons to the community for the community-based learning activities, (5) helping to identify diversity rubrics for assessing the student work samples, and, (6) helping identify evaluation tools to assess the student work samples. Faculty developers do not need to be the campus experts in each of the diversity areas, but in concert with librarians, they can guide faculty to important resources, give personal assistance, or serve as brokers to the appropriate on- and off-campus personnel who are considered the diversity content experts.

CREATING COMMUNITY LEARNING EXPERIENCES

AS DIVERSITY BECOMES FULLY INTEGRATED into the university curricula, faculty will continue to expand their traditional courses to reflect these diversity issues, especially in the area of community-based learning experiences. In order to provide greater opportunities for interactions with diverse communities, raise awareness of diverse communities, and create opportunities for students to achieve diverse student learning outcomes, faculty will need to integrate community engagement projects within their course curricula. Integrating community engagement projects into a course requires time and expertise that are beyond many faculty members' experiences. Faculty developers can serve to support faculty members in identifying diverse student learning outcomes specifically related to community engagement. They also may help in identifying appropriate community-based partners, in educating students and community partners on liability issues related to community engagement, and, in helping faculty understand how to assess and grade students on the community engagement experience.

Many campuses create "service learning" offices where faculty developers serve the campus needs. Other campuses create offices that blend together the faculty development professionals who assist faculty with teaching and learning issues, all community engagement issues, and all assessment. Portland State University is an example of a campus that is designed in the latter format. The PSU Center for Academic Excellence is the campus office that provides assistance for all teaching and learning issues, community-based learning, and assessment. The message to faculty is that these three components are blended, each as important as the other, and each an important factor in the overall course design and delivery (http://www.oaa.pdx.edu/cae).

Developing Technology Options

THE ROLE OF TECHNOLOGY IS BEGINNING to change how students learn and, likely, will transform student learning experiences in the future. The recent improvements in information and computer technologies are likely to continue to develop at an ever increasing pace—especially in the area of sophisticated content-oriented software—which will enable institutions of higher education to further integrate technology into the core of the educational process. Newman and Scurry (2001) emphasized this point in a recent article:

> As the inexorable improvement in digital technology continues, and we gain a better understanding of how to use it, we will experience further improvements in the capacity, reliability, cost effectiveness and ease of use. Soon it will be impossible, even with great effort, to achieve the same learning results without the use of technology that we can achieve with it.

Diversity issues must be addressed as courses become more dependent on electronic delivery. The diversity of the learner is an important component in this format. Diversity may mean differences in age, socioeconomic and learning styles of students. For example, many adult learners who cannot attend classes due to work and family obligations may be able to take advantage of educational opportunities provided by asynchronous course delivery. With asynchronous or hybrid delivery, a combination of face-to-face and distance education, students are able to maintain their employment and/or familial responsibilities as well as meet their academic responsibilities.

Faculty development professionals can provide very important services in the electronic environment by providing faculty with skills to create an environment that achieves the expected student learning. Developers can assist the faculty in answering such questions as:

- What can the student learner achieve in the face-to-face environment that is impossible in the electronic environment?
- What can the student learner achieve in the online environment that would be impossible in the face-to-face environment?
- Are there "hybrid" settings that combine face-to-face and online settings that can be both educationally successful and cost effective?

The answers to these questions, coupled with specific student learning outcomes, can guide the electronically oriented learning activities and the pedagogies that will shape the type of educational settings in which students will learn and faculty teach. Faculty developers and instructional designers working in concert can provide indispensable support for faculty teaching in this environment.

Partnering with Librarians

Students coming to college arrive with limited library skills, yet understanding how to use library resources is an essential part of every student's education. Today, and especially in the years ahead, access to library resources will be ubiquitous—from home, places of work, the library itself, almost anywhere that computer access is available. However, there may be obstacles to achieving effective access to library resources.

- Students holding full-time employment may not have the time or opportunity to have a physical presence in the library.
- Students who do not have access to technology when off-campus will not be able to take advantage of the ubiquitous library resources.
- Students who did not receive "training" in using technology to access the library resources may find the electronic library options intimidating, off-putting, or impossible.

Faculty development professionals play an important role in helping students achieve the greatest use of library resources. Because of their relationship with both faculty members and librarians, faculty development professionals can arrange and broker sessions that the librarians conduct for faculty, for students, and for individual classes.

Also, the more faculty developers work with librarians in faculty development activities, the more likely librarians will be invited to participate with faculty members in course development. For example, at Portland State University, faculty are encouraged to integrate diversity issues into their courses. The faculty development office (Center for Academic Excellence) conducts a diversity series addressing specific ways faculty can design a new course or redesign an existing curriculum to include diversity issues. Including librarians in these sessions serves to link faculty members with librarians and provide a forum for librarians to articulate all the services they can provide for the faculty and the students.

Developing Learning Communities and Assessing Learning

As higher education evolves, institutions will continue to experiment with alternative learning environments. These environments may encourage students to learn independently; for example, students working independently in electronic environments or on individualized learning programs. The focus on student-centered learning environments may mean that students learn more from each other rather than from the instructor or the course materials. This codependent environment may be through peer learning formats on campus independent of ongoing instructor presence. To meet student and institutional needs, these environments also may assume different credit hour formats, meeting times, and grading options.

As educators "test" and "assess" student learning within these different formats, diversity will be an important factor. Among students, different learning styles, different ethnicities, and student abilities will need to be addressed. Therefore, the instructor cannot assume that teaching in a nontraditional format will enable all students to be successful. Matching student capabilities and interests with alternative learning formats can be beneficial to the overall environment as well as those with needs to be addressed. For example, if a course is community based and there are students with disabilities, the faculty member needs to address these issues with the students prior to introducing the community-based class or community-based course component.

Faculty development professionals have a very important role in assisting with these nontraditional courses and helping faculty address the diversity variables within these alternative formats. For example, Portland State's motto is "Let Knowledge Serve the City." In efforts to achieve this motto, approximately 6,700 junior and senior students per year are working in the community with community organizations, businesses, or partners. These students study in 250 courses each year. Many of the community partners comprise diverse populations that are not familiar with PSU students and vice versa. Toward the beginning of the term a faculty development professional participates in each course assisting the students and the community partner with intercultural communication skills. These activities serve to raise student and community partner awareness about the benefits of interacting with diverse individuals as well as providing skills to help achieve this success.

Aligning Rewards with Commitments

Institutional commitment to diversity appears in institutional mission statements across the country. Most often this commitment is expressed as creating an environment that encourages diversity among its faculty and staff while also integrating diversity into the curricula. It is not clear to many faculty *how* to meet the diversity goals stated in the institutional mission statement. Faculty development professionals can be an important resource by assisting faculty to incorporate diversity into their research and their course curricula. They also can help faculty document these activities for purposes of promotion, tenure and merit.

Faculty developers can offer tremendous assistance in helping develop course curricula that weave diversity throughout. Integrating diversity into a course curriculum often reflects a scholarly approach to the classroom and student-centered learning (Morey and Kitano 1997). As faculty document these approaches to creating a multicultural curriculum and integrating diversity into their scholarship, promotion and tenure committees will begin to recognize and value these activities as part of institutional change.

Diversity, Institutional Change, Faculty Development and Student Success

As demographics change across the country and institutions of higher education make efforts to address these changes, it is imperative that administrators and faculty take the initiative to create an environment that encourages success. Success will be reflected and measured in the following increases: diverse student recruitment, retention and learning achievement, educational access, diverse faculty recruitment and retention, career placement and community engagement.

The role of faculty development professionals is critical within this ever-changing environment. Faculty development professionals are those campus-based individuals who provide the necessary support to faculty, staff, and administrators toward achieving these goals. Professionals within the field of faculty development accept the responsibility that their skills will be in increasing demand as institutions of higher education strive to meet the expectations of students, faculty, administrators, and community members.

•

Devorah Lieberman is vice provost and special assistant to the president at the Center for Academic Excellence, Portland State University.

Alan E. Guskin is codirector and senior scholar for the Project on the Future of Higher Education, distinguished university professor, and university president emeritus, Antioch University.

REFERENCES

Banks, J. A. 1994. *Multiethnic education: Theory and practice,* 2d ed. Boston: Allyn and Bacon.

Carter, D. J. and Wilson, R. 1997. Minorities in higher education. *Fifteenth annual status report 1996–1997.* Washington, D.C.: American Council on Education.

Desruisseaux, P. 1997. Foreign enrollment rises slightly at colleges in the United States. *Chronicle of Higher Education* (12 December).

Hurtado, S., Milem, J., Clayton-Pederson, A., and Allen, W. 1999. *Enacting diverse learning environments: Improving the climate for racial/ethnic diversity in higher education 26(8).* Washington, D.C.: ERIC Clearinghouse on Higher Education and George Washington University.

Lieberman, D., and Guskin, A. (in press). The essential role of faculty development in the "new higher education model." In *To improve the academy,* ed. C. Wehlburg, Vol. 21. Boston, MA: Anker Publishing.

Light, R. 2001. *Making the most of college: Students speak their minds.* Cambridge, MA: Harvard University Press.

Marchesani, L. S., and Adams, M. 1992. New directors for teaching and learning, 52. In *Promoting diversity in college classrooms: Innovative responses for the curricula, faculty, and institutions,* ed. M. Adams, 9–19. San Francisco: Jossey-Bass.

Morey, A. I., and Kitano, M. K. 1997. *Multicultural course transformation in higher education: A broader truth.* Boston: Allyn and Bacon.

Nettles, M. T., and Perna, L. 1997. *The African American education data book: Higher and adult education.* Vol. 1. Fairfax, VA: The College Fund/United Negro College Fund.

Newman, F., and Scurry, J. 2001. Online technology pushes pedagogy to the forefront. *Chronicle of Higher Education* 13 (July): B7

Office of Human Relations Programs in Collaboration with Associates at the University of Maryland, College Park and the Association of American Colleges and Universities. 1998. *Diversity blueprint: A planning manual for colleges and universities.* Washington, D.C: Association of American Colleges and Universities.

Smith, D. G. 1998. http://www.diversityweb.org/Digest/SP98.

Snyder, T. D. 1997. *Digest of education statistics.* U.S. Department of Education, National Center for Education Statistics. NCES 98-015. Washington, D.C.: U.S. Government Printing Office.

Suzuki, B. H. 1984. Curriculum transformation for multicultural education. *Education and Urban Society* 16(3): 294–322.

Suzuki, L. A., Ponterotto, J. G., and Meller, P. J., eds. 2001. *Handbook of multicultural assessment.* 2d ed. San Francisco: Jossey Bass.

U.S. Bureau of the Census. Current Population Reports Series. 1998. *Population profile of the United States: 1997.* Washington, D.C: U.S. Government Printing Office, pp. 23–194.

U.S. Department of Education. National Center for Education Statistics. 1995. *The condition of education.* Washington, D.C.: U.S. Government Printing Office.

·3

COMPUTING
the VALUE *of*
Teaching Dialogues

Peter Magolda
MIAMI UNIVERSITY

Mark Connolly
UNIVERSITY OF WISCONSIN—MADISON

The world of knowledge

takes a crazy turn

When teachers themselves

are taught to learn

—Bertolt Brecht from his play
 The Life of Galileo

◆

*D*uring the summer of 1998, Peter attended a weeklong computer technology institute sponsored by his university. The institute's purpose was to introduce new campus technological advances in the hope that faculty would infuse these technologies into their classrooms. Throughout the week, participants learned technical skills (e.g., managing still images, streaming audio, and video files) and discussed topics such as the pros and cons of incorporating computer-mediated communication into college courses. One session, focusing on a course-management software package, interested him. It promised professors, among other things, the ability to create online discussion boards, initiate virtual chats with students, generate class rosters, and post online surveys and tests. Influenced by the ubiquity of computers and their seeming potential to deliver and redefine teaching, Peter decided to adopt these new innovations.

Following the institute, Peter tinkered with and tweaked his graduate-level education seminars courses (Stevens 1988) to meld these new digital advancements with his more conventional pedagogy. He created a Web site, uploaded course documents, e.g., syllabus, and added an online journal and Internet research assignments. He did not expect students to notice these changes, but they did. In fact, these *minor* modifications dramatically altered the rhythm of the seminar, disoriented students' ways of knowing, and shifted the classroom power dynamics, upending this educational experience for his students and him.

In this chapter, we use Peter's experiences of infusing new computer technologies into a seminar he taught exclusively for graduate teaching assistants (TA) in 1999 to initiate a frank and honest discussion about what it means to teach. (The concept of *teaching* throughout this chapter describes not only what happens in the classroom, but course and curriculum design.) This case study context is particularly relevant because the seminar format encouraged participants to engage in ongoing in-person and online conversations about teaching. Such dialogues are few and far between in higher education, and typically lack depth and duration. Lee Shulman, President of the Carnegie Foundation for the Advancement of Teaching, has argued for making teaching "community property"—that is, improving teaching practice by ending the solitary nature of college teaching by fostering community conversations about what constitutes good teaching (Shulman 1993). Conversation is a crucial component of every type of professional practice. Parker Palmer (1998) explains:

> No surgeon can do her work without being observed by others who know what she is doing, without participating in grand-round discussions of the patients she and her colleagues are treating. No trial lawyer can litigate without being observed and challenged by people who know the law. But professors conduct their practice as teachers in private. We walk into the classroom and close the door—figuratively and literally—on the daunting task of teaching. When we emerge, we rarely talk with each other about what we have done, or need to do. After all, what would we talk about? (p. 8)

We agree with Shulman's and Palmer's assertions that teaching is perhaps the most insular of all the public professions. Higher education needs to initiate public and communal conversation with colleagues about the craft of teaching. This chapter models and articulates the benefits of a public dialogue about teaching and how it can enhance college teaching and student learning.

Instructors are the focus of this chapter. Too often when rare public conversations about teaching occur, dialogues about instructors are eclipsed by student difficulties (e.g., they do not try hard enough), teaching techniques (e.g., how to grade group projects), and disciplinary knowledge. Typical approaches to helping faculty change their teaching dwell on the *how* and *what* of teaching, placing center-stage teaching techniques (Boice 1996; Davis 1993; McKeachie 1999), students, and subject-matter competencies. From this point of view, effective teaching is more about what one does and less about how (or whether) one sees oneself as a teacher. An introspective emphasis, focusing on, for example how instructors' self-understanding (i.e., who one is as a teacher) influences the learning process, plays a supporting role at best in these teaching conversations.

Teachers are dissuaded from talking about teaching because the university in general does not value teaching as much as research. Talking about teaching is often seen as a waste of time or suggests a lack of scholarly purpose (Clark 2001). Such dynamics discourage teachers from talking about teaching in general and their roles in the educational process in particular. This chapter brings these two issues closer to the center or axis of college teaching. High quality teaching requires instructors to connect with students, employ effective teaching techniques, possess disciplinary expertise, and most important understand themselves—especially the unconscious and habitual attitudes, assumptions, and values that guide their pedagogy. It is this latter issue of self-understanding with which instructors must grapple before they focus on other important teaching issues.

System Error: Case Study Overview

ALL GRADUATE STUDENTS TEACHING THE UNIVERSITY'S Career Development and the College Student seminar for the first time concurrently enroll in an advanced education seminar that I (Peter) teach. The seminar examines college teaching (e.g., philosophy of teaching, curriculum, evaluation) and career development issues (e.g., college choice, selecting an academic major). The seminar objectives are to (1) assess, develop, and enhance seminar participants' skills as instructors, (2) enhance seminar participants' career development expertise, and (3) identify and discuss pedagogical issues in higher education. The Boyer Commission (1998) report entitled *Reinventing Undergraduate Education: A Blueprint for America's Research Universities* concluded that graduate apprentice teachers benefit from seminars that encourage ongoing discussions about teaching, mentoring, supervision, and classroom challenges. The origins of this on-the-job seminar grew out of a perceived need for ongoing and substantive support for graduate apprentice teachers, based on the assumption that good teaching is related to formal preparation for teaching roles (Fuhrmann and Grasha 1983; Shulman 1987; Weimer 1990).

Throughout the semester, seminar participants (in addition to teaching their undergraduate career development seminar) attended the weekly instructor seminar, developed an individualized contract that articulates a teaching philosophy, course goals, and specific implementation strategies, wrote and posted a weekly reflective online journal entry for peers to read, visited another instructor's seminar for one session and wrote an assessment of their colleague's educational environment, read two books about teaching, and submitted a comprehensive teaching portfolio. Three paragraphs from the syllabus offer glimpses of course expectations, pedagogy, and technological enhancements:

> I created a web site for the seminar. We will make use of this site throughout the semester. It will be the primary means through which we communicate with each other between class meetings. The web site includes the syllabus, all electronic closed-reserved readings, weekly assignments, handouts, and assignment guidelines. The site also contains a discussion board and chat-room where seminar participants can post questions or comments or engage in virtual discussions. These online exchanges can easily be read by all seminar participants, which should enhance the quality of our in-class discussions. Seminar participants should visit the site on a regular basis—especially before each class meeting.

> Based on my belief that learning only takes place when learners discuss issues, share perceptions, disagree when necessary, and listen to each other, I expect everyone to share their candid thoughts and listen carefully to others' perspectives. Because we will explore together the teaching and learning process, I hope that we can create a comfortable learning environment. This requires reading in advance of the discussion so that everyone can bring ideas, comments, reactions, and questions to the discussion. This kind of learning environment should enable us to engage in genuine in-class and online dialogues about pedagogy and career development by reviewing the multiple perspectives that exist in the literature, reflecting

on our own experiences and beliefs, and listening to the experiences and beliefs of other seminar participants.

Learning only takes place when it is connected to learners' experiences. Thus, discussing abstract concepts of teaching in a sterile classroom environment is not an optimal setting to achieve our goals. Engaging in real teaching and learning, while simultaneously familiarizing oneself with the professional teaching and learning literature is more meaningful. Your teaching responsibilities coupled with the seminar readings will enable us to integrate theory and practice.

I had taught this seminar numerous times prior to 1999 and was well acquainted with the challenges that typically unnerve novice instructors. New teaching assistants struggled to balance their roles as teachers and learners, give and receive feedback (especially negative feedback), and respond to disgruntled students. Their desire to "do good," as we say in the Midwest, overshadowed all other teaching-related issues as instructors strove to establish interpersonal competence (e.g., being liked and respected by students), intellectual competence (e.g., being a disciplinary expert), and technical/administrative competence (e.g., calculating grades). Lively in-class and out-of-class discussions, applied and theoretical readings, and collaborative assignments provided seminar participants opportunities to unpack, examine and develop these three competencies. I intended seminar participants to use the course-management software as a communal vehicle to accomplish their aims.

Conceptually, the seminar blended digital innovations with a more conventional pedagogy, educational theory with practice, and high expectations with a supportive learning environment. Operationally, however, the whole was dramatically different from the individual parts. Soon after the semester began, the computer-enhanced pedagogy altered students' performances, changed in-class and online communication patterns, advantaged a new subculture of students, and created pockets of resistance. This revised pedagogy collided with students' expectations—resulting in an educational experience worthy of recounting and analyzing.

For example, electronic tools that I asked students to use increased seminar interactivity. I encouraged seminar participants to use the electronic discussion board to unpack the wide range of emotions—excitement, fear, confidence, doubt—they expressed during our initial class meeting. Embedded in these instructors' emotion-filled recollections of their first days as college teachers was a series of worrisome questions about teaching—questions almost identical to ones Sandstrom (1999) asked himself as he prepared to embark on his first college teaching experience:

> Will any of these students feel as excited about this course as I do? Will they find the topics and readings interesting? Will they get involved in the discussions? Will they see the course as useful and worthwhile? Will they think that I am a good teacher? (p. 517)

Participants in the teaching seminar sorted out mixed feelings and answered these questions using the online journal as well. Although my seminar's students obtained some useful outcomes, some seminar participants perceived this technology-enhanced interactivity as impersonal, awkward, and time-consuming. Traditional seminar discussions involved in-person give-and-take exchanges, but online journaling and discussion board postings required one to communicate at length without any feedback. These time-consuming, online exchanges limited seminar participants' ability to *read* social cues, e.g., aural or visual. Online journals or discussion board entries allowed users to revise and edit their comments before they introduced them to the public; for some, this became a near-obsession. Seminar participants struggled to find a balance between full attention and excessive attention. Simply stated, interactive behavioral norms dramatically changed.

The course-management software encouraged self-directed learning by allowing seminar participants to pace and sequence their own learning. Instructors, at their leisure, explored the many career development Web sites available on the Internet. Such efforts enhanced their disciplinary expertise, increased their confidence, and actively engaged them in constructing knowledge. Instructors developed individualized online learning sequences that were compatible with their learning style. Most instructors appreciated the abundance of easily accessible resources (which they readily shared with their peers). The course-management software acted as a gateway to a wealth of educational knowledge that each instructor assimilated in a unique way. Despite these benefits, outcomes were not always positive. The seemingly unlimited amount of information overwhelmed some instructors. During seminar gatherings, melding instructors' self-directed learning discoveries with their own teaching experiences, and my seminar agenda, e.g., required readings, spawned awkward interactions.

The online discussion boards provided forums for participants to teach one another (e.g., allowing instructors access to peers' philosophy statements or journal entries). The course-management software reinforced my pedagogical belief that all seminar participants (including me) should be both teachers and learners. The software especially benefited seminar participants who labored over writing, because it allowed them access to their peers' online papers. Comparing their work with peers' work on an identical assignment offered struggling students concrete ways to improve their writing. Publicly, seminar participants lauded this innovation that encouraged them to teach and learn from each other. Privately, they confessed that allowing peers easy access to their work (and vice versa) created much angst, adding additional layers of complexity to the already challenging written assignments.

My use of instructional technology in the seminar also changed participation patterns. Prior to initiating these changes, I recognized and accepted the fact that my participation expectations advantaged extroverted students. Extroverts dominated class discussions while introverts were less active (much to the bewilderment and dismay of extroverts). Often, introverted students used their written assignments to contribute to the learning community. Prior to the introduction of the course-management software, their peers did not have access to these offerings. With the advent of the seminar Web site, many introverts regularly used the online discussion board because it provided them a forum to present their ideas carefully and thoroughly. Some extroverts shunned this virtual medium, favoring face-to-face interactions. Introverts' contributions to the learning community became more obvious and central—radically upending the privilege and power dynamics previously held by extroverts. Because this new Web-based pedagogy privileged those who preferred to express themselves in writing, written communication became as influential as oral communication, thus altering the character of seminar participation.

Disenchantment with the course-management software provoked seminar participants to recognize the connection between their individual learning style preferences (e.g., assimilators who focus on *what* questions; convergers who focus on *how* questions; accommodators who focus on *what-if* questions; and divergers who focus on *why* questions) and satisfaction with the seminar. Participants better understood their preferences for ways of *perceiving* (e.g., concrete experience favoring personal involvement and feelings versus abstract conceptualizations favoring building and analyzing theory) and ways of *processing*, ranging from active experimentation to reflective observation. These realizations created a paralysis for some as they attempted to offer recommendations to alter the seminar to suit the learning styles of all participants.

These curricular changes exposed procrastinators. Previously, seminar participants could postpone completing their written and reading assignments until the night before our weekly meetings. So long as participants completed their work before the start of each class, they remained in good standing. New technology-related expectations required participants to evenly distribute their course preparation times to participate regularly and consistently between formal class meetings. They needed to regularly post discussion board reactions to the required readings on the discussion board days before our weekly seminar gathering. Procrastinators, rather than post comments at the last minute, opted to not participate, leading some of their peers to conclude that the nonparticipants were not invested in the seminar.

A digital divide between *technogeeks* and *technophobes* emerged, based on familiarity and comfort with technology. Technology-savvy participants embraced these new expectations, while many participants less familiar and comfortable with computers withdrew.

A sampling of online, anonymous, midsemester survey responses capture participants' varied reactions to the seminar:

I enjoy using the discussion board; it is only as useful as those who decide to participate.

The online discussions helped me to clarify some of my own thoughts and consider what other people have to say.

I posted things [on the discussion board] sometimes just to post and it doesn't really mean anything. It is also hard for me to sit and read everything everybody writes.

I often forget about the online discussion. I understand the purpose of it though; I'm just worried about how much the responses (or lack there of) count in participation.

At first, I hated it. But it is really very useful. I wish I had the time to read everyone's comments, but it's not possible.

Postings are not my preferred learning method—I much prefer class discussion. BUT, I do think posting helps me to get my thoughts straight and discuss them in some depth before I get to class—this is a good thing.

I know that this technology is a helpful way to do this, but when you're already spending a lot of time on writing journal entries, it can be quite time-consuming to be sharing your lesson plans, and clever websites you've found, as well.

The course-management software became a lightning rod of sorts—attracting open disapproval and criticism, thus diverting attention from other important aspects of the teaching and learning processes. The more we talked explicitly about ways to make optimal use of this new technology, the more ossified some participants' oppositional views became.

In theory, these digital advances benefited me as the instructor. The advances broadened my teaching roles and provided me new and different ways to connect with students. In practice, however, my teaching roles inside and beyond the classroom narrowed. Reading students' online comments prior to seminar meetings made me privy to concerns about assigned readings and (mis)interpretations of them. This allowed me to think carefully about students' perspectives prior to class meetings and redesign the seminar agenda (e.g., bring in additional resources) to optimally address these issues. Although students' online commentaries better prepared me for class, once class began, I tended to dominate and micromanage the seminar agenda and discussions, which were previously tasks shared among class participants.

Similarly, anonymous online surveys provided me ongoing feedback about participants' learning style preferences and satisfaction level with the seminar. Faced with an abundance of formative feedback, I tended to over-tinker with the structure and flow of the seminar. As it did with students, the seminar became a small part of my daily routine, dramatically increasing my preparation and disrupted my teaching rhythms.

Elbow (1986) noted, "Students seldom learn well unless they give in or submit to teachers. Yet they seldom learn well unless they resist or even reject their teachers" (p. 65). During our weekly teaching conversations, these teaching assistants who were my students grappled with the realization that their undergraduate students simultaneously submitted to and resisted them. Resisters especially frustrated TAs who were thrust into the authority role. This submission-resistance tension was ever present throughout the instructor seminar. Teaching assistants wanted to learn, please me, work hard, and express their frustrations candidly. Simply acquiescing to my agenda was not a viable option, nor was assuming the role of resister. Seminar participants struggled to reconcile these conflicting and contradictory feelings.

I, too, struggled with this submission-resistance tension. I had carefully crafted a graduate course based on professional judgments and analysis of previous students' feedback and suggestions. I did not want to simply surrender this agenda to a small core of resisters, nor did I want to automatically dismiss genuine concerns that differed from my views.

Throughout the semester I used the online and in-person discussions about teaching to systematically scrutinize my teaching of this seminar. I concluded that the gap between what I preached and practiced was wider than I wanted to privately (let alone publicly) acknowledge. I concluded that who I am an as instructor had a powerful influence on the seminar dynamics and students' learning acquisitions. Ironically this was a foundational premise of the seminar—a premise I had overlooked when augmenting the curriculum with digital innovations. These dilemmas forced me to reflect upon the class I had designed and consider how issues of power, privilege, learning styles, collaboration, critical thinking, intellectual development, and diversity, intersected with my core pedagogical beliefs, which affected the structure of the seminar and student learning. What's a professor to do?

Abort and Retry

End-of-semester evaluations by seminar participants revealed that despite semester-long tensions centering on the infusion of the course-management software into the curriculum, most agreed-upon learning outcomes were met. Participants were generally satisfied with the seminar, although their feelings about the course-management software were tepid at best. Some students' galvanized opposition to the course-management software masked other equally important seminar assets and liabilities. Despite these mostly positive reviews, an unsettling tone permeated these evaluative comments:

> Re-evaluate the purpose and effectiveness of the virtual exchanges during the first half of the course I did find comfort and use for the online discussions, during second half, it became something I had to and I didn't really gain much.

> At times, I felt as though it was a ton of work, considering the fact we were all teaching a course for the first time and had a lot of preparation for that.

It's my own fault, I did not utilize the online journal entries or the class discussions as well as I could have. I think the lack of involvement here was group-wide, so it made it difficult to really learn from the experiences of one another.

The course-management software, in my opinion, was a worthwhile addition to the seminar because it enhanced the overall teaching and learning experience. Despite ongoing student resistance, introverted students, typically on the margins, were more involved. Procrastinators learned to distribute their schoolwork more evenly between seminar meeting intervals. The software greatly increased the possibilities for participants to teach and learn from each other and provided new ways for individuals to selfdirect their learning. The software blurred in-class and out-of-class learning; communal teaching and learning were no longer restricted to our weekly gatherings. I remained steadfast in my commitment to the continued use of the software, but recognized the need to challenge the status quo.

As I mentally replayed the semester, I traced much of my discomfort to the gap between my espoused and enacted values. In this particular instance, my "do as I say, not as I do" style of teaching in this seminar was not worthy of emulation. This realization was particularly troubling because first-year college teachers often attempt to emulate their own instructor's teaching approaches (Fink 1984).

A second source of discomfort had to do with the kind of tinkering I used during the planning and implementation of the seminar. My initial decision to incorporate the course-management software into the seminar reflected my desire to tinker (i.e., make small and manageable changes) with my familiar teaching practices. Stevens (1988) described two different kinds of "tinkerers": reactive and reflective. *Reactive tinkerers* changed their teaching to solve a particular problem by adopting a technique or trick (e.g., trying "think-pair-share" activities with seemingly bored students), and when the technique did not work, the reactive tinkerers often give up. *Reflective tinkerers* instead tinker regularly and almost playfully, seeking not necessarily to solve problems but to engage in a kind of continuous improvement, knowing that one never solves instructional problems permanently and for all groups.

Reactive tinkerers are like computer users who run into a problem and download a utility that they expect to help them. If it solves their problem or meets their need, they press ahead. But if it does not, they uninstall it and either give up or search for something else. Reflective tinkerers instead view teaching as "open-source code" and themselves as programmers with a capacity for building their own innovations. And although they too may borrow tools and others' utilities, they are willing to "reverse engineer" an approach that does not work and perhaps use it in a different context. As with computing, those who can construct and evaluate their own approaches have greater flexibility (and perhaps satisfaction!) than those who must rely on programs or applications devised by others that may or may not accommodate their particular circumstances.

The origins of my technological alterations to the seminar exemplified reflective tinkering. Yet, once the seminar commenced, I adopted a reactive tinkering mode once students' problems with the course-management software appeared. I did not, as Stevens (1988) observed, give up; instead, I became fixated on solving this instructional problem.

I wanted to abort and retry—embracing a reflective tinkering stance and temper my yearning to solve problems. I resisted traditional fixes such as trying to persuade future students to alter behaviors, tinkering with teaching techniques, altering disciplinary content, or blaming the course-management software for my woes. Improving this particular teaching experience rested principally with me (i.e., my assumptions about teaching and learning, interacting with students, delivering disciplinary content, and structuring seminars) as I pondered the question, If I were to reconceptualize this seminar to make use of the lessons learned from the semester-long experience, how might I approach this change process and what might it look like?

Troubleshooting Help Center

Teaching is a very lonely profession. It's one thing to know there are other teachers, but it's another thing to hear their frustrations and understand what they are going through. I liked how the class provides me a forum to talk about teaching.

One TA, in her end-of-semester evaluation wrote this comment when listing seminar assets. Indeed, a unique aspect of the TA seminar was that it provided ongoing opportunities for teachers to discuss teaching with peers. After the seminar concluded, I no longer had a sounding board to help me interpret and better understand seminar dynamics. As a response to this realization, I invited a colleague (Mark), whose scholarly agenda focuses on college teaching, to engage in numerous after-the-fact dialogues (Palmer 1993,

1998; Shulman 1993) with me about college teaching, acting as a sounding board and critical friend. In the remainder of this chapter, we (Peter and Mark) synthesize our conversations about teaching and generate eight lessons learned about college teaching that are embedded in the case study. It is our hope that readers, too, will engage in a similar public dialogue about their teaching.

THINK DIFFERENT: A CASE ANALYSIS

IN RECENT YEARS A POPULAR COMPUTER company's slogan has been *think different*. In this section we heed this advice and use the case study as a springboard to reflect on and "think different" about teaching.

Gillespie (1996) articulates the value of stories and cases in initiating and maintaining reflections about the practice of teaching:

> By beginning with an event description and then watching as it is transformed into a story with commentary and then again into a case with commentary we attempt to open up possibilities for ourselves and our readers, especially those who endeavor to encourage reflection and dialogue about teaching on their campuses.... The employment of case and story frequently reveals layers of meanings, large-scale assumptions about knowledge, imagination, and action in the context of contemporary institutions (p. 49).

Hutchings (1993) identified four benefits of teaching cases: "Cases put permission in the air to talk about teaching ... cases recognize and honor the experiences of teachers ... cases can help reconnect process and content ... cases foster a view of teaching that leads to improvement" (p. 14). To invoke this "think different" process and initiate a dialogue about teaching, this analysis centers on eight teaching realizations that dominated our postseminar reflective conversations about the case study in particular and college teaching in general. This analysis provides us an opportunity to talk about teaching, connects the process and content of teaching, reveals the layers of meaning and assumptions we gleaned from the case study analysis, and fosters a view of teaching that will hopefully lead to high quality college instruction.

Eight Realizations about Teaching
1. Technology—Does Not (Always) Compute

THE FIRST AND THE MOST OBVIOUS ASPECT of the case is the allure of technology as a solution to education's vexing problems. These days, college professors, such as Peter, are faced with the dilemma of how to leverage technology to improve their teaching and students' learning. Deciding whether to use technology in a university classroom is no longer a viable option. With the camel's nose under the tent, so to speak, it is difficult, if not impossible, to justify keeping it out. Technology can be genuinely useful to solve problems that contemporary teachers encounter. It provides a means of communicating with students who spend less time on campus, and a means of communication between students and faculty, whose lives are busier and more complex than ever.

Often, technology is marketed to faculty as an instrumental solution to nagging instructional problems (e.g., keeping track of student work). Yet, as the case study illustrates, solving instructional problems does not necessarily solve educational problems. Although faculty may think that technology can help them check off items on their to-do list of instructional problems, the process is more analogous to a game of Whack-a-Mole—pound down one problem and certainly another (if not more) will emerge in its place. Higher education's fixation on efficiency encourages teachers to think of instructional complications as problems to be eliminated using technological solutions rather than as opportunities for teachers and students to talk about the ends and means of education (as though more *efficient* instruction were always more *effective*). And when teachers' inflated expectations for using technology to make teaching and learning more efficient are not met, they can become disillusioned with any effort to improve teaching.

The sirens' song of technology made it difficult for Peter to resist infusing it into his graduate seminar. Soon after the seminar commenced, Peter realized that enhancing teaching was more complicated than adding technology to his pedagogical recipe, stirring, and then hoping the new concoction was more palatable than before. Needed are hardy recipes that satisfy both the instructional and educational appetites of faculty and students.

Too often, as the case study reveals, the seminar participants treated technology as the main course rather than a condiment. When designing the seminar, Peter intended to position the scholarship of teaching and career development in the foreground and locate technology in the background, which did not happen.

How will technology enhance students' understanding of the process of college teaching and career development? Posing and answering this kind of question prior to making even *minor* technological change would likely increase the probability that technology's role in the seminar would remain a critical and supporting one. It is imperative that professors know how technology fits with pedagogical beliefs about teaching and learning in order to integrate it effectively in their classrooms.

2. World Wide Web Networks

A SECOND REALIZATION SUGGESTED BY the case study is that the enterprise of teaching is best characterized as a complicated, intertwined Web of educational interactions rather than a series of discrete instructional activities. A *simple* and seemingly independent alteration of one variable (i.e., incorporating course-management software in a seminar) rippled powerfully throughout all seminar participants' learning experiences, including the instructor's learning. Treating the course-management software as a disconnected strand of instruction limited Peter's ability to recognize its influences on other aspects of the teaching enterprise and vice versa. Likewise, a student's *discrete* resistance to, for example, the required online journal expectation affected the learning of others. Instructors' (and students') ability to see the whole, the parts, and the interrelationships of this entangled web of teaching is of paramount importance.

In higher education, untangling the networking labyrinth can overwhelm and fatigue faculty, often leading to a paralyzing sense of hopelessness. One strategy for fending off this sort of inertia/paralysis is for educators to compartmentalize the murky whole into unambiguous and digestible dichotomies. Palmer (1998) eloquently names these dichotomies and their liabilities for educational communities. Palmer argues that higher education institutions subtly compel educators to separate their head from heart and separate facts from feelings. This leads to minds that do not know how to feel and hearts that do not know how to think. It also leads to bloodless facts that objectify the world and raw emotions that reduce truth to how one feels on any given day.

Peter based his decision to adopt course-management software on a logical evaluation of facts (e.g., students' increased familiarity with technology will enhance their professional effectiveness). While designing the TA seminar, he underestimated the affective dimensions of this decision. Palmer (1998) also argued that educators frequently separate theory from practice. Unfortunate outcomes are theories that are disconnected with life and practice that is void of understanding (we return to this issue later in our analysis). Peter did not theoretically ground his implementation of the course-management software. He neglected to ask how this new practice would dovetail with his foundational theories that guided his pedagogy; this disenfranchised some students.

The most grievous dichotomy Peter created when implementing the curricular changes involved the students and him. Peter altered the curriculum with minimal input from students. Such actions, however inadvertent, conveyed symbolically an antiquated educational dichotomy to seminar participants—the teacher as the omnipotent authority and students as recipients of the teacher's knowledge. This dichotomous thinking dampened students' investment in the seminar.

There are very few simple, discrete, and dichotomous aspects of college teaching. Understanding the organic whole of teaching and the web of beliefs and behaviors of faculty is essential.

3. Power Surge

A THIRD REALIZATION GLEANED FROM the case study is that teaching is a political act with power, as is any collective activity that involves participants obtaining, developing, and exercising power in pursuit of competing outcomes (Birnbaum 1988). Instructors' personality and beliefs about teaching and learning are a powerful influence on the curriculum and student learning. Peter's decision to infuse technology into the curriculum was an ideological decision based on his beliefs, values, and ideas about teaching. Initially Peter treated the decision as an apolitical, neutral and technical task. Oppositional students quickly reminded him his decision was a political and value-driven decision. Other seminar participants also reminded Peter that they too had ideological views about teaching and learning (and were not bashful about sharing them). These oppositional views clashed with the instructor's views, which incited occasional power skirmishes.

Elbow (1986) argued that there is an inescapable power relationship in any institutional teaching situation. This case study supports Elbow's claim. As the seminar instructor, Peter wielded power by setting the seminar agenda, which influenced his presentation of disciplinary information and shaped students' behaviors. Peter deemed technology to be important and he had the political power to advance this agenda and act. Student resistance was a not-so-subtle reaction to the inevitable power inequities between instructors and students—a powerful pointed reminder that embody all educational activities entail political struggles between groups with different aims.

Creating apolitical classrooms and level playing fields between students and instructors is a frequently espoused educational goal that is seldom attained. Instead of striving for this mythical balance of power, it might be prudent for instructors to devote their energies to *thinking ideologically* and initiating dialogue with students about these ideologies. One way to uncover these ideologies is to critically examine classroom discourses (e.g., ways teachers and students talk to each other, how much one-way teacher talk occurs, instructors' views on subject matter, the degree to which students are free to disagree, the degree to which students talk to and work collaboratively with each other). Who decides what learning opportunities should be? To what goals are the learning activities directed? Who benefits from these learning activities? Asking and answering these kinds of questions will likely bring to the forefront of instructors' consciousness the webs of political intricacies that typically ensnarl students and faculty (Shor 1992).

Power and politics are not necessary evils in college classrooms. Sandstrom (1999) reminds readers that instructors' power can promote a common good:

> I became increasingly aware of how I could use my authority to promote conditions that encouraged students to participate actively in discussions, to grapple with challenging issues, to think creatively and critically, to understand and appreciate diverse perspectives, and to form thoughtful and just relationships with one another (p. 526).

4. Processing Cycles

A FOURTH REALIZATION GLEANED FROM the case study is that it is imperative for an instructor to "know thyself" through self-reflection (Brookfield 1995; Brunner 1994; Clift, Houston, and Pugach 1990; Centra 1993; Grossman 1999; Valli 1992). "Arguing for self-reflection and analysis has an 'apple pie and ice-cream quality to it.' It is a point with which few would take exception. Yet, self-reflection may be the most difficult task we try to do as teachers" (Grasha 1996, 50).

Although an integral part of faculty life is thinking, it is seldom directed toward the self. By first learning and understanding themselves as teachers, professors are better equipped to extract and apply new knowledge; learn from, and assist students in their personal and professional endeavors; and manage the politics of teaching. Engaging in a self-reflective process can reveal the ideological assumptions that are deeply embedded in teaching practices. Self-reflection offsets faculty members' predilection for operating without much attention to the underlying processes that guide and direct teachers' actions (Grasha 1996).

Often, faculty members' disciplinary expertise can lure them into mechanically performing their teaching duties without a high degree of mindfulness or self-reflection. This autopilot mode often leads instructors to ignore how their values shape classroom practices. Faculty members' reluctance to place themselves at the epicenter of teaching discourses (in part due to a fear they will be perceived as egotistical, selfish, or narcissistic) exacerbates these dynamics. The self-reflection that we advocate is not a technique or a set of procedures or a learned skill or competency. It is an idiosyncratic, personal process of identifying and questioning internal assumptions that shape the solutions teachers generate.

Two TAs' comments in their end-of-the-semester seminar evaluations convey the struggles and benefits of this reflective process.

> This class has been a struggle, but a worthwhile struggle, throughout this past semester. I say struggle, because there were times where the extra effort involved in this course seemed overwhelming along with planning and teaching. Yet when I reflect back on the various assignments, I not only see why they were necessary, I can also see why they were beneficial in my own learning experience. I was forced to reflect at times when I thought I didn't have the energy to do so, yet from these reflections came energy to continually strive to improve my teaching.

> I found the opportunity to reflect upon my own values and that which shall guide my teaching to be very valuable. I am the type of person who relies on my actions to speak to my values rather than speaking about them. Yet I found our reflection on them to be extremely important.

In the case study, Peter failed to reflect critically on the effects of his teaching and ponder questions such as, Are these technological changes compatible with my core values? or What kind of teacher do I want to become as a result of these changes? This complicated students' ability to fully optimize the teaching and learning experience. The case study reminds readers that it is crucial for faculty members to develop habits of identifying and critically analyzing assumptions behind their practice.

Brookfield (1995) encouraged the discovery of tacit beliefs about teaching and learning through critical reflection, an act he described as "hunting assumptions." However, rather than seeking to simply improve instructional performance, critical reflection on teaching practices has two distinctive purposes: (1) understanding "how considerations of power undergird, frame, and distort educational processes and interactions" and (2) questioning "assumptions and practices that seem to make our teaching lives easier but actually work against our own best long-term practices" (Brookfield 1995, 8). Applying Brookfield's critical reflection process to the case study, Peter's power allowed him to implement his assumption that technology would enhance the educational experience for all seminar participants (including himself). Students, who took exception to this assumption, perceived that these technological enhancements worked against their long-term best interests.

A teacher's actions are defined and influenced by a personally constituted array of beliefs, values, and expectations that may or may not be informed by formal educational theories (Clark and Peterson 1986). Teachers regularly rely on personal theories about the connections between teaching and learning not only for making everyday decisions such as infusing technology into instructional methods, but also for making sense of teaching-related interactions and situations, including understanding students' resistance. The case study reveals several of Peter's personal theories.

In discussing a variant of personal theories called theories of action, Argyris and Schön (1974) distinguished between theories of action of which the "personal theorist" is aware and can articulate (e.g., Peter's espoused theories) and the theoretical frames that are unarticulated yet nevertheless implicit in one's actions (e.g., Peter's theories-in-use). An implicit theory, as such, is constructed by *reading* a person's actions and inferring a system of tacit understandings—the theory-in-use—within which the actions make sense. For example, examining Peter's requirement that students read each other's journal entries, one might conclude he teaches using an implicit theory that students can learn from each other, not just from the instructor. What makes these implicit theories problematic, however, is that their relationship to everyday educational decisions can be so transparent, their validity is taken as self-evident, despite the fact they often are shaped by habit, tradition, and precedent, and adopted in an uncritical way (Carr and Kemmis 1986). From our perspective, the personal theories of college teachers is the sort of knowledge instructors need to possess in order to teach well.

Argyris and Schön (1974) argue that the primary reason for surfacing one's tacit theories-in-use is to improve performance. That is, one can employ a different (and ostensibly better) map of the way things work only after first exposing the current (and perhaps flawed) map on which one is unconsciously relying. The key to improving performance lies in uncovering the discrepancies between a person's theory of action, which is his/her explanation of how to interpret and direct a situation, and his/her theories-in-use, which are inferred from his/her actions in that situation. The goal is to better understand one's implicit beliefs about teaching and learning. In many ways Peter's initial decision to use the course-management software reflects his desire to tinker with his familiar teaching practices—that is, altering the role of technology in his seminars in small and manageable ways rather than on a large scale.

5. Network Protocol

A FIFTH REALIZATION GLEANED FROM the case study is that faculty need to invite students to become educational collaborators (i.e., cocreators and coimplementers) in the learning experience, not simply passive recipients of it. This necessitates faculty networking with students and sharing power with them to develop a suitable protocol for collaboration. Baiocco and DeWaters (1998) speak to the value of these student-teacher partnerships:

> Effective teaching is a shared enterprise, where both the teacher and student take some degree of responsibility for the learning process and establishing work standards. The process may be initiated by the teacher, who outlines the expectations for the students, but it continues to emerge over time through mutual feedback (p. 144).

It is a prudent course of action to involve all learning community members in the educational process because it enhances educational interactions, incorporates the interests of both parties, and promotes learning. Baxter

Magolda (1992) offers three principles—validating students as knowers, situating learning in the student's own experience, and defining learning as mutually constructing meaning—that serve as a constructive guide for genuine collaboration.

Validating students as knowers necessitates those in power, e.g., professors, relinquish power, by inviting the less powerful, e.g., students, to join in thinking and talking about the educational process. Concurrently, the less powerful must realize that they too have voices, and permission to express their views (and continually seize these opportunities). In the case study context, codesigning the use of the course-management software or negotiating online assignments are two examples of how Peter might have implemented this first principle. Had TAS been validated in offering their hesitations about online work, perhaps the perceived conflict of learning technology and learning to teach could have been resolved more productively. A collaborative agreement on how to merge Peter's interests and TAS' interests would have easily offset the time spent on conflict centering on the educational utility of the course-management software.

Baxter Magolda's (1992) second principle—*situating learning in the student's own experience*—necessitates that the more powerful welcome the less-powerful stakeholders' *real life* experiences and meaning-making into the process. Often, those with minimal power or influence are not permitted to bring their life experience into the change process because these experiences are perceived as irrelevant. This principle intertwines students' experiences with course content, placing course material in familiar context (Beidler and Beidler 1993). Chalmers and Fuller (1996) articulate the benefits of implementing this ideal:

> Students bring a wealth of knowledge, experience, and skills to university. They may not be able to apply this immediately in the university learning context, but this does not diminish its value. Teachers who can identify and use their students existing knowledge and skills are likely to increase their motivation, application of knowledge and understanding (p. 50).

In this case study, all seminar participants had a wealth of knowledge about teaching and learning—from the vantage point of both a long-time student and first-time teacher, as well as from growing up with technology. Peter did not solicit from students their existing knowledge about and everyday use of technology and its intersection with teaching and learning. This oversight undermined an ongoing collaborative opportunity for students and Peter.

Baxter Magolda's *learning as mutually constructing meaning* principle suggests that learning will result from a dialogue where all stakeholders' voices are considered. This principle does not advocate, for example, instructors abdicating their expertise or knowledge; rather instructors infuse their knowledge and expertise in the context of students' perspectives—bringing it to the dialogue, but not imposing it unilaterally. To avoid imposing knowledge, the more powerful must shun the role of omnipotent authority.

Seminar participants were active contributors in the seminar but were shut out of the design process. Throughout the semester students expressed themselves, built on each other's knowledge, and explored multiple perspectives and the mutual construction of meaning. Peter provided teaching assistants opportunities to negotiate ways to modify his plan to better meet their needs, but he did not aggressively pursue their input. This contributed to the disenfranchisement of some students. It is critical for all seminar participants to contribute actively to the collective learning effort, breaking traditional roles of teacher/learner and necessitating that faculty and students become both active learners and instructors. "Students are not just receivers of knowledge orchestrated by an outside authority but they also produce it through group interaction" (Grasha 1996, 266).

A centerpiece of the TA seminar was to reach consensus about the question, What is good teaching? Struggling collaboratively with the issues that arose around technology would be one way to model the practice of good teaching. Validating students as knowers, situating learning in the student's own experience, and defining learning as mutually constructing meaning are collaborative means to generate conversation with students. Giroux (1988) argued that it is imperative for teachers to make students an integral part of the educational experience, celebrating their voices, and allowing them to construct their own meaning. Making better use of Peter's knowledge of students' preexisting levels of comfort would have helped him greatly. Genuine collaboration requires teachers to cross borders and begin to negotiate realms of meaning, social relations, knowledge, and values—no easy task.

Professors' personal and professional values shape the entire educational experience; students' values, too, shape the experience, either through resistance or through collaboration. Genuine collaboration invites students to mutually shape classroom learning interactions. Professors establishing and maintaining these collaborative network protocols is more productive than shaping the educational experience through stimulating resistance.

6. Conflict Error

As THE CASE STUDY SUGGESTS, college classrooms are lightning rods for conflict because they provide space for diverse individuals with divergent views to interact. Accepting rather than repressing conflict is an important consideration for those who desire healthy collaborative educational communities. It is essential for teachers and learners to engage in respectful dialogue and exchange, active listening, and embrace learning from multiple perspectives. Conflict needs a public space in which to flourish. Gamson (1993) speaks to the benefits of accepting conflict and difference:

> [Higher education communities] must develop ways for members to disagree with one another without losing the respect of other members. People in colleges and universities are notoriously uncomfortable with conflict. We run away from it or stomp it into the ground. We deny it or over-dramatize it. ... dealing with conflict ... requires respect and civility. It does not ask that parties love or even like each other, just that they continue interacting (p. 6).

Collaborative dialogue needs to include conversations about celebrating difference and accepting conflict as a way of life. In this case study, multiple sources of conflict emerged between TAS and Peter, between extroverts and introverts, between techno-savvy and techno-phobic students, between students with differing learning styles, and between procrastinators and non-procrastinators. While Peter effectively used the course-management software to provide students opportunities to explore career development and teaching issues, Peter did not use the online and in-person exchanges as opportunities for seminar participants to mediate conflict or to explore the conflict that arose from the differences. It could have been an invaluable vehicle for students for learning to disagree and respect one another. Disagreements are effective learning tools. Out of disagreement comes new information, other ways to view a situation, leading to more complex understanding and ethical practices. Educational communities must accept rather than repress conflict and provide members the necessary human relation skills that will result in civil, collaborative interactions. As Palmer (1987) argues, educators should welcome creative conflict to correct our biases and prejudices about the nature of great things.

7. Morphing

ANOTHER LESSON EMBEDDED IN this case study centers on the relationship between theory and practice in college teaching. Traditionally, postsecondary education has tended to view *theory* as something apart from, and applied to, *practice*. In this view, theory is about knowledge (the domain of the academicians), and practice is about action (the domain of the "real world"). However, we take exception to this theory-practice dichotomy. Schön (1983, 1995) describes higher education's view of the relationship between thinking and doing—or its epistemology of practice—as "technical rationality," which sees sound professional practice as solving instrumental problems through the application of scientific theory and technique. Schön adds,

> As one would expect from the hierarchical model of professional knowledge, research is institutionally separate from practice, connected to it by carefully defined relationships of exchange. Researchers are supposed to provide the basic and applied science from which to derive techniques for diagnosing and solving the problems of practice. Practitioners are supposed to furnish researchers with problems for study and with tests of the utility of research results. The researcher's role is distinct from, and usually considered superior to, the role of the practitioner (1983, 26).

Similarly, Palmer (1998) criticizes higher education for cleaving to an "objectivist myth," which relies in part on the belief that answers to complicated real-world problems are best generated using rigorous scientific methods. According to Palmer, this view of truth-knowing and truth-telling has four major elements:

- *objects* of knowledge that reside "out there" somewhere, pristine in physical or conceptual space, as described by the facts in a given field;
- *experts*, people trained to know these objects in their pristine form without allowing their own subjectivity to slop over onto the purity of the objects themselves;

- *amateurs*, people without training and full of bias, who depend on the experts for objective or pure knowledge of the pristine objects in question;
- and *baffles* at every point of transmission—between objects and experts, between experts and amateurs—that allow objective knowledge to flow downstream while preventing subjectivity from flowing back up (pp. 100–1).

The danger associated with separating theory from practice is evident in students' comments from their end-of-semester evaluations.

In the beginning of the seminar, we need to be "instructed" on how to handle typical problem situations (e.g. how to handle people who need to drop due to poor attendance/grades; motivating students with regards to external distractions such as sunny weather). Theory should be introduced later in the term.

I'm just not sure about all the theoretical discussion. I truly believe that it's important to get into that stuff, but I wish it had served as an introduction to a much more in-depth discussion of actually teaching the course, which we didn't really get to at all. As I was working on my syllabus, I realized that I really had no particular tools with which to write it, other than the model of previous syllabi. Other than having a better sense of educational philosophy, I don't feel prepared to teach the course.

What I'm saying here is that the theoretical aspect is important, but approaching the seminar from that perspective made it difficult at times for instructors to feel comfortable just talking about what we did and how it worked or didn't work—I sometimes felt like those conversations were taking away from the discussion of the theoretical concepts, and that shouldn't be how the seminar feels.

Throughout the semester, Peter worked hard to combat TAs' propensity toward artificially separating theory from practice, by, for example, requiring students to concurrently read and discuss "how-to-teach" texts (McKeachie 1999; Gullette 1984; Brinkley et al. 1999) and theoretically-oriented teaching texts (e.g., Palmer 1998; Baxter Magolda 1999). Students responded favorably to the eclectic collection of readings that valued theory and practice and responded to students' diverse learning styles, but viewed them as separate entities.

Unfortunately, when Peter infused the course-management software into the seminar, he, like his students, inadvertently and artificially separated theory from practice, embracing a technical rationality perspective about using technology to improve the learning process. College teachers tend to fare better at improving or changing their teaching when they see *themselves*, and not only academic researchers of teaching, as a source of instructional knowledge that can be both practical and credible. This is also true when these teachers interact with students and provide them opportunities for them to be researcher-practitioners.

8. No Tech Support

AN EIGHTH AND FINAL REALIZATION gleaned from the case study is that teaching is too often seen as a *technical* rather than as a *practical* activity. By this, we refer to a distinction made by Aristotle in the *Nicomachean Ethics* between productive activity (*poiesis*) and practical activity (*praxis*). Defined simply, *poiesis* is a kind of making or instrumental action, the aim of which is to produce some object or artifact. The type of reasoning appropriate for this kind of "making action" is *techne*, or what today might be called technical expertise. Carpentry, cooking, and other forms of making might be considered paradigm cases of *poiesis* (productive activity) guided by *techne* (technical skill), leading to an outcome, which is a thing or object.

In contrast with "making action" is "doing action," or *praxis*, which is guided by *phronesis*, or practical wisdom. This kind of practical activity is concerned not with the production of an object or a state of affairs, but rather with how one conducts one's life and participates as a member of society. As Schwandt (2001) explains,

> [*Praxis*] is about doing the right thing and doing it well in interactions with fellow humans. It is an activity that leaves no separably identifiable outcome as its product, hence the end (aim) of the activity (i.e., being a 'good' human being, teacher, doctor, lawyer, etc.) is realized in the very doing of the activity. This is the kind of activity from which one cannot 'rest'— unlike ... poiesis, it is not an activity one can set aside at will (p. 207).

Phronesis, then, is the practical-moral reasoning that is constitutive of *praxis*. Phronesis, sometimes called practical wisdom or practical judgment, is principally a moral disposition to act truly and rightly. It is a kind of reasoning that is characterized by "flexibility, attentiveness (understood as including alertness and sensitivity), matters of character and experience, and the ineliminability of ethical considerations" (Smith 1999, 331). Or, as Schwandt describes it, "Phronesis is intimately concerned with the timely, the local, the particular, and the contingent (e.g., 'What should I do *now*, in *this* situation, given *these* circumstances, facing *this* particular person, at *this* time?')" (p. 208).

When teaching is framed as a kind of *poiesis*, or technical activity, theory about teaching and learning can be produced apart from the activity that it is to guide and then applied algorithmically to that activity to achieve fixed ends. But in any account of teaching as *praxis*, making sense of contextual particularities and balancing competing moral ideals arises from a kind of reasoning—*phronesis*, or practical-moral judgment—in which neither theory nor practice is privileged over the other. Teaching is indeed a practice, then, when its practitioner "combines practical knowledge of the good with sound judgment about what, in a particular situation, would constitute an appropriate expression of this good" (Carr 1995, 71).

Changing teaching practices is possible when those who comprise a community of practice adopt different language to either extend or upset their prevailing understandings of what the practice is. From this view, moving those who think about teaching as a technical, instrumental activity toward a notion of teaching as a practice will occur as they begin to reshape, through critical conversations, the language which constitutes their practices (McEwan 1995).

Perhaps the most important aspect of seeing teaching as a kind of *praxis* that requires practical judgment is that it begins to provide a language for discerning and appreciating the moral dimensions of teaching. As Palmer and others (Tom 1984; Sockett and LePage 2002) point out, teachers are often encouraged to consider their classrooms as technical rather than moral areas, and their tendencies to use *technical vocabulary* precludes any use of a *moral vocabulary* for understanding and extending their teaching.

Logging-Off

This chapter is more than a richly described idiosyncratic case study of technology-gone-awry in a classroom and a retrospective sense-making analysis of the experience. The case study illuminates the daily challenges many professors encounter when teaching college students, highlighting pervasive missteps that diminish the potential for optimal teaching and learning.

An overarching lesson learned as a result of this case study analysis is the value of reflective dialogue about teaching and learning that focuses on the *teacher*. Peter's dialogue with his students as well as his dialogues with Mark brought to the forefront of both authors' consciousness eight important issues for college professors to consider that have implications well beyond technology to include issues such as networking, power, self-reflection, collaboration, conflict, theory *and* practice, and moral aspects of teaching. Too often faculty members metaphorically focus on the trees, unable to see the forest or the relationship between the trees and forest. Often professors dichotomize the educational enterprise, creating either/or options that seldom ameliorate problems educators hope to overcome. Faculty members shun discussions about power and politics in their classrooms, while simultaneously attempting to create conflict-free educational zones (that merely repress rather than resolve conflicts). Often, faculty members allocate disproportionate amounts of their time to technical and mechanical aspects of teaching, often at the expense of contemplating equally important philosophical and moral issues.

A first place for faculty to look to improve college teaching is within— rather than look externally to change students, disciplinary content, or teaching techniques. A natural extension of this internal self-reflective process is genuine dialogue with colleagues about teaching with students, which allows for shared meanings to emerge, integrates multiple perspectives, and uncovers and examines core assumptions about *teaching* and *learning* for teachers. For as Bertolt Brecht wrote, "The world of knowledge takes a crazy turn when teachers themselves are taught to learn."

•

Peter Magolda is an associate professor in the Department of Educational Leadership, Miami University, Oxford, Ohio.

Mark Connolly is a researcher at the LEAD (Learning through Evaluation, Adaption, and Dissemination) Center, University of Wisconsin—Madison.

References

Argyris, C., and Schon, D. A. 1974. *Theory in practice: Increasing professional effectiveness*. San Francisco: Jossey-Bass.

Baiocco, S. A., and DeWaters, J. N. 1998. *Successful college teaching: Problem-solving strategies of distinguished professors*. Boston: Allyn and Bacon.

Baxter Magolda, M. B. 1992. *Knowing and reasoning in college: Gender-related patterns in students' intellectual development*. San Francisco: Jossey-Bass.

———. 1999. *Creating contexts for learning and self-authorship: Constructive-developmental pedagogy*. Nashville: Vanderbilt University Press.

Beidler, P. G., and Beidler, G. M. 1993. What's your horse: Motivating college students. *Journal on Excellence in College Teaching* 4:9–26.

Birnbaum, R. 1988. *How colleges work: The cybernetics of academic organization and leadership*. San Francisco: Jossey-Bass.

Boice, R. 1996. *First-order principles for college teachers: Ten basic ways to improve the teaching process*. Bolton, MA: Anker.

Boyer Commission on Educating Undergraduates in the Research University. 1998. Reinventing undergraduate education: A blueprint for America's research universities [online]. Available: http://www.notes.cc.sunyb.edu/pres/boyer.nsf.webform/VIII

Brinkley, A., Dessants, B., Flamm, M., Fleming, C., Forcey, C., and Rothschild, E. 1999. *The Chicago handbook for teachers: A practical guide to the college classroom*. Chicago: University of Chicago Press.

Brookfield, S. D. 1995. *Becoming a critically reflective teacher*. San Francisco: Jossey-Bass.

Brunner, D. D. 1994. *Inquiry and reflection: Framing narrative practice in education*. Albany, NY: State University of New York Press.

Carr, W. 1995. *For education: Towards critical educational inquiry*. Buckingham, England: Open University Press.

Carr, W., and Kemmis, S. 1986. *Becoming critical: education, knowledge, and action research*. London; Philadelphia: Falmer Press.

Centra, J. A. 1993. *Reflective faculty evaluation: Enhancing teaching and determining faculty effectiveness*. San Francisco: Jossey-Bass.

Chalmers, D., and Fuller, R. 1996. *Teaching for learning at university: Theory and practice*. London: Kogan Page.

Clark, C. M., ed. 2001. *Talking shop: Authentic conversation and teacher learning*. New York: Teachers College Press.

Clark, C. M., and Peterson, P. L. 1986. Teachers' thought processes. In *Handbook of research on teaching*, ed. M. C. Wittrock, 3d ed. 255–96. New York: Macmillan.

Clift, R. T., Houston, W. R., Pugach, M. C., University of Houston, and U. S. Office of Educational Research and Improvement. 1990. *Encouraging reflective practice in education: An analysis of issues and programs*. New York: Teachers College Press Teachers College Columbia University.

Davis, B. G. 1993. *Tools for teaching*. San Francisco: Jossey-Bass.

Elbow, P. 1986. *Embracing contraries*. New York: Oxford University Press.

Fink, L. D. 1984. *The first year of college teaching*. San Francisco: Jossey-Bass.

Fuhrmann, B. S., and Grasha, A. F. 1983. *A practical handbook for college teachers*. Boston: Little Brown.

Gamson, Z. 1993. The destruction and re-creation of academic community: A personal view. *ASHE Open Forum* 6:4-5, 7.

Gillespie, M. L. 1996. Stories, cases, and practical wisdom. *Innovative Higher Education* 21 (1): 49-66.

Giroux, H. A. 1988. *Schooling and the struggle for public life: Critical pedagogy in the modern age*. Minneapolis: University of Minnesota Press.

Grasha, A. F. 1996. *Teaching with style: A practical guide to enhancing learning by understanding teaching and learning styles*. Pittsburgh: Alliance Publishers.

Grossman, P. L. 1990. *The making of a teacher: Teacher knowledge and teacher education*. New York: Teachers College Press Teachers College Columbia University.

Gullette, M. M. 1984. *The Art and craft of teaching*. Cambridge, MA: Distributed for the Harvard-Danforth Center for Teaching and Learning Faculty of Arts and Sciences Harvard University by Harvard University Press.

Hutchings, P. 1993. Windows on practice: Cases about teaching and learning. *Change* 25 (November/December): 14-21.

McEwan, H. 1995. Narrative understanding in the study of teaching. In *Narrative in teaching, learning, and research*, eds. H. McEwan and K. Egan, 166-83. New York: Teachers College Press.

McKeachie, W. J., with Gibbs, G., Laurillard, D., Chism, N. V. N., Menges, R., Svinicki, M., and Weinstein, C. E. 1999. *Teaching tips: Strategies, research, and theory for college and university teachers*, 10th ed. Boston: Houghton Mifflin.

Palmer, P. 1987. Community, conflict, and ways of knowing: Ways to deepen our educational agenda. *Change* (September/October): 20-5.

Palmer, P. J. 1993. Good talk about good teaching: Improving teaching through conversation and community. *Change* 25 (November/December): 10-3.

———. 1998. *The courage to teach: Exploring the inner landscape of a teacher's life*. San Francisco: Jossey-Bass.

Sandstrom, K. L. 1999. Embracing modest hopes: Lessons from the beginning of a teaching journey. In *The social worlds of higher education: Handbook for teaching in new century*, eds. B. A. Pescosolido and R. Aminzade, 517-29. Thousand Oaks, CA: Sage.

Schön, D. A. 1983. *The reflective practitioner: How professionals think in action*. New York: Basic Books.

———. 1995. Knowing-in-action: The new scholarship requires a new epistemology. *Change* 27 (November/December): 27-34.

Schwandt, T. A. 2001. *Dictionary of qualitative inquiry*, 2d ed. Thousand Oaks, CA: Sage.

Shor, I. 1992. *Empowering education: Critical teaching for social change.* Chicago: University of Chicago Press.

Shulman, L. S. 1987. Learning to teach. *AAHE Bulletin* 40 (November): 5–9.

———. 1993. Teaching as community property: Putting an end to pedagogical solitude. *Change* 25 (November/December): 6–7.

Smith, R. 1999. Paths of judgement: The revival of practical wisdom. *Educational Philosophy and Theory* 31:327–40.

Sockett, H., and LePage, P. 2002. The missing language of the classroom. *Teaching and Teacher Education* 18:159–71.

Stevens, E. 1988. Tinkering with teaching. *Review of Higher Education* 12:63–78.

Tom, A. R. 1984. *Teaching as a moral craft.* New York: Longman.

Valli, L. 1992. *Reflective teacher education: Cases and critiques.* Albany, NY: State University of New York Press.

Weimer, M. 1990. *Improving college teaching: Strategies for developing instructional effectiveness.* San Francisco: Jossey-Bass.

·4

TEACHING and LEARNING in Different Academic Settings

A doctor is a doctor wherever he may be, but a professor is a professor only if employed by a college or university. This close connection with one type of institution means that the structure of the institutions and the nature of academic work have always interacted with each other.

(Light 1974, 17)

Laurie Richlin
CLAREMONT GRADUATE UNIVERSITY

Bettina J. Casad, Shannon Hensley, June K. Hilton, and Jeffrey T. Williams

◆

For a satisfying and successful academic career, faculty members need to find their best "fit" with institutional missions and expectations, and with student abilities and needs. This chapter describes the four primary types of higher education institutions, with background on their history and institutional missions, student profiles, and faculty workloads. It is written to provide future and current faculty members with ideas of what an academic job would like be at different institutions, particularly how they would need to spend their time to be successful.

ACADEMIC WORKPLACES

INSTITUTIONS

SINCE 1971, THE CARNEGIE FOUNDATION for the Advancement of Teaching has provided a taxonomy of higher education institutions (most recent: www.carnegiefoundation.org/Classification/CIHE2000/background.htm), which has been revised several times. Beginning with the 2000 classification, the taxonomy is based on the number and types of degrees institutions offer. The most recent prior scheme included, as well, the amount of federal support as a basis for classification of research universities and classified baccalaureate colleges by admissions selectivity, but these criteria have been dropped because they were not useful and because they led to inappropriate competition among institutions to move "up the Carnegie Classification" (McCormick 2000, 3).

As shown on table 4.1, the 2000 Carnegie Classification of 3,941 United States' institutions includes 1,669 associate's colleges (42%), 606 baccalaureate colleges (15%), 611 master's colleges and universities (16%), and 261 doctorate-granting/research universities (7%), as well as 755 specialized institutions (for instance, theological seminaries, schools of art, medical schools, etc.) and 28 tribal colleges and universities (19% and 1%, respectively). Associate's colleges (community, junior, and some technical colleges) offer almost exclusively associate's degrees and certificate programs, although some institutions are included that awarded bachelor's degrees as less than 10% of the degrees given. Baccalaureate colleges include *liberal arts* and *general* categories, depending on whether they offer more or less than half their degrees in liberal arts fields, and *baccalaureate/associate's colleges,* in which the majority of conferrals are below the baccalaureate but bachelor's degrees accounted for at least 10%. Master's colleges and universities offer a wide range of baccalaureate programs as well as master's degrees. The doctorate-granting institutions are divided into the categories of *intensive,* which award at least 10 doctorates per year across three or more disciplines or at least 20 doctoral degrees per year overall, and *extensive,* which award 50 or more doctoral degrees per year across at least fifteen disciplines.

Although one use of the classification can be the determination of institutional mission, the Carnegie Foundation cautions:

> Because of its emphasis on institutional "functions," the Classification is widely interpreted as differentiating colleges and universities with respect to mission. In this respect, one of the Classification's strengths is its grounding in objective data on institutional behavior: to the extent that it differentiates institutions by mission, it is mission as revealed in institutional action (McCormick 2000, 1).

TABLE 4.1
Distribution of Higher Education Institutions

Category	Total (% of institutions)	Public (% of category total)	Private not-for-profit (% of category total)	Private for-profit (% of category total)
All Institutions	3,941 (100.0%)	1,643 (41.7%)	1,681 (42.7%)	617 (15.7%)
Associate's Colleges	1,669 (42.3)	1,025 (61.4)	159 (9.5)	485 (29.1)
Baccalaureate Colleges	606 (15.4)	91 (15.0)	499 (82.3)	16 (2.6)
Baccalaureate Colleges—Liberal Arts	228 (5.8)	26 (11.5)	202 (88.6)	0 (0.0)
Baccalaureate Colleges—General	321 (8.1)	50 (15.6)	266 (82.9)	5 (1.6)
Baccalaureate/Associate's Colleges	57 (1.4)	15 (26.3)	31 (54.4)	11 (19.3)
Master's Colleges and Universities	611 (15.5)	272 (44.5)	331 (54.2)	8 (1.3)
Master's Colleges and Universities I	496 (12.6)	249 (50.2)	246 (49.6)	1 (0.2)
Master's Colleges and Universities II	115 (2.9)	23 (20.0)	85 (73.9)	7 (6.1)
Doctoral/Research Universities	261 (6.6)	166 (63.6)	93 (35.6)	2 (0.8)
Doctoral/Research Universities—Extensive	151 (3.8)	102 (67.5)	49 (32.5)	0 (0.8)
Doctoral/Research Universities—Intensive	110 (2.8)	64 (58.2)	44 (40.0)	2 (1.8)
Specialized Institutions (Seminaries, Medical, etc.)	766 (19.4)	67 (8.7)	593 (77.4)	106 (13.8)
Tribal	28 (0.7)	22 (78.6)	6 (21.4)	0 (0)

SOURCE: From the print version of the 2000 Carnegie Classification. Obtained from www.carnegiefoundation.org/Classification/CIHE2000/Tables.htm.

TABLE 4.2
Number of Higher Education Institutions by Number of Students, Fall 1999

NUMBER OF STUDENTS	ALL INSTITUTIONS			RESEARCH			DOCTORAL			MASTER'S			BACCALAUREATE			2-YEAR			SPECIALIZED		
	ALL	PUB	PRI	ALL	PUB	PRI	ALL	PUB	PRI	ALL	PUB	PRI	ALL	PUB	PRI	ALL	PUB	PRI	ALL	PUB	PRI
Up to 999	1,593	178	1,415	1	0	1	3	1	2	21	0	21	365	11	354	723	144	579	480	22	458
1,000–4,999	1,507	746	761	4	1	3	21	4	17	281	80	201	493	95	398	576	534	42	132	32	100
5,000–19,000	730	604	126	50	23	27	75	46	29	244	186	58	21	16	5	330	329	1	10	4	6
20,000 or more	128	118	10	71	62	9	14	14	0	11	11	0	1	1	0	30	30	0	1	0	1
Total	3,958	1,646	2,312	126	86	40	113	65	48	557	277	280	880	123	757	1,659	1,037	622	623	58	565

SOURCE: U.S. Department of Education

We *can* extrapolate that faculty members' activities reflect their institutions' reward structures and, therefore, that the categories do represent institutions' actual, if not stated, missions.

Because each data-gathering agency collects information in its uniquely defined categories, it is not possible to give an exactly comparable picture of faculty members and students across institutional types. Some currently available data were collected prior to the reclassification of the Carnegie scheme, some are more concerned with the public/private division, and many, including the National Science Foundation and U.S. Department of Education, recently have changed their reporting categories as well.

Table 4.2 displays the range of colleges and universities by the number of students they enroll. There are approximately as many small institutions with fewer than 1,000 students as there are medium-sized institutions with between 1,000 and 4,999 students. The greatest bulk of the smaller institutions are private, while the medium-sized ones are evenly divided between public and private. Research universities are moderate-size (5,000 to 19,000 students) and large (20,000 or more students), with only a five research universities enrolling under 5,000 students. Two-year and specialized institutions tend to be small or moderate in enrollment.

STUDENTS

THE 2000 CENSUS REPORTS OVER fifteen million students currently enrolled in higher education. Table 4.3 shows that, as in other recent years, female students outnumber male students in all categories of institution, both full-time and part-time. As students get older, they are more likely to attend college on a part-time basis. This information will be discussed, later in this chapter, for each institutional type.

Table 4.4 displays college enrollment by race and ethic group, comparing 1980 and 1999 enrollment figures. The only category that declined in enrollment is white males. The greatest enrollment gains were by Hispanic and Asian students. Table 4.5 shows the proportion of undergraduates receiving federal, institutional, and state financial aid.

FACULTY

TABLE 4.6 DESCRIBES THE DEMOGRAPHICS of faculty members by institutional type, including sex, race, age, highest degree, and base salary. There remains 2:1 ratio of men to women across all institutions, with a 3:1 ratio in public research and private doctorate-granting universities. The bulk of the American faculty is white, non-Hispanic, between the ages of forty and fifty-nine, with doctoral degrees. Salaries vary widely, with more salaries over $69,000 being paid at universities than colleges. This information will be discussed, later in this chapter, for each institutional type.

Table 4.7 displays the distribution of full-time and part-time faculty members by gender and ethnicity across the different types of institutions. Average salaries by gender and institutional type are shown in table 4.8.

Table 4.9 describes faculty activities by institutional type, including numbers of faculty members, hours worked per week, hours and percentages of time spent on teaching and research/scholarship, and numbers of courses taught. Faculty members at all types of institutions report spending high percentages of time on their teaching, with only research university faculty spending more of their time on research/scholarship than on teaching. As would be expected, faculty members teach fewer courses at universities than at colleges. This information will be discussed, later in this chapter, for each institutional type.

ASSOCIATE'S DEGREE COLLEGES

THE ASSOCIATE'S DEGREE COLLEGE (ADC) CLASSIFICATION includes community and junior colleges and technical institutes that offer almost exclusively associate's degrees. According to Phipps, Shedd, and Merisotis (2001), the new categorization scheme is problematic because it lumps together 1,669 institutions, which account for more than all of the doctoral/research, master's colleges, and baccalaureate colleges combined. In addition, the new classification includes only accredited and degree-granting institutions, excluding over 700 two-year institutions that participate in Title IV student aid funds. Phipps, et al., conclude that it would be more useful to include the remaining two-year institutions, such as certificate-granting and allied health institutions, in order to contribute to policy discussions regarding the broader spectrum of schools. Recognizing this limitation, we focus here exclusively on ADCs, where most upcoming faculty will find employment.

HISTORY

THE FIRST PRIVATE TWO-YEAR COLLEGE in the United States was established in 1851. It opened as part of a reform movement providing more of the population with access to higher education (Williams 1989). The first formal discussions about two-year colleges were spurred by economic downturns near the beginning of the twentieth century. When a convention of small Baptist colleges in Texas and Louisiana recognized that insufficient funding and lack of student support would not allow their numerous small colleges to remain open, the president of Baylor University, Reverend J. M. Carroll, suggested that the smaller colleges take students only for their first two years of course work, while Baylor would educate students for their last two years. Thus, each school could survive by limiting the number of faculty members and students.

At the same time, the American university system began to place greater emphasis on research and many university presidents looked to restructuring the university as a whole. The presidents of the University of Michigan, University of Minnesota, and University of Chicago proposed that university education would concentrate on the development of new knowledge and theories while collegiate education would concentrate on developing general education in the arts and sciences. They went on to suggest that collegiate instruction either be a function of secondary education, instituting the thirteenth and fourteenth grades, or that it be a function of the small liberal arts colleges.

William Rainey Harper, president of the University of Chicago, in conjunction with J. Stanley Brown, superintendent of Joliet Township High School, implemented an experimental postgraduate high school program. The experimental program became Joliet Junior College, paralleling the first two years of a university. Founded in 1901 with an initial enrollment of six students, it is America's oldest public community college. Today, Joliet Junior College serves more than 10,000 students in credit courses and 21,000 in noncredit courses, and offers associate's degrees, career education, adult education, and literacy programs.

The extension of high school to include the thirteenth and fourteenth grades was not widely accepted, but the junior college movement worked well with university restructuring from state to state (Ratcliff 1994). Initially, the purpose of the junior college was to serve as a transfer school where students could remain near home and receive a low-cost, general education for their first two years of college. However, as the educational needs of communities changed so did the responsibilities of the junior college. Thus, it created the need for a more *community*-based college.

TABLE 4.3
College Enrollment by Age

	ALL	Undergraduates at 2-Year Institutions		Undergraduates at 4-Year Institutions		Graduate Students	
		Full-time	Part-time	Full-time	Part-time	Full-time	Part-time
Male							
15–24	66.3%	83.3%	54.2%	85.4%	45.5%	39.0%	10.2%
25–44	29.6	14.1	42.6	13.5	49.0	47.6	71.6
45 and older	4.5	2.4	9.2	1.1	5.6	3.5	18.3
Enrollment	6,682,000 (43.6%)	969,000	685,000	3,090,000	776,000	546,000	617,000
Female							
15–24	60.2%	79.4%	35.9%	85.5%	35.4%	41.9%	10.7%
25–44	32.4	18.6	50.3	13.2	54.3	49.5	63.7
45 and older	7.5	1.9	13.9	1.2	10.6	8.6	25.7
Enrollment	8,632,000 (56.3%)	1,225,000	1,002,000	3,609,000	1,046,000	772,000	1,029,000
Total Enrollment	15,313,000	2,193,000	1,688,000	6,698,000	1,822,000	1,268,000	1,645,000

NOTE: The figures are based on a Census Bureau survey of 60,000 households conducted in October 2000. The statistics may differ from enrollment data compiled by the U.S. Department of Education because of differences in survey methodology. Because of rounding, figures may not add up to 100%.
SOURCE: *The Chronicle of Higher Education*

The evolution from junior college to community college has been widely debated. One theory holds that the Great Depression created the need for vocational and technical training (Karabe 1989) while another maintains that vocational training was already a function of the early two-year colleges (Ratcliff 1994). Today, the functions of two-year colleges vary from institution to institution. Most junior colleges are not strictly transfer schools. They often provide vocational training in many fields. Larger community colleges offer an array of programs to meet the needs of the current trends in vocational training as well as offering traditional two-year degrees. Furthermore, the rise of technical colleges and technical institutes (many of which are left out of the Carnegie classification) has followed the changing demands of the labor market for trained personnel in a variety of fields.

The 1960s and 1970s saw the creation of 568 new community colleges, almost half the total number in existence today. The rapid increase in new colleges created a demand for new experts in the management and leadership of these schools. Dynamic programs in community college leadership were introduced at the graduate level to prepare leaders for these schools.

MISSION

THE EARLY PURPOSE OF JUNIOR COLLEGES was focused on general liberal arts studies (Phillippe 1999). However, the mission of today is focussed not only on the provision of low-cost, local baccalaureate preparation, but also on remedial, occupational, and general education. ADC shared mission elements are access, with equity and inclusion for all learners. Open admissions policies and low tuition costs have attracted more than half of the nation's ADC undergraduates (Phillippe 1999). Beyond these fundamental concepts, however, there are widely disparate views of what the mission of the associate's college is or should be. There is considerable diversity among ADC structures, offerings, and their relationships with the communities in which they are located. Social, economic, and demographic shifts have led to increased competition and differentiation among the ADCs.

The average in-state tuition for public community colleges in most states is less than the average cost of a high-end personal computer (Phillippe 1999). In 1997/98, California had the most affordable associate's degree, costing on average a total of $750 (about $11 per unit), while New Hampshire had the most expensive associate's degree at $6,035. During that academic year, tuition and fees at public two-year institutions averaged less than half of those at public four-year institutions and averaged one-tenth of private four-year institutions' tuition and fees. Across the United States, tuition and fees for public community colleges average $1,518 per year.

The debate over the two-year college mission is not a new one. The past thirty years have seen a shift towards vocational education services and the curriculum at these institutions has become much more occupationally and technically oriented. Questions about mission have been raised for over two decades (see, for example, Cross 1981). Cohen (1985) argued that collegiate/academic transfer should be the core function of ADCs. Clowes and Levin (1989), on the other hand, question whether associate's colleges are leaving higher education. They argue that these schools should identify career education aimed at older employed students as their core function, leaving collegiate and remedial education, and community service as marginal functions.

More recently, a new and powerful trend has emerged within the ADC, intensifying the debate. There has been a growing shift on the part of the colleges to become involved in offering economic development services, such as contract training, small business development, and local economic development planning (Dougherty and Bakia 2000). The expansion of these functions is tied both to the colleges' responsiveness to the needs of their communities and also by economic necessity resulting, in part, from a growing trend for academically oriented students to go directly to four-year schools, bypassing ADC academic transfer programs.

The newer programs tend to differ substantially from traditional programs in revenue sources, types of students, and organizational culture. In addition, they draw limited administrative resources away from the traditional programs. Some argue that because of this broadening of activities, the associate's colleges have become less effective as they lack a clear purpose and do not serve any particular group of clients (students, businesses, or government) as well as they might. In addition, critics hold that this development undermines the ability of the associate's colleges to handle the traditional task of preparing citizens and not just workers. A recent study of faculty members at associate's colleges (Brewer 1999) indicates that growth of these activities in preference to traditional academic and occupational missions has led to fragmentation of the institutions, dissatisfaction of faculty members, and disputes over the allocation of scarce resources.

There are twenty-eight tribal colleges in the United States. In the past, these colleges had been termed two-year institutions, but under the new

Carnegie classification, tribal colleges have a distinct category (see table 4.1). Since tribal colleges typically do not offer baccalaureate degrees, we will include them as ADCs. Most of the tribal colleges were created in the 1960s and 1970s to provide a general education at the postsecondary level to the residents of reservations and to engage the Native American culture. Tribal colleges generally serve people living in geographically isolated areas. Most of these schools have small student bodies that are predominantly American Indian, are chartered by one or more tribes, have open admissions policies, and all started as two-year institutions (AIHEC 1999). Some of the colleges now offer four-year degrees, but their primary function remains to offer associate's degrees (Phillippe 1999).

And, finally, some associate's degree colleges are now becoming involved with the educational institutions before and after them, awarding credits (and soon degrees) to high school students and offering bachelor degrees to their own students. Most ADCs have become collegial partners with baccalaureate institutions and research universities. Currently, associate's colleges find themselves with multiple missions as they adapt to the needs of their client groups. Perhaps the best definition of associate's colleges' mission at this time is that given in *The Knowledge Net* (AACC 2000) that the mission is to serve and to create a climate for change.

STUDENTS

> The students I teach in the morning tend to be coming straight out of high school, while the students I teach in the evenings tend to be coming straight from work. You have to be a better teacher if you teach at an ADC (third year faculty member).

> Many of the students I've taught in the past have returned to visit after transferring to four-year institutions. They tell me that they are better prepared than many of the students who had already spent two years in the university (fifth year faculty member).

COLLEGE ENROLLMENT OBVIOUSLY WILL FOLLOW demographic trends just as college programs will mold to the demands of the students. This is demonstrated by the 149% increase in the number of students enrolling in ADC programs over the last century. In 1979 the number of eighteen year olds in the American population reached an all-time low (Cohen and Brawer 1996). Associate's colleges responded to the subsequent decline in numbers by

TABLE 4.4
College Enrollment by Racial and Ethnic Group

Group	All	Men	Women	Public 4-Year	Private 4-Year	Public 2-Year	Private 2-Year
Native American							
1980	83,900	37,800	46,100	29,000	7,900	45,200	1,800
1999	145,300	58,500	86,800	55,700	17,500	68,400	3,700
Asian							
1980	286,400	151,000	355,200	117,200	44,900	122,500	1,800
1999	909,700	435,300	474,400	370,100	183,800	344,300	11,500
African American							
1980	1,106,800	463,700	643,000	38,200	196,100	437,900	34,600
1999	1,640,700	603,000	1,037,700	614,600	347,400	637,700	41,000
Hispanic							
1980	471,700	231,600	240,100	156,400	60,200	249,800	5,300
1999	1,316,600	562,300	754,400	393,200	188,200	704,500	30,600
White							
1980	9,833,000	4,772,900	5,060,100	4,243,000	2,031,500	3,413,100	145,400
1999	10,262,500	4,539,900	5,722,600	4,286,900	2,305,300	3,507,900	162,500
International							
1980	305,000	210,800	94,200	143,800	97,100	60,300	3,700
1999	516,400	291,600	224,800	249,300	186,400	76,700	4,000
Total							
1980	12,086,800	5,868,100	6,218,700	5,127,600	2,437,800	4,328,800	192,600
1999	14,791,200	6,490,600	8,300,600	5,969,900	3,228,600	5,339,400	253,300

SOURCE: U.S. Department of Education

expanding their programs to attract older students interested in career changes, improving skills, or simply for personal interest. In the fall of 1999, there were 30 ADCs with an enrollment of more than 20,000 students at each one. In comparison to research universities that have a total of 71 schools each with more than 20,000 students, it appears as though the enrollment at ADCs is insubstantial. However, there are 330 ADCs with an enrollment between 5,000 and 19,000 students (see table 4.2).

In two-year institutions as well as other institution types, there is a substantial age difference between students attending full-time and those attending part-time (see table 4.3). Most full-time students are of traditional age (between fifteen and twenty-four years), while a substantial number of part-time students are of nontraditional age (over twenty-five years old). In ADCs, there are actually more students attending part-time than full-time. Approximately 50% of the students attending part-time are of nontraditional age, indicating that they already are in the work force and/or attending to families. Faculty must take this into account when working with students at all institutions, but, in particular, with students at ADCs.

By 1978, women finally were represented equally among all college students, largely due to an increase in women at the ADC level. Since that time, women have represented the majority of associate's degree earners. By 1999, there were approximately two million more women than men in college (see table 4.4). Part of the increase may reflect various state welfare reform efforts. At least half of the ADCs offer the Welfare to Work program, providing job training to welfare recipients and noncustodial parents (Phillippe 1999). These job seekers can receive on-the-job training, academic instruction, job-specific instruction, and job-placement assistance, as well as childcare, while part of the Welfare to Work program.

The percentage of minority students at ADCs also has risen steadily. In the fall of 1999, 34% of all the students attending associate's colleges were minority students (table 4.4). In fact, of all ethnic minority students in higher education in the United States, 47% were attending a two-year college. As the demands for education change within a community due to the changing cultural and social composition, the mission of the ADCs evolve to better suit the clients (Mellander and Robertson 1992).

According to Cohen and Brawer (1996), the change in number of underrepresented students is attributable to several factors, an important one of which is the availability of financial aid. For many years after World War II state and federal aid was strictly categorical, mainly benefiting people of low economic standing, war veterans, and minority groups. However, in the 1970s this type of financial aid was expanded with the goal of providing equal opportunity to anyone seeking an education regardless of socioeconomic background, race, sex, or ability (Cross 1971). According to the College Board's annual survey, the cost of attending public two-year institutions rose 5.8% in 2001, but 57.7% of the students receive some sort of federal financial aid—grants, loans, or work-study for tuition that is still comparatively low (see Brownstein; table 4.5).

The open door policy is exemplified by the range of cultures, economic background, and academic ability represented by the student body of ADCs. For example, 51.4% of the students at public two-year institutions were first-generation students in 1995, contributing to the diverse student body (Phillippe 1999). As for academic ability, in 1991 the average ACT composite score was 17.0 for students planning to attend an associate's college, whereas the national average was 20.6 (National Center for Education Statistics 1993). This type of data has been presented many times over, demonstrating the lack of academic preparation common among ADC students. Community colleges also serve a higher percentage of students with disabilities than any other institution type. In particular, 37% of students attending community colleges in 1995 had learning disabilities (Phillippe 1999). However, faculty members from community colleges report (personal interviews) that they have found less difference in preparedness between community college students and university students than would be expected. Because some of their students certainly need remedial education, remedial classes and writing centers are available. The faculty report that their students are engaging and challenging.

Additionally, the traditional 2+2 transfer path is no longer the most important among ADC students' educational goals. Only 6% of baccalaureate graduates earned an associate's degree (Palmer and Pugh 1993). A similar study documents that many students enroll in ADCs with no intention of receiving an associate's degree (Cejda and Kaylor 2001).

Faculty Life

There's a stigma that surrounds community college professors. People say we 'just' teach—as if teaching is something a professor should be ashamed of (fifth year faculty member).

THERE ARE MANY IMPORTANT DISTINCTIONS between ADC instructors and other higher education faculty. At the same time that the ADC student body has come to better represent the community in which it exists, so does their faculty. In particular, the number of women and minorities hired by these institutions has increased substantially in the last thirty years (Finkelstein et al. 1998). The faculty at public ADCs is comprised of 45.3% women—the highest percentage of women compared to other institution types (table 4.6). However substantial the increase in minority employment over the past thirty years may be, the faculty at public ADCs is a disproportionate 85.5% white faculty. This is not an unusual figure as minority status in academia is about the same across institutional types.

The percentage of faculty at ADCs with graduate degrees increased from 6% in 1941 to 22% in 1984 (Monroe 1972; Ottinger 1987, respectively). In 1993, only 16.6% of the full-time faculty had PH.D.s, 63.9% had master's degrees, 11.9% had a bachelor's degree, and 5.4% had less than a bachelor's (table 4.6). Historically, ADC faculty members did not hold doctoral degrees because the early instructors were drawn from high school teachers. A faculty member can be hired for a tenure track position at a tenure-granting ADC with a master's degree. Faculty members who are hired while writing a dissertation are not typically asked to finish their doctorate. One faculty member stated that, "As a matter of fact, my colleagues told me that the school would prefer that I not finish my dissertation, because they would have to pay me more if I did" (personal interview). However, this is not the situation for all junior faculty at ADCs. Another junior faculty member, who received tenure at her institution, is finishing her dissertation. She reports feeling positive pressure from her colleagues to do so and there is a growing feeling at her college that a master's degree is not enough (personal interview).

There is no doubt that financial instability contributes to the continued hiring of master's degree holders, rather than doctorates. However, ADCs also hire people for instructional positions who have less than an M.A., which has little to do with finances. In particular, the schools hire people, regardless of their educational background, with technical skills that run parallel to the needs of local industry. Most, if not all, these people occupy adjunct positions. The overall number of part-time faculty positions increased threefold between 1960 and 1984, as a response to an increase in the number of students and the hiring of practitioners to teach in some professional areas. ADCs employ the largest proportion of part-time faculty compared to other types of

TABLE 4.5

Proportion of Undergraduates Receiving Financial Aid 1999–2000

Type of Institution	Any	Grants	Federal Aid			Institutional	State
			Loans	Work-Study	PLUS*		
Public							
Less-than-2-year	25.3%	23.4%	6.1%	0.7%	0.3%	4.5%	6.4%
2-year	20.7	17.2	7.0	1.3	0.1	4.1	13.6
4-year	46.4	24.4	38.5	4.6	3.5	17.4	18.1
Not Doctorate-Granting	47.6	27.8	36.7	5.1	2.2	13.0	20.2
Doctorate-Granting	45.7	22.4	39.6	4.3	4.3	19.9	16.8
Private, Nonprofit							
Less-than-4-year	57.7%	40.9%	36.7%	6.8%	7.0%	32.8%	19.6%
4-year	56.6	24.7	48.2	13.4	7.1	46.7	22.3
Not Doctorate-Granting	58.1	27.2	48.2	11.7	6.6	44.0	24.6
Doctorate-Granting	54.3	20.9	48.3	16.0	7.9	50.8	18.9
Private, For-Profit							
Less-than-2-year	80.1%	64.0%	54.1%	0.6%	.07%	6.1%	4.1%
2-year and above	80.4	45.6	72.4	1.1	8.6	8.0	12.9
Total	39.1%	23.1%	27.9%	4.1%	2.9%	15.4%	16.1%

SOURCE: U.S. Department of Education   * Parent Loans for Undergraduate Students

institutions (table 4.7). There is no disparity between genders or ethnicities regarding who is teaching full- or part-time: approximately half of each group teaches part-time. Unlike other sectors of higher education, it is not uncommon for faculty at an ADC to have taught part-time for several years prior to receiving a full-time position.

More than half of the faculty members at ADCs make less than $40,000 per year (table 4.6). However, this figure includes part-time faculty as well as full-time faculty with, and without, academic rank. In the academic year 2000/01, the average annual income for full-time ranked professors at public ADCs was $57,785 (table 4.8). This is lower than their counterparts at other institution types, but this gap has narrowed over the years (Phillippe 1999). The pay increases for faculty members has prompted ADCs to hire more adjunct faculty rather than full-time faculty, creating more teaching positions while substantially lowering the institutional cost per teacher. This widespread practice is not without its critics. ADCs are facing numerous retirements of administrators and faculty members whom have been working since the 1960s when many of the ADCs were formed (Phillippe 1999). The question for the future will be whether the institutions fill the faculty positions with full-time faculty or multiple part-timers.

A primary difference between ADC faculty and those who teach at other institution types is that faculty members at ADCs devote a higher proportion of time and energy to teaching rather than research or keeping abreast in their field (Palinchak 1972). On average, full-time faculty spend 46.9 hours per week working, while spending 32 of those hours teaching (table 4.9). Compared to faculty members at research universities, ADC professors spend fewer hours working, but more time in the classroom. Professors at research universities are granted time for research by a reduction in teaching responsibilities and the help of teaching assistants (TAs), while professors at associate's colleges do not have access to TAs and are typically not offered time off for research. Additionally, 36.6% of the full-time faculty members at ADCs teach five or more courses per academic term, thereby lengthening their office hours and spending more hours in preparation and grading (table 4.9). It is not that ADC professors do not have time to work on scholarship in their fields. More likely, they do not spend time on research because they do not receive incentives for publications and they do not have a pool of graduate students to help with their research and teaching. However, publication is not usually a tenure requirement at ADCs.

Teaching and Learning

> Although I don't formally participate in faculty development, I spend a considerable amount of energy on developing my teaching abilities. My institution just doesn't offer enough formal feedback, so I have to talk with other teachers to see if they're doing something that I should try out (third year faculty member).

TEACHING IS THE PRIMARY RESPONSIBILITY of faculty at ADCs. The student to faculty ratio at public ADCs is about 18:1, while the independent schools' ratio is 10:1 (Phillippe 1999). Although the numbers are appealing, we must keep in mind that these figures include full- and part-time faculty. Students of part-time faculty do not have as much interaction with their professors. Part-time faculty members keep fewer office hours, if any at all, and their committee and advisory responsibilities are minimal, thereby hindering the relationships between students and instructors while increasing the work load of full-time faculty.

Like other institution types, ADCs rely on the traditional lecture format (Phillippe 1999). However, alternative teaching methods are encouraged. Research on learning styles has caused instructional staff to reconsider the traditional methods of teaching students. More than ever, instructors are experimenting with cooperative and collaborative methods, as well as student-centered learning environments. In addition to the pedagogical techniques surrounding learning, instructors are encouraged to use technology in the classroom. Technology can come in the form of computer and projector use, overhead projector use, teleconferencing, and so forth.

Experience with distance education courses is a particular plus when seeking a full-time position at an ADC. ADCs are more likely to offer non-face-to-face courses than other institutions (U.S. Department of Education). Distance education includes using a computerized system, TV-based format, or any other non-face-to-face method. Surveys show that the overall teaching load for those teaching distance education is somewhat higher than those not teaching distance education (U.S. Department of Education). Distance education is taught by faculty regardless of status, gender, or ethnicity. Faculty members at ADCs are more likely to teach distance education courses than their counterparts at other institutions. Distance education courses are usually taught as overload courses in addition to the regular teaching schedule. Full-time faculty members who teach distance education earn approximately

$1,700 above their base salary (U.S. Department of Education). According to the surveys, although faculty members teaching distance education have heavier workloads, they are just as likely to indicate that they are very happy with their workloads.

Faculty development programs are usually available at two-year colleges. A national sample of community colleges shows that 93.1% of the colleges surveyed provide financial support for conference attendance and 87.7% have teaching consultants who conduct workshops on campus for the improvement of teaching and learning. Some form of sabbatical leave is available to improve teaching and learning at 63.1% of the colleges surveyed (Murray 1999). However, the survey suggests that there is a lack of enthusiasm for faculty development. The perks that are mentioned are nearly universal, but the main problem reported is that faculty participation is too low to warrant additional services.

BACCALAUREATE COLLEGES

THIS CLASSIFICATION REPRESENTS A NUMBER OF DIFFERENT types of institutions with varying historical roots. While some of these institutions may trace their origins back two centuries or more (as many liberal arts colleges do) and retain a commitment to an education based largely, if not solely, in the liberal arts, others have evolved from the more recent emergence of community/associate's colleges to grant at least some baccalaureate degrees. Still others began as liberal arts colleges but as a result of changing educational philosophies or the need to expand enrollment, branched out beyond the traditional liberal arts to include professional programs.

HISTORY

AT THE BASE OF WHAT WE now call baccalaureate colleges lay some critical events occurring within higher education dating back to the nineteenth century. Changes in curriculum, the appearance of agricultural schools, and the evolution of large doctorate-granting institutions forced the small colleges established across much of the early American republic in the late eighteenth and early nineteenth centuries, particularly in rural communities, to become more self-conscious about their own place in American higher education. If universities would provide graduate degrees and agricultural schools would provide practical education, these smaller colleges sought to retain a baccalaureate education with a limited curriculum based around the liberal arts,

TABLE 4.6
Faculty Demographics by Type of Institution

	ALL	RESEARCH		DOCTORAL		COMPREHENSIVE		PRIVATE LIBERAL ARTS	PUBLIC 2-YEAR
		PUBLIC	PRIVATE	PUBLIC	PRIVATE	PUBLIC	PRIVATE		
SEX									
Male	353,000 (66.8%)	76.7%	69.1%	69.9%	76.4%	66.1%	64.9%	61.1%	54.7%
Female	176,000 (33.2%)	23.3%	30.9%	30.1%	23.6%	33.9%	35.2%	38.9%	45.3%
RACE									
White, non-Hispanic	457,000 (86.5%)	88.0%	83.7%	87.5%	84.1%	82.7%	91.3%	90.0%	85.5%
Black, non-Hispanic	27,000 (5.2)	2.8	5.0	3.1	4.9	9.1	3.5	5.4	6.2
Hispanic	14,000 (2.6)	2.2	2.1	2.5	3.7	2.6	1.6	1.3	4.1
Asian/Pacific Islander	28,000 (5.2)	6.9	9.0	6.1	7.1	5.1	3.3	2.8	3.3
American Indian/ Alaskan Native	3,000 (0.5)	0.1	0.2	0.8	0.2	0.5	0.2	0.5	1.0
AGE									
Under 40	110,000 (20.7%)	22.5%	30.0%	29.4%	25.2%	18.0%	18.8%	23.0%	16.8%
40–59	350,000 (66.3)	63.8	55.8	63.3	60.4	69.8	64.8	63.7	73.0
60 or Older	69,000 (12.9)	13.7	14.2	12.7	14.5	12.1	16.4	13.3	10.3
HIGHEST DEGREE									
Doctoral	284,000 (54.0%)	70.8%	63.7%	62.6%	58.2%	68.1%	60.8%	58.4%	16.6%
Professional	58,000 (11.1)	17.0	24.9	20.1	29.4	4.3	7.7	3.2	2.3
Master's	156,000 (29.7)	10.6	10.2	16.1	10.5	26.4	29.3	35.3	63.9
Bachelor's	21,000 (4.0)	1.6	1.1	1.3	1.9	1.1	2.1	3.1	11.9
Less than Bachelor's	6,000 (1.2)	0.1	0.1	<.05	<.05	0.2	0.1	<0.5	5.4
BASE SALARY									
Under $40,000	225,000 (42.6%)	40.0%	22.5%	35.8%	30.0%	44.7%	52.0%	66.0%	56.9%
$40,000–$69,000	241,000 (45.5)	57.0	44.0	46.8	44.7	50.9	42.1	30.6	41.8
$70,000–$99,999	43,000 (8.2)	16.5	16.5	11.6	17.6	4.9	4.6	2.8	0.9
$100,000 or More	20,000 (3.7)	6.5	6.5	6.2	7.7	0.4	1.4	0.5	0.4

SOURCE: U.S. Department of Education, National Center for Education Statistics (NCES), National Study of Postsecondary Faculty (NSOPF), 1993. The information for this table was prepared by NCES in September 1996. There is an additional category of "Other" representing 5% of full-time faculty in a range of specialized institutions. Additional data are available at http://nces.ed.gov/pubs2001/digest/ch3.html

including Latin, philosophy and mathematics (Hawkins 1999). With this determination, the *liberal arts* college, as we know it, was born. Liberal arts schools championed the classical subjects as central means for the production of "well-rounded" students, by which they generally meant ones infused with religious ideals, breadth of knowledge, and an ethic of social service.

Mission

Early liberal arts colleges had at least two foundational aims. First, drawing upon nineteenth-century political theory on the integral role of education in the formation of good citizenship and the preservation of democracy, liberal arts colleges, like all institutions of higher education at the time, tried to equip their students for civic participation. However, until the second half of the nineteenth century, most universities could manage only relatively small student bodies, leaving the majority of students to attend one of the many smaller liberal arts colleges. In terms of sheer numbers, then, liberal arts colleges significantly contributed to the political aims of the young republic.

A second crucial aim for early liberal arts colleges focused on religious instruction. The need for an educated clergy to support America's expanding population led Protestant denominations to establish colleges to prepare their recruits for the ministry. Furthermore, mandatory chapel and church attendance, along with a curriculum culminating in a senior seminar on moral philosophy, ensured that students not interested in pursuing a career in the ministry would at least be imbued with strong religious ideals.

However, the twentieth century brought a host of challenges, and with them, significant changes to liberal arts colleges. What is more, the reorganization that ensued fundamentally influenced the development of the general baccalaureate college.

In the quest to expand enrollment, coupled with a theological and social commitment to greater pluralism, many church-related liberal arts colleges dissolved their official religious connections and eliminated mandatory chapel attendance in the early to mid–twentieth century. At the same time, liberal arts colleges, whether religiously affiliated or not, expanded their curriculum, permitting students greater freedom in the choice of courses and majors, while simultaneously instituting general education programs to ensure exposure to a range of disciplines. Thus, while liberal arts colleges moved away from the limited curriculum of classical education, they attempted to retain the concept of "well-rounded" students by exposing them to a number of fields of study, all with the intention of fostering critical and analytical skills that could be applied across the range of disciplines.

All of these changes made liberal arts colleges appear strikingly similar to their research and comprehensive university counterparts. But supporters of liberal arts colleges pointed to the small student body, lower student-faculty ratio, close interaction between students and faculty, and the sense of shared community as essential characteristics that set them off from other types of institutions.

Nevertheless, liberal arts colleges declined during the twentieth century as a percentage of the total number of institutions of higher learning from 40% in 1950 to roughly 25% by 1970. They also declined in the number of students they taught, accounting for only 8% of college students by 1970 (Hawkins 1999). The number of students now taught by liberal arts colleges may in fact be as low as 3% (Pace and Connolly 2001).

As a corrective measure, many colleges began offering more programs for students in vocational areas such as business, education, engineering, and the health fields, thereby drawing themselves away from a singular focus on the liberal arts fields of the sciences, humanities, and social sciences. This movement away from the liberal arts marked the transition for many schools toward general baccalaureate colleges, a transition further facilitated by changing student interests. The numbers of students majoring in vocational areas has increased dramatically at baccalaureate colleges in recent years. Students majoring in basic liberal arts fields at the most selective liberal arts colleges declined from 80% in 1983–86 to only 57% in 1997/98, whereas majors in professional fields rose from 12% in 1983–86 to 29% by 1997/98 (Pace and Connolly 2001).

Despite the many adaptive changes, baccalaureate colleges as a whole now represent only 16% of institutions of higher education (table 4.1). Still, their proponents believe that the benefits accruing from their smaller size and residential emphasis allow them to occupy a special niche within higher education, enabling them to survive in an increasingly competitive market.

STUDENTS

Our school tends to draw extremely high achieving applicants, not only inside the classroom, but also outside it. This can be both a blessing and a curse. On the one hand they are extremely well rounded, with interests stretching beyond their studies. On the other hand, their classwork some-times suffers because of their other interests (fourth year faculty member).

THE AMAZING DIVERSITY CHARACTERISTIC of baccalaureate colleges pre-vents generalized remarks about students and their lives at these types of schools. For instance, while many small baccalaureate/associates degree col-leges draw heavily from students already residing within the community, lib-eral arts and general baccalaureate colleges draw a far larger percentage of their students from outside the local community. Nevertheless, despite clear differences, it is possible to draw at least some tentative and general conclu-sions about students at baccalaureate colleges. Table 4.2 shows that more than half of baccalaureate colleges list enrollments between 1,000 and 4,999 stu-dents. Further, only 2% of these schools have enrollments over 5,000, com-pared with 45% for master's degree colleges and universities, and 96% for re-search universities. This relatively small size frequently results in personal interaction with faculty; a feature that can be attractive to younger students away from home for the first time, not to mention comforting to their par-ents who desire a quality education for their children but worry that they might not receive close attention at a large university (Astin 1999).

A second problem for establishing firm conclusions about baccalaureate colleges lies in the available statistical data. Tables 4.3 and 4.4 note important data concerning the student population but are divided into categories that combine several different kinds of institutions. We therefore must tread care-fully in making any conclusions from such data in relation to baccalaureate colleges. Nevertheless, since baccalaureate colleges represent approximately 50% of the private four-year and 10% of the public four-year colleges and uni-versities, we can at least make some qualified remarks, particularly in relation to table 4.4. Here we see that in terms of racial and ethnic groups, white stu-dents continue to significantly outnumber all others at both public and pri-vate four-year institutions. We also find dramatic increases over the twenty-year period from 1980 to 1999 in terms of minority enrollment across the board. For instance, at private four-year institutions, the number of Hispanic students more than tripled while the number of Asian students quadrupled.

One of the most imposing barriers to attendance at many baccalaureate colleges, especially the more prestigious liberal arts colleges, continues to be the considerable monetary commitment. Many students and their families may be expected to pay over $35,000 per year in tuition, board and other ex-penses at some of the more prestigious colleges. In spite of the high cost, only

TABLE 4.7
Full-time and Part-time Faculty by Gender, Ethnic Group, and Type of Institution

	ALL	RESEARCH		DOCTORAL*		COMPREHENSIVE		PRIVATE LIBERAL ARTS	PUBLIC 2-YEAR	OTHER**
		PUBLIC	PRIVATE	PUBLIC	PRIVATE	PUBLIC	PRIVATE			
NUMBER										
Full-time	560,393	137,532	38,953	58,054	20,655	83,041	37,508	47,586	102,463	34,601
Part-time	416,024	35,762	14,769	25,539	18,017	48,401	36,709	32,970	170,092	33,765
MEN										
Full-time	63.7%	70.5%	73.9%	66.7%	63.6%	61.7%	63.3%	62.2%	50.1%	67.9%
Part-time	52.2%	55.2%	60.3%	49.6%	58.6%	46.5%	59.1%	44.0%	51.8%	54.3%
WOMEN										
Full-time	36.3	29.5	26.2	33.3	36.4	38.3	36.7	37.9	49.9	32.1
Part-time	49.7	44.8	39.8	50.4	41.4	53.5	40.9	56.1	48.2	45.8
NATIVE AMERICAN										
Full-time	0.7	0.5	0.2	1.3	0.7	0.5	1.2	1.1	0.8	0.6
Part-time	1.0	1.9	—	2.3	0.4	1.2	0.5	0.2	1.0	0.2
ASIAN										
Full-time	5.8	8.5	7.0	6.0	9.2	5.9	3.7	2.9	3.4	4.6
Part-time	3.2	4.6	2.5	3.1	7.1	5.5	1.7	3.2	2.3	2.9
AFRICAN AMERICAN										
Full-time	5.1	3.2	3.7	3.9	4.4	7.4	4.5	6.4	6.0	7.1
Part-time	4.5	2.9	3.3	3.6	3.4	4.1	2.7	6.9	5.3	4.6
HISPANIC										
Full-time	3.3	3.4	3.5	3.0	3.9	3.6	2.7	1.6	4.6	1.3
Part-time	3.7	3.5	4.3	3.1	2.3	3.8	2.0	3.1	4.8	2.0
WHITE										
Full-time	85.1	84.5	85.6	85.8	81.8	82.6	87.8	88.1	85.3	86.4
Part-time	87.6	87.1	89.9	87.9	86.8	85.5	93.1	86.7	86.6	90.3

SOURCE: U.S. Department of Education, 1999 National Study of Postsecondary Faculty

* Includes medical schools   ** Includes public liberal arts, private 2-year, religious, and other specialized colleges and excludes medical schools

56% of students at private four-year colleges receive some kind financial aid (table 4.5), leaving nearly half of the students to fund their education through a combination of family support and/or private employment. For many students, this simply becomes impossible, especially in families with multiple children in college at the same time. In fact, Breneman (1994) argues that high tuition may be a contributing factor in the decline of middle- and lower-class student enrollment.

However, those students who do choose liberal arts colleges have some advantages over larger schools: smaller class size, residential living that facilitates lasting relationships, and personal contact with faculty. Astin (1999) notes students in liberal arts colleges more often finish their bachelor's degree and go on to graduate school than students at other types of institutions.

FACULTY LIFE

> I would say that I end up working about sixty hours a week between teaching, research, and service. I've seen a number of colleagues burn themselves out working seven days a week. I just knew this wasn't for me. So I try to take off at least one day a week to pursue other activities (second year faculty member).

GETTING A FULL-TIME JOB AT BACCALAUREATE colleges has never been easy, especially for minority applicants. Despite gains over the last two decades in the numbers of women and racial minorities, white males still dominate the faculties at these schools (table 4.6). On the bright side, the liberal arts wing of the baccalaureate colleges do rank second behind only the public comprehensives in the percentage of women on their faculty. They also rank second in the percentage of black faculty members. However, many of the positions available to women and people of color are part-time. Table 4.7 indicates that women hold more part-time than full-time positions at liberal arts colleges and that this is true almost without exception across the various minority groups.

Salary comparisons for the year 2000/01, shown in table 4.8, indicate that salary levels for faculty at baccalaureate colleges generally rank lower than those of their colleagues at comprehensive and doctoral-granting institutions, yet higher than colleagues at community colleges. On average, full professors at public and private baccalaureate institutions received $64,365 as compared to their cohorts at doctoral universities who averaged $89,848 and comprehensives who averaged $69,917. However, when the averages within baccalaureate colleges are broken down, it becomes clear that these figures hide quite distinct variations among the types of schools that constitute the category. Professors at private independent colleges make considerably more ($74,031) than their counterparts at public institutions ($62,059), while faculty members at church-related schools receive more than $17,000 less per year than their colleagues at private independent schools. Interestingly, this disparity between church-related and private independent/public schools closes considerably at both comprehensive and doctoral institutions where salaries at some church-related schools exceed those at public institutions.

Of course, an important factor in salary consideration is regional variation. Salaries at baccalaureate institutions in the Northeast, for instance, on average rank substantially higher than the West, followed by the North Central region with the South lagging behind (DeNeef 1995). Much of the difference results from cost of living variations, but even these differ within regions.

Despite lower pay, faculty members at liberal arts colleges seem more satisfied with teaching undergraduate students than their colleagues at research and comprehensive universities (Finkelstein, Seal, and Schuster 1998). This may be the case, in part, because the institutions tend to be smaller and, therefore, faculty members have greater opportunity to get to know the students more personally inside and outside the classroom.

Faculty life at all types of institutions requires heavy commitments in terms of time and energy and this is no less true for baccalaureate colleges. Administrators at baccalaureate colleges increasingly expect faculty members to excel at both teaching and research. Full-time faculty members generally teach about six courses per year, although some may teach as many as eight to ten, depending on the school (table 4.9). Aside from this, faculty members also must find time to publish and perform committee work if they hope to obtain tenure. Recent studies show that faculty at private liberal arts colleges spend on average 63% of their time on teaching and just under 19% on research (table 4.9). By comparison, teaching time ranks second highest at liberal arts colleges behind only associate's degree colleges. On the other hand, faculty members say they spend nearly as much time as their colleagues at master's universities on research, despite spending more time teaching.

Some of the most important issues for faculty members at baccalaureate colleges center on the very characteristics that distinguish these schools: a small student body, typically rural location, and a tight-knit community. While all of these have their strengths, they also can present problems for some. For instance, many new faculty members frequently find the transition from their graduate programs at major universities to the small and often geographically (and frequently professionally) isolated liberal arts college difficult. Faculty members often choose to take a position at a liberal arts college because of the lower faculty to student ratio, the focus on teaching with less emphasis on research (although, this varies by institution), and the "ability to make a difference" in the lives of students and the institution as a whole (Wilson 2000). These findings speak to the quality of life that new faculty intend to find on the campuses. While some of these expectations are met, others are not, and this can leave many scholars feeling frustrated. Many new faculty members admit surprise when they find students they believe inadequately prepared for college. Others complain of a petty and overly obtrusive senior faculty or poorly equipped facilities (Wilson 2000).

Of course, no school is perfect and the problems that confront faculty at baccalaureate colleges simply mean that faculty members interested in working at this type of school should carefully consider the school's strengths and weaknesses. At the same time, they should consider whether their skills, as well as personal and professional interests, match with the expectations of the particular baccalaureate institution.

TEACHING AND LEARNING

> I really can't say that I've integrated technology into my teaching in any
> great way. I'm not someone who puts his syllabi online or sets up chat
> rooms to discuss course material (second year faculty member).

BACCALAUREATE COLLEGES TYPICALLY TRY to take advantage of the small faculty/student ratios to encourage close interaction between faculty members and students. While lecturing remains a standard practice within the baccalaureate system, seminar-style discussion, faculty supervised independent research, and even student participation in faculty research projects all represent opportunities for alternative teaching and learning experimentation (Finkelstein, Seal, and Schuster 1998; Smallwood 2002).

However, baccalaureate colleges have resisted exploring one area of teaching and learning that has undergone tremendous growth in recent years: distance learning through online courses. One scholar estimates that

TABLE 4.8
Average Faculty Salaries by Type of Institution and Gender 2000–01

Type of Institution	Professor			Associate Professor			Assistant Professor		
	All	Public	Private	All	Public	Private	All	Public	Private
Doctoral Institutions	$89,848	$84,007	$107,663	$62,446	$60,571	$70,314	$52,671	$50,635	$60,853
Comprehensive Institutions	69,917	68,828	75,143	55,347	54,886	57,832	45,334	45,147	47,045
Baccalaureate Institutions	64,365	62,059	74,031	50,253	50,811	54,933	41,667	42,311	44,774
2-Year Institutions With Academic Ranks	57,785	57,932	54,628	47,150	47,323	45,052	41,192	41,575	32,368
All	78,912	76,147	93,244	57,380	57,071	62,188	47,358	47,195	51,727
Men	80,860	77,971	95,467	58,941	58,583	63,962	49,015	48,726	54,121
Women	71,419	69,145	84,100	54,638	54,362	59,110	49,015	48,726	54,121

	All	Public	Private
2-Year Institutions Without Academic Ranks	46,039	46,020	47,460
Men	47,114	47,112	48,230
Women	44,942	44,930	46,205

SOURCE: U.S. Department of Education

only 10% to 15 % of America's colleges and universities have yet to implement significant online programs. The overwhelming majority of these are liberal arts colleges (Carnevale 2001). The most common explanation for this is the value most baccalaureate colleges place on retaining small student populations who maintain residence on or near campus. This format, they believe, continues to appeal to enough prospective students that, at least for the foreseeable future, most baccalaureate colleges will retain a residential approach to learning and forego distance education.

But while largely rejecting online education, baccalaureate colleges have taken other steps toward implementing new technology into the classroom. Many faculty members routinely use computer and Internet technology to publish course syllabi, provide reading assignments, encourage student research, and organize discussion groups. Further, through implementing Web-based research projects, faculty members have introduced greater diversity in terms of the resources students can draw from in their work (Olsen 2000). Beyond this, some professors have begun to integrate software into their courses that allows students to explore and experiment in different areas of study, thereby moving the student from passive learner to active investigator. As more and more research reveals that students learn in different ways, the ability to diversify teaching styles through active learning techniques will become increasingly essential.

It is likely that new faculty members at baccalaureate colleges will be expected to incorporate basic computer and Internet technology into their classrooms (for instance, online chat rooms and Internet research projects). Just how far this requirement will extend remains uncertain. Many colleges openly acknowledge the need to integrate new technology that will enhance both the teaching and learning process, in reality most have yet to incorporate a standard rule for what technology they should use, or have established a means to evaluate how well faculty members incorporate this technology into the classroom (Kiernan 2000). As a result, the use of technology has not yet become a clear criterion in evaluating good teaching or included in coherent promotion and tenure review. Because of this, it is less likely that younger faculty members will have a material interest in working to incorporate new technology into their teaching. Even so, their own professional training, creativity, and personal interest lead many to experimentation.

MASTER'S LEVEL INSTITUTIONS
HISTORY

> My campus developed as part of changes in the state's plan for the higher
> education system in the mid-1940s. A major emphasis of our school is to
> train the state's public school teachers (second year faculty member).

THE ORIGINS OF MASTER'S LEVEL (previously called *comprehensive*) institutions can be traced back to the early nineteenth century in response to the needs of society to train teachers. When mandatory primary and secondary education became law, the need arose for normal schools and teacher colleges to prepare teachers. In the 1830s, Massachusetts was the first state to establish *normal schools* to train common-school teachers. The mission of these noncollegiate institutions, to educate common-school teachers, assumed that students needed to prepare in the basic subjects that they would teach. The establishment of normal schools gradually spread throughout many of the states and territories of the United States throughout the second half of the nineteenth century. Many felt that these schools were adequate for preparing teachers (Finnegan 1991); the prevailing wisdom assumed that teacher training did not require a college education. During this same time however, a group also arose who insisted that teacher-training schools were foreign in origin since they were modeled after Prussian and French institutes. They believed this European system was a "curse" (Finnegan 1991) on the American system. In some states, these proponents won. Eighteen state colleges (mostly located in New England) of the present 611 master's degree institutions began as academies that offered a curriculum of practical subjects in addition to teacher education instruction. Normal schools did not die out, however, and by the beginning of the twentieth century, 103 normal schools had been established throughout the country.

The transition from noncollegiate to collegiate and then to baccalaureate education for primary and secondary school teachers progressed in stages from the late eighteenth century through the first third of the twentieth century. Finnegan (1991) cites five factors that encouraged the evolution of the normal schools into teachers colleges: (a) the rapid increase in the number of primary and secondary students that necessitated more teachers; (b) the turnover of teachers in primary and secondary schools, which made it desirable to stabilize the profession; (c) the demand for collegiate and secondary school academic standards, resulting in the beginning of the voluntary accreditation movement; (d) the propagation of voluntary associations of higher education administrators by institutional type; and (e) the upgrading of the curriculum of the normal schools through the development of education theory and practice.

Teacher training was not the only goal of master's level institutions. As the United States entered the age of the Industrial and Technological Revolution, it became necessary to train people in the occupations resulting from this revolution. Institutions that disseminated applied knowledge became critical and the Morrill Acts of 1862 and 1890 resulted. Basically, these acts called for the donation of federal land to each state and territory for the development of a school that would "provide the population with a practical education that had a direct relevance to their daily lives" (Place 2000). The first three states to accept the 1862 Morrill Act were Iowa, Vermont, and Connecticut after President Lincoln signed the bill into law on July 2, 1862. By 1870, thirty-seven states had instituted a program for teaching agriculture, mechanical arts, and military tactics (Place 2000). In all, there are 105 land-grant colleges and universities stemming from the 1862, 1890, and 1994 federal legislation (Place 2000).

Mission

Teaching at a master's level institution provides the best of all worlds (second year faculty member).

THE ORIGINAL MISSION OF THE MASTER'S level institutions was set forth in the Morrill Acts. The First Morrill Act (1862) charges a land-grant college or university to "teach agriculture, military tactics, and the mechanical arts as well as classical studies so that members of the working classes could obtain a liberal, practical education" (Place 2000). Since that time, land-grant institutions have broadened their mission to encompass programs of "on-campus instruction, research, and off-campus extension work in many areas beyond the initial educational needs of the agricultural and industrial classes" (Place 2000). Thus, not all the land-grant colleges and universities remain as master's level institutions. Many have been reclassified as Carnegie research institutions. The mission of the remaining land-grant and other master's degree level institutions continues to be a commitment to student learning with an emphasis on knowledge, problem-solving, and career/professional preparation; faculty-staff cooperation in meeting student needs; and connections

TABLE 4.9
Faculty Activities by Type of Institution

	ALL	RESEARCH		DOCTORAL		COMPREHENSIVE		PRIVATE LIBERAL ARTS	PUBLIC 2-YEAR
		PUBLIC	PRIVATE	PUBLIC	PRIVATE	PUBLIC	PRIVATE		
Full-time Instructional Faculty and Staff	528,000 (100%)	139,000 (26.4%)		82,000 (15.4%)		133,000 (25.2%)		38,000 (7.2%)	110,000 (20.8%)
Hours Worked Per Week	52.5	57		54.4		52.1		52.5	46.9
Hours Spent Teaching	28.6 (54.5%)	21.4 (37.6%)		25 (45.7%)		31.3 (60%)		33.4 (63.7%)	32 (68.8%)
Hours Spent on Research/Scholarship	13 (24.7%)	22.8 (40%)		16.6 (30.6%)		11 (21.1%)		10 (18.8%)	4.3 (9.2%)
Credit courses taught by faculty with undergraduate courses only		PUBLIC	PRIVATE	PUBLIC	PRIVATE	PUBLIC	PRIVATE		
1	16.0%	34.4%	40.9%	20.6%	22.1%	11.5%	11.3%	9.9%	12.3%
2	23.2	42.9	37.2	34.0	40.8	20.8	21.2	21.6	13.9
3	23.6	14.5	7.9	27.6	25.0	31.9	31.2	35.0	15.3
4	20.0	6.1	7.4	13.3	6.5	26.7	26.1	20.7	21.9
5 or more	17.2	2.1	6.5	4.5	5.5	9.2	10.2	12.9	36.6
Credit courses taught by faculty with both undergraduate and graduate courses		PUBLIC	PRIVATE	PUBLIC	PRIVATE	PUBLIC	PRIVATE		
2	42.3%	58.9%	67.6%	48.3%	40.5%	25.0%	17.6%	22.1%	
3	32.2	29.9	22.8	31.3	36.6	34.0	45.7	21.7	
4	16.1	5.5	7.4	14.6	12.1	25.7	27.6	37.0	
5 or more	9.5	5.7	2.2	5.8	10.8	15.3	9.1	19.3	

SOURCE: U.S. Department of Education, National Center for Education Statistics (NCES), National Study of Postsecondary Faculty (NSOPF), 1993. The information for this table was prepared by NCES in September 1996. There is an additional category of "Other" representing 5% of full-time faculty in a range of specialized institutions. Additional data are available at http://nces.ed.gov/pubs2001/digest/ch3.html

between academic and student life (Associated New American Colleges 2000). To this end, they offer both baccalaureate and master's degrees, the latter being more professional than academic in nature. These are not research-focused institutions and most offer few, if any, doctoral degrees. Slightly more than half are public, most often controlled by the states, but a few are run by municipalities (table 4.1).

STUDENTS

> Many of the classes offered in my department now have sections scheduled for after 5:00 P.M. This is specifically done to address the needs of working students (first year faculty member).

As with the previous institutional types, it is difficult to generalize about students in master's degree institutions, because the institutions themselves vary considerably in size, population, and community. This variety in size is reflected in table 4.2. Master's level institutions comprise approximately 23% of all institutions with enrollments under 1,000 students. This number rises to 32% for institutions with enrollments between 1,000 and 5,000. For larger institutions, the numbers drop significantly (3% for schools with enrollments between 5,000 and 20,000 and <.1% for enrollments greater than 20,000). Although this range makes it difficult to generalize, there are some commonalities about students at master's degree institutions. First, many students are "place-bound," unable to leave the area to attend an alternate university, because of family, work, and other outside responsibilities. Students are career oriented, somewhat older on average than most college-age students, and more likely to be full time workers (Dalbey 1995).

Some type of financial aid is received by 47.6% of students in public, master's level institutions and by 58.1% of students in private schools (table 4.5). Master's level institutions base their finances on enrollment and, therefore, focus on student needs and interests (Smith 1979). This attention to student interests allows master's level institutions to be attractive to students from a wider range of backgrounds.

FACULTY

> Time management is definitely an issue. You must plan your time wisely between lesson planning, assessment, research, and community service (second year faculty member).

FACULTY MEMBERS IN MASTER'S DEGREE institutions represent the second largest number in higher education (table 4.7). One out of five full-time faculty members teaches in either a public or private master's level institution. The same proportion holds true for part-time faculty members. They are predominantly white (approximately 85%) and more than half are male (62.5% for full-time faculty and 52.8% for part-time faculty). It appears that only in public master's level institutions are the majority (53.5%) of part-time faculty women.

Faculty members also spend a substantial amount of time in teaching each week, spending 33.1 hours (60% of hours/week) versus 21.4 (37.6%) at research institutions. While they are committed to teaching, they are increasingly pressured to conduct research, especially if they are to achieve tenure and promotion. Recent data on faculty activities (table 4.9) show that 11 hours (21.1%) of faculty time are spent on research at master's degree institutions. The vast majority of faculty members at master's level institutions share a deep commitment to their disciplines and to the teaching profession (Youn 1992).

Faculty members typically teach three to four courses per semester, and most teach introductory, lower-level courses on a regular basis (table 4.9). Teaching is a priority at these institutions, and administration looks for faculty committed to the "belief that less-privileged, less-prepared students have the same rights to excellent education as more privileged students do" (Dalbey 1995). However, many faculty members (over 66%) reportedly believe that admission policies are too lenient; this opinion may be motivated by a desire for students requiring less classroom assistance (Henderson and Kane 1991).

Research is becoming increasingly important at master's level institutions, and faculty members are regularly expected to engage in some form of scholarly research. Due to the competitiveness of the job market, research expectations are now much more rigorous than they used to be (Dalbey 1995). Unfortunately, these changes have not resulted in reductions in teaching loads. Faculty members' workload is made somewhat easier by the fact that master's level institutions have a much broader understanding than other institutions of what constitutes research; thus, their faculty may be involved in writing textbooks and producing books for popular audiences. (Dalbey 1995).

While faculty members are given heavy teaching loads and little research time, they rarely benefit from graduate student assistants (Henderson and

Kane 1991). Due to this disparity between research expectations and teaching loads, several studies suggest that faculty at master's level institutions have a lower level of job satisfaction that faculty members at other four-year institutions (Youn 1992; Henderson and Kane 1991).

Faculty salaries (table 4.8) at master's level institutions vary from approximately $70,000 for full professor to $35,000 for instructor. A new faculty member can expect to earn $45,000 as an assistant professor and $55,000 for associate professor status. Private institutions continue to pay more than public and this gap continues to increase (Smallwood 2001). Women continue to earn less than their male counterparts in all ranks (table 4.8).

Teaching and Learning

> I am able to get to know my students. Nothing is more rewarding than the big 'Ah Hah' from a student once they understand (second year faculty member).

The fact the so many students are commuters affects classroom behavior. Commuter students have family responsibilities not experienced by residential students (Chapman et al. 1999). Simply because a commuter student enrolls in college, does not free them from responsibilities at home. For some students, juggling school and home life becomes difficult because of the extra preparation needed for college course work and/or added responsibilities at home (Chapman et al. 1999). Many commuter students either work a full-time job or work as many as twenty-five to thirty hours per week, part-time. These workloads may impose limitations on such things as a student's studying time, participation in campus activities, opportunities to meet with professors, work on group projects, and get additional help. Thus, students find it difficult to find time to do their coursework outside of the classroom. Travel time to and from campus is another issue for commuter students. Chapman, et al., (1999) report that obstacles, such as lack of parking, inclement weather, and car problems can add to the problems of being a commuter and affect how often a student is able to reach campus.

Class sizes at master's level institutions tend to be smaller than those at research institutions. Lower-division courses typically range in size from twenty-five to forty while upper-division courses are significantly smaller, ranging in size from ten to twenty (Snyder and Hoffman 2002). Due to the emphasis placed on student learning, smaller class sizes are in keeping with the mission of master's level institutions.

The number of distance education offerings is increasing at all public institutions, including master's level institutions. The number of formal enrollments in distance education courses at two-year and four-year institutions had grown from 753,640 in 1994/95 to 1,343,580 enrollments in college-level, credit granting distance education courses, and 1,632,350 enrollments in all distance education courses. For public four-year institutions, enrollment in all distance education courses was approximately triple in 1997/98 (711,350) what it was in 1994/95 (234,020). Enrollment growth was somewhat less at these public four-year institutions for college-level, credit-granting distance education courses, with 452,600 enrollments in 1997/98 (Bradburn 2002). These offerings allow students the flexibility of enrolling in classes with minimal required attendance at class sessions. Some distance education classes are held in virtual classrooms where students meet at a specified (synchronous) time, while others allow students to receive coursework and assignments at their convenience (asynchronous). In fact, the newest modes of distance education make possible forms of interaction that may have benefits *not* available in face-to-face instruction (Sherron and Boettcher 1997; Turoff 1999). For instance, asynchronous online conferencing may increase class participation by giving students who would be reluctant to contribute to a face-to-face discussion more time to think about the issues raised by other students and formulate their comments in response. Also, keeping transcripts of online course sessions allows students with limited English proficiency the opportunity to read the actual words of the instructor and other students several times to cement their understanding of the material (Turoff 1999). Distance education courses fit well with the mission of master's level institutions allowing them to meet the needs of students who have many outside responsibilities.

Support Systems

My orientation consisted of an all-day meeting prior to the opening of school. Whatever I needed to know about effective teaching, curriculum, and faculty development I either learned from my department chair or other colleagues (second year faculty member).

Most faculty members at master's level institutions do not have the assistance of graduate students as either teaching or research assistants. They are often under extreme time constraints to grade papers, prepare lessons and exams, and conduct research on their own.

Technology for teaching is readily available at most of these campuses. Bradburn (2002) reports:

> Computer resources were associated with the likelihood of teaching any non-face-to-face classes. Instructional faculty and staff who rated their institution's computing resources as poor were less likely than others to teach any non-face-to-face classes (5% versus 9–11%), and their rating of computer resources was also associated with their likelihood of teaching any computer-based classes. Also, respondents who had Internet access both at home and at work were slightly more likely than those who did not have Internet access at home to teach any non-face-to-face classes. This pattern was also found for teaching any primarily computer-based classes. Institution type and size were related to teaching any non-face-to-face classes. Instructional faculty and staff at public 2-year institutions were more likely than those at doctoral institutions or private liberal arts colleges to teach any non-face-to-face classes (12% versus 5–8%). This pattern was also found for teaching any computer-based classes. Also, faculty at institutions with larger FTE enrollments were less likely than their colleagues at institutions with fewer students enrolled to teach any non-face-to-face classes.

Approximately 12.4% of the faculty at master's level institutions report teaching an average of 1.5 distance education classes (Bradburn 2002).

DOCTORAL/RESEARCH UNIVERSITIES

HISTORY

THE MODERN AMERICAN RESEARCH UNIVERSITY has an extensive lineage that can be traced back to the University of Berlin, founded in 1809 by Wilhelm von Humboldt. At Humboldt's university, there was a unique and innovative partnership between research and teaching during a time when the sciences were blooming and other disciplines had just begun to grow. Based on the classical wisdom of Aristotle and Plato, scholars believed that only a step-by-step process (research) would produce the new knowledge they desired. The University of Berlin became a site of world education where the substance of historical disciplines was brought to life in the minds of researcher students and professors. This yielded not only enlightenment for old areas of study, but also produced new ones. This spread rapidly to America as a place where romantic ideals were embraced and took on a wider meaning.

With German universities as the ideal, the United States developed Johns Hopkins University in 1876, "modeling itself on the nineteenth-century German doctor seminar, [which] evolved into one that emphasizes combining doctoral training, including classes and research apprenticeship, with the highest level of scholarship" (Lipset 1994, 219). Because of Johns Hopkins and its followers, "graduate education achieved a stable American presence during the last two decades of the nineteenth century, when awarding the PH.D. became a laudable academic goal" (Gumport 1999, 400). By 1900, the number of schools granting doctorates had grown to fourteen, with a total of 300 doctoral degrees awarded (Gumport). By this time, American universities like Harvard and Yale began to take the lead in the global educational economy. Fewer students were going to Europe for their education, opting to study at research institutions in the United States. The scientific element of German learning was embodied in the United States research institution as the students taught each other through critically engaging the text and discussing theoretical concepts with one another (Lipset).

The number of doctoral/research universities in the United States has grown substantially since the establishment of Johns Hopkins University in 1876. Currently, there are 261 institutions classified as doctoral/research universities, comprising 6.6% of all institutions of higher education in the United States. (table 4.1). The majority (63.6%) of doctoral/research universities are public. As of the 2000 Carnegie classification, the 261 doctoral/research universities are divided between 151 (3.8%) *extensive,* which awarded 50 or more doctoral degrees per year across at least fifteen disciplines, and 110 (2.8%) *intensive,* which awarded 10 doctoral degrees per year across three or more disciplines, or at least 20 doctoral degrees per year overall.

Mission

MUCH OF THIS CONSTRUCTIVE SCIENTIFIC (and philosophical) learning would have been virtually impossible without the financial support of individuals and the government. Just as Germany counted on industry and the state for educational funding at the onset and throughout the development of the Industrial Revolution, American research universities relied on the same kind of support. The Carnegie and Rockefeller families were at the head of individual philanthropic giving to academic research institutions. In fact, "in

1934, Rockefeller Foundation grants constituted a large portion of foundation giving to research in higher education (35%), to the social sciences (64%), and to the natural sciences (72%)" (Gumport 1999, 404). Such funding from individuals, charitable foundations and the United States government continues to draw students and faculty to universities throughout the United States.

Research universities in the United States were established to provide a venue for scholars to conduct research projects funded by endowments from private foundations and industry. Eventually—particularly for military defense purposes—the federal government became the primary sponsor of scientific research in universities. The government began to view universities as a valuable resource, providing education and research training to promote economic growth, national security, and healthcare. In 1995, the federal government allocated $17.1 billion for basic research, comprising 58% of universities' research funding (Gumport 1999, 415). Private industry was the second largest source for research funding, providing about $7.5 billion in 1995 (Gumport). Institutions also provided their own support for research, ranking third at $3.4 billion in funding in 1995 (Gumport).

Research universities conduct half of the United States' basic research (Gumport 1999). However, distribution of research expenditures is hardly equitable across institutions and disciplines. Out of the 261 doctoral/research universities, the top 100 (38%) institutions receive more than 80% ($15.6 billion) of research and development funds (Gumport). Federal research funding favors the "hard" sciences, with over 80% of allocations divided among the life sciences (54%), engineering (16%), and physical sciences (11%). Only 6% of federal funding goes to the behavioral and social sciences (Gumport).

In addition to meeting many of the basic research needs of the United States, doctoral/research universities educate many of the country's future scholars. The purpose of doctoral/research universities is to integrate teaching and research in the education of undergraduate and graduate students (Gumport 1999). They provide a broad liberal arts education to undergraduates and specialized training for graduate students. They emphasize the advancement of knowledge, the ability to make independent judgment, and critical thinking among students. Faculty members are expected to contribute to student development by engaging in original scholarship and integrating their production of new knowledge with the classroom.

STUDENTS

> The students here are pretty ethnically diverse. There is a large Asian
> American population and a growing number of Latino students. The age
> of the undergraduates is pretty traditional, between 18 and 22 years. The
> graduate students are mostly under 30, with a few exceptions. Students are
> academically prepared for college and are in the top 10% of their class
> (second year faculty member).

TO UPHOLD THE STANDARDS ESPOUSED in the missions of doctoral/research universities, students admitted to doctoral/research universities tend to be at the top of their high school classes. For example, the University of California system guarantees admission to any of its nine campuses to students who graduate in the top 4% of their high school classes (Schmidt 2001). A national survey of faculty indicated educators at doctoral/research universities had greater satisfaction with the quality of their undergraduate students compared to faculty at master's and associate's colleges (Finkelstein, Seal, and Schuster 1998).

Although the category of doctoral/research university has the fewest number of institutions except for tribal colleges (table 4.1), it has the highest student enrollment (table 4.2). Just over half (55.5%) of all institutions with an enrollment of 20,000 or more students are research universities. Of these research universities, 62 (87%) are public institutions. The majority (66.3%) of doctoral universities have an enrollment of between 5,000 to 19,000 students. Of these doctoral universities, 46 (61.3%) are public institutions. The average research university is a large public institution with an enrollment of at least 20,000 students. The average doctoral university is also public, but somewhat smaller than most research universities with an enrollment of 5,000 to 19,000 students.

Included in the large enrollment at research/doctoral universities are graduate students. As shown in table 4.3, the greatest proportion of graduate students is between the ages of twenty-five and forty-four. Although older students are more likely to attend graduate school part-time, males and females are equally likely to attend part-time. In 1999, the majority of graduate students were Caucasian (69%), and 12.5% of students were from other countries, 8% African American, 5% Hispanic, 5% Asian American, and 0.5% American Indian (table 4.4).

Students traditionally sought a graduate education for the sake of advancing their intellectual knowledge. Some suggest that today more individuals seek graduate education to advance their professional careers. A large percentage of incoming students indicate they are attending college to get a good job (70.3%) or to make more money (69.8%) (Higher Education Research Institute 2001). Graduate students are less likely to be viewed as the future intellectual leaders and are more likely to be viewed as valuable assets to the advancement of universities' prestige (Gumport 1999).

Financing graduate education is becoming more difficult as federal support for graduate training is decreasing (Gumport 1999). In 1999, 45.7% of students at public and 54.3% at private doctorate-granting institutions received some type of federal financial aid (table 4.5). To help finance education, it is becoming more common for students to receive financial support by working with faculty on sponsored research (Gumport). This is beneficial to faculty members wishing to advance their research and to students wishing to gain research experience. However, as a result, the faculty/student relationship has shifted from a mentor/apprentice model to an employer/employee relationship (Gumport). The new model of faculty/student relationships has contributed to the increased time it takes to finish doctoral degrees. The median length of time for doctoral degree completion across disciplines has increased from 5.6 years in 1970 to 7.2 years in 1995 (Gumport, 417).

FACULTY

> At one department in a midwestern university, there was only one African American female who has been there for ten years and is still single. I wanted to live and work in a metropolitan area where I can meet someone and start a family. It is also important to work at a university where you can learn from the people around you. The faculty members here are good and are doing a lot of research. I can learn a lot from them (second year minority professor).

THE MAJORITY OF FACULTY MEMBERS at doctoral/research universities are Caucasian males over the age of 40 (table 4.6). The highest percentages of faculty at doctoral/research universities (55.8% to 63.8%) are between the ages of 40 and 59. The second largest age group (22.5% to 30%) is 40 years old and younger. Fewer than 15% of faculty members at doctoral/research universities are 60 years old or older. Males outnumber females more than 2:1 in private research universities and public doctoral universities. The ratio is even greater in public research universities and private doctoral universities where males outnumber females 3:1. The predominate racial group is Caucasian, ranging from 83.7% to 88% of faculty at doctoral/research universities. Asian and Pacific Islander is the next largest racial group, with the highest percentage (9%) employed at private research universities. There is a higher-than-average percentage of Asian and Pacific Islanders across public and private doctoral/research universities (7.28%), compared to the average percentage at the other institution types (3.6%). African Americans are the third largest racial group represented among doctoral/research university faculty members, with the greatest percentages at the private institutions. Hispanic and American Indian/Alaskan Native faculty members are the least represented groups among doctoral/research universities.

The modal faculty member at a doctoral/research university has a doctoral degree and works full-time at a public institution (tables 4.6 and 4.7). Faculty members are more likely to hold a doctoral or professional degree and less likely to have a master's or bachelor's as their highest degree than faculty at other types of institutions. Although the average faculty member works full-time, there is a significant gender difference in full- and part-time status. Men are more likely to work full-time, especially at public doctoral/research universities. Women are more likely to work part-time, especially at public doctoral/research universities.

The average faculty member at a doctoral/research university earns between $40,000 and $69,000 annually (table 4.6). The second greatest percentage of faculty earn $40,000 or less. Doctoral/research universities pay higher salaries at all ranks and institution types (public or private), compared with master's, baccalaureate, and associate's colleges. However, a faculty member's salary depends on their rank, their institution type (public or private), and often their gender (table 4.8). As expected, salaries increase with rank from the assistant professor to the full professor level. In addition, private universities pay higher salaries than public universities. Finally, men tend to earn higher salaries than women, especially at the rank of full professor.

One reason doctoral/research universities pay faculty members higher salaries is the institutions' ability to obtain external funding. However, as federal funding has become limited, the institutional climate has become marked by competition (Argon 1995; Gumport 1999). There is competition among universities in securing federal funds, as well as receiving high national rankings and attracting eminent scientists and promising students (Gumport). With the advent of the information age, prospective students have access to information about universities and can more easily draw comparisons (Haviland 2001). There is increased pressure for universities to identify the learning outcomes and benefits students would obtain through attending their university (Haviland). The competitive spirit among the doctoral/research universities has put more pressure on universities, and thus faculties, to be highly productive.

Responsibility for securing external funding for research lies primarily on the shoulders of the individual faculty members. Regardless of one's ability to obtain funding, faculty members are expected to maintain an active research program and publish their work (Lipset 1994). There is also competition among faculty within universities to receive recognition for their research. The reward structure of the tenure system has shifted, assigning more value to research and publications than to effective teaching (Lipset 1994; Noll 1998).

Despite their teaching demands, new faculty members at doctoral/research universities are still able to devote time to research. Table 4.9 shows that faculty at doctoral/research universities spend more time on research than teaching, compared with comprehensive universities, liberal arts and two-year colleges. The typical ratio of time spent on research, teaching, and service is 50%-40%-10%, respectively, however, this can vary depending on the institution and one's career stage. A new assistant professor may spend more time preparing for classes than is the norm at a doctoral/research university. A national survey of faculty shows that compared with their actual effort, faculty members would prefer to spend more time on research, professional growth, and consulting and less time on teaching, service, and administration (Finkelstein et al. 1998).

The climate of doctoral/research universities has become increasingly competitive, with higher faculty workloads and higher expectations for research productivity. Faculty at doctoral/research universities report working more hours a week on average, 54.4 to 57, than faculty at other types of institutions (table 4.9). Despite pressure and workload, many faculty members remain productive. In their longitudinal study of new faculty at a doctoral/research university, Olsen and Sorcinelli (1992) found that within the first five years of employment, 40% of new faculty had a nontextbook published and almost 100% had at least one journal article published, with a five year average of 10.5 articles each (p. 18). Remarkably, 75% of the faculty members in the study said that they were happy with the quality of their research (Olsen and Sorcinelli, 18). Tenured faculty members usually enjoy many benefits within the doctoral/research university setting. Faculty members who are "stars" within a doctoral/research university usually receive higher salaries, funds for research facilities, summer pay, travel allowances, housing and even lighter teaching loads (Lipset 1994). While some doctoral/research universities have salary caps within certain disciplines, perks are a way to lure faculty members to a university (Lipset).

Not surprising is the level of stress that faculty members at research institutions face. Olsen and Sorcinelli (1992) found that 71% of faculty reported being "very stressed" in their work lives (p. 22). Many faculty members cited lack of collegiality within their department as a problem, especially a lack among tenured faculty. They also stated that they received little praise from other campus faculty members and campus administration (Olsen and Sorcinelli). This type of work stress leads many newer faculty members to develop chronic health problems, loss of stamina and weight gain (Olsen and Sorcinelli). Surprisingly, faculty members at doctoral/research universities tend to retire later than their colleagues at other types of institutions (Lipset 1994). One way in which faculty members can lighten their workloads is by recruiting scholarly students to assist in their research. Faculty members at doctoral/research universities who are successful in their fields are attractive to promising students wishing to work with them (Lipset).

Teaching and Learning

> I love teaching, but I do not want it to overwhelm me. I must dedicate more of my time to research (second year faculty member).

Although doctoral/research universities rhetorically emphasize teaching, faculty members understand that salary increases and tenure are based mostly on research. Faculty members do not become "stars" at a research university because of their teaching; it is due to their research (Lipset 1994). Nevertheless, faculty members are expected to teach effectively while producing original research (Noll 1998). For faculty members who have not been tenured, this is an increased pressure. Although they are expected to be good teachers, their tenure will not be heavily based on their teaching ability (Lipset). Faculty members typically teach one to two courses per semester or quarter (table 4.9). Faculty members usually teach a mix of large undergraduate and smaller graduate courses. New faculty members may teach a greater number of "service" courses, the large introductory undergraduate courses required by students across disciplines. Typically, faculty members at doctoral/research universities spend between one and four hours with undergraduates per week, outside of the classroom, and over five hours a week with graduate students (Olsen and Sorcinelli 1992, 17).

It is a common misconception that undergraduate classes at large doctoral/research universities have hundreds of students and are held in large, impersonal lecture halls. In actuality, classroom size is quite diverse. Classes can range from five-person seminars to 500+ student lectures. Averaged across research and doctoral universities (public and private), the largest percentage of students (45.4%) is taught in classes with 49 or fewer students (U.S. Department of Education 1996). Only 15% of students are taught in classes of 150 or more students (U.S. Department of Education 1996). With the exception of the large lecture classes (150 or more students), master's, baccalaureate, and associate's colleges tend to have larger class sizes than doctoral/research universities (U.S. Department of Education 1996). However, courses at doctoral/research universities may be small because teaching assistants teach many smaller sections of large courses.

Another way universities may try to reduce class sizes while accommodating increases in enrollment is the implementation of distance learning courses. In the 1997/98 academic year, 79% of all public four-year universities (master's and doctoral/research universities) offered distance education courses, an increase from 62% in 1995 (U.S. Department of Education 1999a). However, when faculty were surveyed, only 5% of faculty at public and 4% at private doctoral/research universities indicated they had taught a distance learning course (U.S. Department of Education 2002). With the exception of liberal arts colleges, there are fewer faculty members teaching distance education courses at doctoral/research universities than at the other types of institutions. This pattern holds for the percentage of faculty members who have taught other types of non-face-to-face classes (e.g., computer or TV-based). Eight percent of faculty at public and 6% at private doctoral/research universities have taught non-face-to-face courses (U.S. Department of Education 2002). As enrollment continues to increase, it is likely that distance education will become more widely provided by research university faculty members.

Support Systems

> I have three teaching assistants for my large course. There is a teaching development program here for teaching assistants, however, there isn't a faculty development program for faculty. The attitude here is that once you have a Ph.D. you shouldn't need further development (second year faculty member).

Faculty members at doctoral/research universities usually have support for their teaching in the form of teaching assistants for large undergraduate courses. However, faculty members take less advantage of teaching development activities, which range from informal, committee-led activities to highly funded faculty development centers providing mentors and technical support. When one prospective faculty member asked in her interview about the availability of faculty development programs, she was asked, "Do you *need* more faculty development?" (personal interview).

Some universities have informal programs in which senior faculty are encouraged to collaborate with junior faculty members. Department chairs often try to make sure junior faculty are guided in both their teaching and research.

> There is a big push to use computers in the classroom. Training, such as workshops, is provided for using the new technology that was installed in many of the newer classrooms (second year faculty member).

The technological revolution is said to be a powerful force that will restructure higher education (Finkelstein et al. 1998). Doctoral/research universities lead the way in some areas of teaching with technology and lag far behind in others. A survey of full-time faculty at doctoral/research universities in fall 1998 indicated 98% of instructors had access to the Internet, 77% used email to communicate with students, and 45% used a course-specific Web site (U.S. Department of Education 1999a). These percentages were higher than those of all other institution types. However, when it comes to implementing technology in the classroom, doctoral/research universities trail behind the other types of institutions. Only 10% of faculty at research universities reported the use of computer-aided instruction in the classroom. In addition, only 12.8% of new faculty and 17% of senior faculty at research universities used computational tools or software as an instructional method (Finkelstein et al. 1998).

Discussion

THE WIDE VARIETY IN ACADEMIC SETTINGS MAKES it a challenge for faculty members to find their best institutional fit. Misperceptions of what is expected can lead to misallocation of personal time and institutional resources. Ambiguous criteria and mixed signals can lead to frustration and failure. This is true whether the perceived criteria for success are research productivity or teaching evaluations. Austin and Gamson (1983) found that faculty members' satisfaction with their work was not dependent on their rank, career or chronological ages, length of service, or even salary. Rather, the work itself—how time is spent—is the greatest source of satisfaction. What matters is the match between institutional rewards and the type (if any) of research faculty members want to pursue, their interest in service, and the type of teaching they prefer. Unfortunately, few faculty members know what elements to investigate to find the situation in which they will be most productive. The information provided in this chapter is only a summary. The situations at individual colleges, indeed, in different departments on a campus, will vary.

Because what matters is the match between personal preferences and the institution, rather than any specific quality, prospective faculty members should ask themselves the following questions about how they want to spend their time:

1. Do you want to work with students who need special academic help to provide the support they need to succeed in college? or Do you prefer to work with well-prepared students already motivated in your discipline?
2. Do you want to teach large, introductory courses to give students an appreciation for and grounding in the basics of your field? or Do you want to work with small groups of advanced graduate students interested in expanding the boundaries of knowledge in your field?
3. Are you interested in finding colleagues to collaborate with you on teaching and research? or Do you prefer to work independently?
4. Will you need research assistants to work with you on your disciplinary research? or Would student researchers get in the way of your progress?

5. Do you want to work in a high-tech environment? or Are you committed to high-touch teaching strategies?
6. Do you prefer to spend the majority of your time teaching? or Will you need release time to pursue your research interests?

These choices, in addition to conventional disciplinary preferences, can give faculty members better insight into selecting academic positions in which they, their students, and institutions will thrive.

•

Laurie Richlin is the president of International Alliance of Teacher Scholars and the director of Preparing Future Faculty Program, Claremont Graduate University.

Betinna J. Casad, Shannon Hensley, June K. Hilton, and Jeffrey T. Williams are each graduate students and Preparing Future Faculty Fellows at the Claremont Graduate University.

Preliminary research for this chapter was done as part of the Claremont Graduate University Preparing Future Faculty course "The Academic Profession" during fall 2001. The authors thank their colleagues Lane David, Daniel Grimminger, Alison Kafer, Michael Koppel, Tasha LaDoux, Sara Patterson, Yer Thao, and Amy Hoyt for their contributions.

References

American Association of Community Colleges. 2000. *The knowledge net: Connecting communities, learners, and colleges.* Washington, D.C.: Community College Press.

Argon, J. K. 1995. Securing funding from federal sources. In *The academic's handbook,* eds. A. L. Deneef and C. D. Goodwin, 2d ed., 219–35. Durham, NC: Duke University Press.

Associated New American Colleges. 2000. A primer on the associated new American colleges. www.anac.vir.org.affects students. *Daedalus* 128:1, 77–99.

Austin, A. E. and Gamson, Z. F. 1983. *Academic workplace: New demands, heightened tensions.* ASHE-ERIC Higher Education Report no. 10. Washington, D.C.: Association for the Study of Higher Education.

Bradburn, Ellen M. 2002. *Distance education instruction by postsecondary faculty and staff: Fall 1998.* NCES 2002-155. U.S. Department of Education, National Center for Education Statistics. Washington, DC: U.S. Government Printing Office.

Breneman, W. D. 1994. *Liberal arts college: Thriving, surviving, or endangered?* Washington, D.C.: The Brookings Institution.

Brewer, D. J. 1999. *How do community college faculty view institutional mission? An analysis of national survey data.* Community College Research Center, Institute on Education and the Economy. New York: Columbia University.

Brownstein, A. 2001. Tuitions rise sharply, and this time public colleges lead the way. *Chronicle of Higher Education* (2 November).

Carnevale, D. 2001. As online education surges, some colleges remain untouched. *Chronicle of Higher Education* 47:A41.

Cejda, B. and Kaylor, A. 2001. Early transfer: A case study of traditional-aged community college students. *Community College Journal of Research and Practice* 25: 621-38.

Chapman, L., Munsell, L., and Caldwell, J. 1999. Advising special population: Commuter students at Ohio University. *The Mentor: An Academic Advising Journal* (4 August)

Clowes, D. A. and B. H. Levin. 1989. Community, technical, and junior colleges: Are they leaving higher education? *Journal of Higher Education* 60 (3): 349-55 (May/June).

Cohen, A. 1985. The community college in the American educational system. In *Contexts for learning: The major sectors of American higher education,* ed. The Study Group on the Conditions of Excellence in American Higher Education, 1-16. Washington, D.C.: National Institute for Education.

Cohen, A. M. and Brawer, F. B. 1996. *The American community college.* 3d ed. San Francisco: Jossey-Bass.

Cross, K. P. 1971. *Access and accommodation in higher education.* Paper presented to White House Conference on Youth. *Research Reporter* 6(2): 6-8. Berkeley: Center for Research and Development in Higher Education.

Cross, K. P. 1981. Community colleges on the plateau. *Journal of Higher Education* 52 (2): 113-23 (March/April).

Dalbey, M. A. 1995. What is a master's level university, and do I want to work there? *ADE Bulletin* 111:14-6.

Deneef, A. L. and Associates. 1995. *The academic's handbook.* 2d ed. Durham, NC: Duke University Press.

Dougherty, K. J. and Bakia, M. F. 2000. *The new economic role of the community college.* Community College Research Center. New York: Columbia University.

Finkelstein, M. J., Seal, R. K., and Schuster, J. H. 1998. *The new academic generation: A profession in transformation.* Baltimore: Johns Hopkins.

Finnegan, D. E. 1991. *Opportunity knocked: The origins of contemporary master's level colleges and institutions.* Boston: New England Resource for Higher Education, University of Massachusetts at Boston.

Gumport, P. J. 1999. Graduate education and research: Interdependence and strain. In *American higher education in the twenty-first century: Social, political, and economic,* eds. P. G. Altbach, R. O. Berdahl, and P. J. Gumport, 396–426. Baltimore, MD: Johns Hopkins University Press.

Haviland, D. 2001. Leading change in the research university. [Cited 10 September 2001]. Available from http://www.higher-ed.org/AEQ.

Hawkins, Hugh. 1999. The making of the liberal arts college identity. *Daedalus* 128: 1–26.

Henderson, B. and Kane, W. 1991. Caught in the middle: faculty and institutional status and quality in state master's level institutions. *Higher Education* 22: 339–50.

Higher Education Research Institute. 2001. *The American freshman: National norms for fall 2001.* Los Angeles: University of California Los Angeles.

Karabel, J. V. 1924. Community colleges and social stratification. *Harvard Educational Review* 42:521–62.

Kiernan, V. 2000. Rewards dim for professors who pursue digital scholarship. *Chronicle of Higher Education* 46:A45.

Light, Jr., D. 1974. Introduction: The structure of the academic professions. *Sociology of Education* 47 (1): 2–28.

Lipset, S. M. 1994. In defense of the doctoral/research university. In *The doctoral/research university in a time of discontent,* eds. J. R. Cole, E. G. Barber, and S. R. Graubard, 219–24. Baltimore: Johns Hopkins University Press.

Mellander, G. A. and Robertson, B. 1992. Tradition and transformation: Academic roots and the community college future. In *Prisoner's of elitism: The community college's struggle for stature,* eds. B. W. Dziech and W. R. Vilter. San Francisco: Jossey-Bass.

Monroe, C. R. 1972. *Profile of the community college.* San Francisco: Jossey-Bass.

Murray, J. P. 1999. Faculty development in a national sample of community colleges. *Community Colleges Review* 27 (3): 47–64 (winter).

National Center for Education Statistics. 1993. *Digest of education statistics.* Washington, D.C.: U.S. Department of Education, October.

Noll, R. G. 1998. The American doctoral/research university: An introduction. In *Challenges to doctoral/research universities,* ed. R. G. Noll, 1–30. Washington D. C.: Brookings Institution.

Olsen, D., and Sorcinelli, M. D. 1992. The pretenure years: A longitudinal perspective. *New Directions for Teaching and Learning* 50:15–25.

Olsen, F. 2000. Mount Holyoke looks at how the Web can improve classroom instruction. *Chronicle of Higher Education* 46:A47.

Ottinger, C. A., comp. 1987. *Fact book on higher education*. Washington, D.C.: American Council on Education, ED 284 472.

Pace, C. R. and Connolly, M. 2001. Where are the liberal arts? *Research in Higher Education* 41:1, 53–65.

Palinchak, R. 1973. *The evolution of the community college*. Metuchen, NJ: Scarecrow Press.

Palmer, J. C. and Pugh, M. B. 1993. The community college contribution to the education of bachelor's degree candidates: A case study in Virginia. In *Probing the community college transfer function*, ed. J. Eaton, Washington, D.C.: American Council on Education.

Phillippe, K. A., and Patton, M. 1999. *National profile of community colleges: Trends and statistics*. 3d ed. Washington, D.C.: Community College Press, American Association of Community Colleges.

Phipps, R. A., Shedd, J. M. and Merisotis, J. P. 2002. A classification system for two-year postsecondary institutions. *Education Statistics Quarterly* (fall).

Place, N. T. 2000. *Land grants–Events leading to the establishment of land-grant universities*. In University of Florida, Institute of Food and Agricultural Sciences [Web site]. [Cited 27 April 2002]. Available from http://www.ifas.ufl.edu/www/ls_grant/whatislg.htm.

Ratcliff, J. L. 1994. Seven streams in the historical development of the modern American community college. In *A handbook on the community college in America*, eds. G. A. Baker III, J. Dudziak, and P. Tyler, 3–16. Westport: Greenwood Publishing Group.

Schmidt, P. 2001. Four percent plan in California lifts minority admissions. *Chronicle of Higher Education* 47:A43.

Sherron, G. T., and Boettcher, J. V. 1997. *Distance learning: The shift to interactivity*. CAUSE Professional Paper Series 17. Boulder: CAUSE.

Smallwood, S. 2001. The price professors pay for teaching at public institutions. *Chronicle of Higher Education* 47 (32).

———. 2002. Williams College expands its Oxford-style tutorials, changing the role of professors. *Chronicle of Higher Education* 46:A16.

Smith, H. 1979. Master's level institutions and colleges: Synthesizers of liberal and professional education. *Liberal Education* 64:469–84.

Snyder, T. D., and Hoffman, C. M. 2002. *Digest of education statistics 2001*. U.S. Department of Education, National Center for Education Statistics. NCES 2002-130. Washington, DC: U.S. Government Printing Office.

Turoff, M. 1999. An end to student segregation: No more separation between distance learning and regular courses. Paper presented at the Summary of Invited Plenary for Telelearning 99, November, Montreal, Canada.

U.S. Department of Education, National Center for Education Statistics. 1996. *National study of postsecondary faculty, 1993.* Washington, D.C.

U.S. Department of Education, National Center for Education Statistics. 1999a. *National study of postsecondary faculty.* Washington, D.C.

U.S. Department of Education. 1999b. In *The Chronicle of Higher Education* [Web site]. [Cited 4 February 2002]. Available from http://chronicle.com/weekly/almanac/2001/nation/0102002.htm.

U.S. Department of Education, National Center for Education Statistics. 2002. *Distance education instruction by postsecondary faculty and staff: Fall 1998.* Washington, D.C.

Williams, D. N. 1989. *The survival of private junior colleges.* Los Angeles: ERIC Clearinghouse for Junior Colleges, ED 327 222.

Wilson, A. 2000. *Making the move: the transition from graduate student at a Ph.D.-granting university to new faculty member at a small, private, liberal arts college.* ERIC, ED 446 715.

Youn, Ted I. K. 1992. *The characteristics of faculty in master's level institutions.* Boston: New England Resource for Higher Education, University of Massachusetts at Boston.

·5

TEACHING
and LEARNING
as a
Transactional
Process

I see communication as a

huge umbrella that covers

and affects all that goes on

between human beings.

–Virginia Satir

Martha C. Petrone
MIAMI UNIVERSITY—MIDDLETOWN

◆

S*easoned college instructors will admit* that in any given semester they could teach two classes in almost exactly the same way, with very different outcomes. At the same time, two instructors may teach the same course in very different ways with a similar level of assessed effectiveness. A reality of the teaching and learning process is that no matter how well you plan the course, there are no assurances that what you are attempting to teach in a particular class session will in fact actually be what your students learn. This is due, at least in part, to the interpersonal dynamics or process issues that affect every classroom.

Seminars for new instructors often emphasize the cognitive domain of learning, e.g., selecting the course curriculum and planning the syllabus. Yet, the daily dynamics that encourage students to engage with each other and the instructor have as significant a bearing on teaching and learning (Lowman 1984). While the cognitive dimension has to do with explicit knowledge or "what we are learning," this affective or emotional dimension deals with tacit information or "how we are learning" and "how we feel about our learning." It asks questions about the process of teaching and learning such as:

- Does what happens in the classroom on a daily basis support student learning?
- Is the subject matter accessible to all students?
- Can students learn and succeed more effectively because of the way the instructor and students are relating in this course?
- Do students have a "voice" in a classroom climate where their opinions and viewpoints are acknowledged and accepted?

Fundamental to understanding this interpersonal dynamic is recognizing that teaching and learning is a form of two-way communication occurring in a social system comprised of a range of participants with their own interests, goals, background factors, knowledge, abilities, attributes, and values. Each classroom interaction, whether among students or between instructor and student, is a transaction where constant mutual influence takes place (DeVito 1998). Everyone who is part of the class—whether present or not—is affected in an individual and unique way by what is said and done. In turn, each person in the class no matter how subtly, also affects what is said and done. Take, for example, a situation where a particularly dominant and outspoken student is absent one day. Not only is that student likely to be affected by what she missed in class, it is likely that the classroom dynamics will be affected by her absence. In contrast, consider a student who is very quiet and appears resistant to participate in class discussions or group work. Although appearing to not communicate, this student's behavior will affect the teaching and learning setting.

In this transactional view, teaching and learning does not merely occur as a direct line from the instructor to students. It is a mutual process where teacher learns from students, students learn from teacher, and students learn from each other. It also encompasses what is going on within the instructor, within each of the students in the class, as well as within the larger societal, environmental, academic, or political context where the learning is taking place.

Imagine that everyone in your classroom is wearing a different pair of eyeglasses—each with a prescription allowing them to make sense of the world they live in and the ways they learn in it. These glasses represent their frame of reference evolving from their unique lives, educational experiences, personalities, and identity dimensions such age, gender, class, knowledge, religion, ability, and cultural upbringing. Just as others would not be able to see clearly through your glasses if they were to borrow them, you would not see clearly through theirs. It is only by sharing your perspective and encouraging students to share theirs that you can collectively reach a level of mutual understanding about your respective needs in the classroom environment.

As colleges and universities become increasingly diverse and multicultural, the possibility for variant learning outcomes is amplified. As James Anderson notes, "... it would be naïve to expect that the cultural values, behaviors, and expectations of diverse groups of students are so diluted on campus that their presence doesn't have an impact on classroom dynamics and learning outcomes" (Anderson 1999, 69–76). As instructors, then, it becomes even more important to expand our pedagogy to include the process dimension. As Gloria Ladson-Billings states, "... [critical] pedagogy operates in the realm of the relational and societal. No longer are we referring merely to the knowledge transactions that occur in the classroom but to the larger social meanings that are imparted between and among teachers, students and their social worlds" (Ladson-Billings, 29).

For new instructors, a significant benefit of this wide-lens view is a feeling of release from the myth of perfection. Faculty no longer have to assume the role of the all-knowing expert bestowing truths and wisdom. Although they are expected to have substantial knowledge of subject matter and a functional knowledge of various pedagogical approaches, it is impossible to know the intricacies of each student's experience or the impact of contextual factors. What faculty can do, instead, is to gain authenticity in their teaching by remaining open to their own fallibility.

As Parker Palmer explains, "good teaching cannot be reduced to technique; good teaching comes from the identity and integrity of the teacher." Further, he notes "... a teacher's ability to connect with students and to further connect them to the subject has more to do with being available [to their students] and vulnerable [to their own humanity, both the strengths and limitations]" (Palmer 1998, 10). Gaining authenticity in teaching is a career-long endeavor based on the recognition that who you are and how well you know and trust yourself is fundamental to establishing rapport between you and your students.

Extending beyond the rapport between the instructor and student, faculty can also advance student learning by creating a classroom climate that promotes the open engagement of ideas and the freedom for students to situate them in their own experience (Magolda 1997). Tiberius and Billson (1991) identify the following five characteristics of a teaching and learning environment that fosters alliances between faculty and students:

1. Mutual respect
2. Shared responsibility for learning and mutual commitment to goals
3. Effective communication and feedback
4. Cooperation and willingness to negotiate conflict
5. A sense of security in the classroom

In a classroom climate built upon these five tenets, students are afforded the space to learn to cope with cognitive dissonance and emotional ambiguity leading to greater intellectual and social development (Berger 1979). By attending to process issues, the teaching and learning setting can be a habitat of egalitarianism, respectfulness, and encouragement where students move from a dualistic view in the classroom to participation in relativistic thinking (Perry 1985).

Chapter Overview

The purpose of this chapter is twofold. The first goal, to paraphrase Palmer, is to prompt you to look at your own teaching in order "to determine your own limits and potentials when it comes to dealing with the relation between your subject and your student's lives" (Palmer, 10). The second is to suggest a variety of process management strategies that facilitate classroom dialogue, makes learning more equitable, and creates a safe climate of mutual respect and shared responsibility for all classroom citizens.

It is my hope that the resources in this chapter will assist you in considering, selecting, and implementing approaches to help you better meet the desired educational and developmental outcomes for your students as well as serve as a basis for recognizing and developing your unique teaching style.

Starting with Yourself: Teaching from the Inside Out

Teaching should come from within, not from without. —Hopi proverb

My friend, Harriet, is a well known and sought out facilitator and trainer.[1] When asked about the key to her success, she simply responds, "I really believe the best teachers I ever had, knew who they were. It has taken me a long time but I have a good sense of who I am, warts and all, and I don't try to be anything else when I train."

There is a lot of wisdom in both Harriet's comment and the Hopi quotation. Facilitating the teaching and learning process effectively and comfortably is based on a journey, self-understanding through self-awareness.

Recently, I did a week long, formative peer assessment in two sections of the same course taught by a colleague in his second year of a tenure-track appointment. On the first day, he lectured. In both sections, he had a clear and energetic delivery and mastery of the material. Yet, the students seemed distant and disengaged. Occasionally, when he would leave the lecture and cite some personal examples, the class enlivened, but once he returned to the lecture, energy once again waned. At the same time, the instructor was putting out a tremendous amount of effort. He was working so hard and futilely to get the students involved; I started to feel tired for him! Even more significant is that I did not recognize him while he was teaching this class; he seemed very different from the person I knew outside of this classroom setting.

Just two days later, he taught the same classes using individual exercises and small group work. The contrasts to the previous class meeting were remarkable. There was now a flow of discussion within and among the student groups and between the instructor and students. An air of openness and inquiry permeated the classroom and there was a high level of critical thinking and engagement with the material. The class session seemed to pass quickly and even when over several students stayed after to continue the discussion. This time, I recognized the instructor as the person I knew outside the classroom—his humor, his mannerisms, his personality, and his sense of self were all clearly present.

When we talked afterwards, I asked the him why he thought the second class meeting had gone so well in contrast to the first. He replied, "I guess it is because I feel comfortable doing exercises and facilitating group work, but I *hate* to lecture. I just feel like I am not really giving them what they need and expect in a college experience, if I don't lecture at least once a week. But, lecturing is something I feel obligated to do."

The point of this anecdote is not to suggest eliminating the lecture as a viable means of teaching. On the contrary, for many, lecturing is their forté and students respond in much the same way as the students in the anecdote responded to the class exercises and small group discussion. The point is to highlight the importance of looking at your view of the teaching and learning process as well as your strengths, weaknesses, likes, and dislikes as a teacher and a learner. Through reflective practice based on your identity and integrity, you can make conscious, pedagogical choices and establish clear guidelines about the ways you want to approach teaching and learning in your classroom.

All faculty have an individualized view of the teaching and learning process. Some may teach in the ways they learned best, others in ways they saw modeled by their instructors, and still others try to develop different ways of reaching their students responding to frustration with their educational experiences. Regardless of which of these or other approaches are taken, there can be an underlying *educentric* assumption that there is a best way to impart knowledge. As Palmer explains, it is important to keep in mind that:

> ... it becomes impossible to claim that all good teachers use similar techniques: some lecture nonstop and others speak very little; some stay close to their material and others loose the imagination; some teach with the carrot and others with the stick ... good teachers share one trait: a strong sense of personal identity infuses their work (Palmer, 10).

In addition to examining your own educentricism, it is important to recognize and explore the expectations you hold about the educational preparedness and social/emotional readiness of your students. As Linda Nilson states:

> No matter how bright or mature your prospective students may be, do not expect them to have reached a high level of cognitive maturity in your discipline ... almost all students, especially freshman and sophomores begin a course of study with serious misconceptions about knowledge in general and the discipline specifically (Nilson 1998, 7–8).

Furthermore, instructors cannot assume that students have an innate understanding of the parameters of acceptable behavior within their classrooms.

When instructors explore, not only *what* to teach and *when* to teach it, but also *who* is in their class, and *how* best to facilitate learning, their teaching becomes mindful and adaptive, rather than imitative or reactive. In the peer assessment example, if the instructor had contemplated how lecturing was affecting him as well as the teaching and learning environment, and if he had taken the time to find out more about his students' learning styles and needs, he might not have lectured at all during the entire term.

Beginning Reflective Practice

We must not cease from exploration.
And the end of all our exploring will be to arrive where
we began and to know the place for the first time. —T. S. Eliot

The guided self-inquiry inventory is designed to help you explore your personal perspective on the teaching and learning process. Think of the inventory more as a form of self-exploration than a search for correct responses. Set aside some uninterrupted time and find a peaceful place where you can think about your answers. Pause before you answer each question and really contemplate what you believe, know, or don't know, about each question. As you will see in subsequent sections of this chapter, the information you gain from this exercise can serve as a basis for clarifying your personal boundaries in the teaching and learning setting and your own classroom interaction guidelines.

Guided Self-Inquiry Inventory

1. Who are you as a teacher and a learner?
   · How did you learn to teach?
   · How do you intend to approach your teaching?
   · How do you prefer to approach teaching?
   · What excites you about teaching?
   · What makes you most apprehensive about teaching or learning?
   · In what ways do you learn best?
   · Do you tend to teach the way you learn best?
   · Think about the teachers from whom you learned the most effectively. In what ways did their unique approach to teaching encourage your learning? What are the common characteristics they shared which encouraged your learning?
   · When you have tried to impart knowledge to others whether in a formal classroom setting or informally with a friend or colleague, what approaches make you feel most effective?
2. What are your students' perspectives on learning?
   · How do your students learn most effectively?

- What is the potential range of learning styles that might be represented by the students in your classroom?
- In what ways might you facilitate your classes to meet the varying styles represented?
- How can you learn more about the ways your students learn best?

3. What is your stance on issues of power and authority in the classroom?
   - How do you see issues of power and authority within the classes you teach?
   - Are you more comfortable setting the guidelines for the course or do you prefer to allow the students to generate the course syllabus together with you?
   - What are your personal boundaries in your classroom? In other words, what are the things your students need to know about what you think, feel, or believe about your subject, about your view of appropriate classroom behavior, or about you, personally.
   - How comfortable are you in dealing with conflict in general?
   - When there is a clash or ideas or values within your class, do you feel confident you can handle the situation?
   - In what ways do you want your students to conduct themselves in conflict situations in order for you to feel more comfortable with and in control of the situation?
   - How effective are you at active listening?
   - Do you find yourself correcting or judging your students' viewpoints, rather than listening nondefensively?

4. What barriers or biases do you have which might affect the teaching and learning process?
   - How much information do you know about the various racial, ethnic, gender, sex, class, ability or religious perspectives that might be represented in your classroom?
   - What stereotypes do you hold about each of these groups? (We all have biases and hold stereotypes whether or not we like that we do. If you answer initially that you hold no stereotypes, keep contemplating the question until you can answer it openly.)
   - Might you expect a nontraditional student to be a better student, a Mexican student to speak on behalf of all native Spanish-speaking

students, or a disabled student to need special assistance without asking for it?

· What do you expect your students to know about expectations for academic work before they start your class?

Completing the Guided Self-Inquiry Inventory is a first step on the path of reflective practice. With the unique pressures facing pretenure faculty and teaching assistants also comes the risk that time for reflection on teaching will get relegated to a lesser priority. Attending local, regional, or national conferences on teaching and learning, engaging with colleagues by joining faculty learning communities or through peer assessments, and reading books or articles about teaching and learning representing a variety of perspectives are all ways to continue this important practice. Yet, it is your own recognition of the value of this work that will establish reflective practice as a necessary part of your ongoing faculty development.

Some Beginning Resources

Anthony Grasha. *Teaching with Style*. Alliance Publishers. 1996.
ISBN 0964507110
bell hooks. *Teaching to Transgress*. Routledge. 1994. ISBN 0415908086
Samuel M. Intrator and Parker J. Palmer. *Stories of the Courage to Teach: Honoring the Teacher's Heart*. Wiley, John and Sons. 2002.
ISBN 0787956325
Parker Palmer. *The Courage to Teach: Exploring the Inner Landscape of a Teacher's Life*. Jossey-Bass. 1998. ISBN 0787910589

ACKNOWLEDGING AND VALUING STUDENTS' LEARNING STYLES AND TEMPERAMENTS

There are two ways of spreading light;
to be the candle or the mirror that reflects it. —Edith Wharton

NOW THAT YOU HAVE A CLEARER SENSE OF YOUR OWN VIEWS, it is time to turn to the range of perspectives on teaching and learning represented in your classes. Through the exploration of diverse perspectives, including your own, your students not only gain insight into themselves, but into the different personalities, learning styles, preferences, and background factors represented in the classroom. This exploration also helps to establish a common language for a community of learners leading to a sense of acceptance and belonging for all students.

Two very accessible and useful instruments that help to provide individual student information as well as to promote the recognition of diverse perspectives are the Myer-Briggs Type Indicator (MBTI) and the VARK[2] (Visual, Auditory, Read/Write, Kinesthetic) Learning Styles Inventory. (Myer and Myers 1995). The MBTI is a formal inventory based on statistical analysis, depicting sixteen different categories of personality. A later, but similar instrument, The Keirsey Scale, expands on the work of the MBTI, by identifying four major temperaments corresponding to each of the sixteen personalities (Keirsey 1998). Both of these instruments are used extensively in business/industry and counseling settings to encourage understanding of the behavioral tendencies based on the different types. More significant to this discussion, they are also reliable methods for assessing student learning styles.

The MBTI is based on the premise that four sets of preferences distinguish how people differ from one another—extraversion versus introversion, sensing versus intuition, thinking versus feeling, and judging versus perceiving. A person's personality type is determined by the blend of their preferences from each of these four categories. The following cursory explanation of the preferences may help to give you an initial sense of how they might impact the teaching and learning setting:

- The first category of preference deals with how an individual derives energy from the social environment. *Extraverts* tend to be action-oriented and get energy from interacting with others. Expressing themselves is fundamental to their self-understanding. Often when they participate in class discussion, they are clarifying what they think and feel as they speak. In contrast, *introverts* although often sociable, get their energy from drawing inside and reflecting on the concepts, theories, or ideas discussed in class. They concentrate, formulate, and think before expressing.
- The second set of categories has to do with how people perceive. A student whose preference is *sensing* tends to be detail oriented and prefer facts. They also prefer linear thinking and structured classroom organization. *Intuitive* students on the other hand, draw on their hunches or gut reactions to find relationships

among the facts. Their learning begins with a conceptual framework or "big picture" view.

- The third category of preferences deals with how people form judgments. Students with a *thinking* preference tend to be logical, objective decision makers who focus on the end result or the task at hand. Those with a *feeling* preference tend to approach decision making viscerally, strive for harmony, and consider the impact that decisions have on other people.
- The final set of categories represent how students manage their lives. Those with a *judging* preference tend to be planners and list makers. They focus on the outcome and take action quickly. Deadlines are sacred—assignments are in on time—sometimes early. In contrast, *perceivers* may find it difficult to complete a task due to their natural curiosity and spontaneous nature. They often work on many tasks at once but are easily distracted by new information or the desire to know as much as they can about a subject.

The MBTI provides much more information about personality and learning styles than described above. Yet, as you can see from this basic explanation of the preferences underlying the personality types, with this knowledge, students and instructors alike, can gain sights into their own learning as well as discover ways to work more effectively with others.

The MBTI and the Keirsey Scale, complete with scoring and limited analysis are available online at a variety of sources, some free of charge and others with a small fee. College and university counseling centers generally have trained professionals who can provide, administer, score and interpret the results of hard copies of the MBTI at your request. (See resources at the end of this section.)

The VARK Inventory is a simple but powerful instrument comprised of only thirteen questions but with practical applications to the teaching and learning process. It is especially useful for "students to learn more effectively and faculty to become more sensitive to the diversity of teaching strategies necessary to reach all students."[3] By gaining an understanding of visual, aural, reading/writing, and kinesthetic approaches to learning, students can appreciate their own as well as others' styles and can develop potential interventions to improve their own learning. At the same time, with this information, teachers can better understand ways to develop teaching and learning strategies designed to connect with students from all of the learning styles. The VARK Inventory is available online at www.vark-learn.com.

CASE STUDY:
APPLICATIONS OF THE MYERS-BRIGGS AND VARK INVENTORIES

PERHAPS, THE BEST WAY TO ILLUSTRATE HOW TO USE the information you gain from the Myers-Briggs or the VARK Inventories is through an actual case study. I will use an example of a colleague, Lizz, a tenure-track, assistant professor in computer information technology, who worked for many years as an engineer in industry before she began teaching six years ago.[4]

Lizz' MBTI personality type is that of the "Field Marshall." In behavioral terms, this means that she is extroverted, highly organized, has contingency plans for her contingency plans, and takes and expects action. Her VARK learning scores are 3 for visual, 0 for auditory, 10 for reading and writing, and 7 for kinesthetic. It is common to walk into her office and see her reading sections of five books at a time (reading) to get the information she will put in the detailed lecture notes she passes out to her students (writing). It is equally common to hear her voice frustration from attending a meeting where she has to listen intently for a prolonged period. Not only is listening (auditory where her score is 0) a challenge for her, she has to do it while sitting still which opposes her kinesthetic learning needs.

Lizz teaches a liberal-education course entitled "Introduction to Computer Concepts and Programming." Since there are multiple sections of this course, a common syllabus exists for all classes. One of the requirements for the course is a writing assignment. When Lizz first began teaching the course, she assigned a research paper simply because that was what she was accustomed to from her education and engineering experience. The papers she received were abysmal. Not only was the quality of the work poor, it was a toss up whether the students disliked writing them more than she disliked grading them.

The next year, Lizz discovered the MBTI. Now, during the first week of each semester, she has the students take the test online. In addition to sharing their personality types with her, they now write [much more effective and interesting] papers based on their results. They answer questions such as:

- In what ways does the description of your personality type fit or not fit you?

- What is your opinion of studying personality types?
- What can you learn from knowing your own and other's types?
- In your ideal university, how would your courses be taught?

Following this assignment, the entire class has a short discussion about where they might find personality types useful whether in professional careers or on a daily basis with their families. During that discussion Lizz also shares her own personality type and students discuss how their types interface with it.

By knowing her students' individual personality types, Lizz now adapts her teaching in appropriate ways. She encourages extroverted students to ask questions and talk through a new assignment. For more introverted students, she sits next to them while the class is working on the new project and talks through the instructions with them face-to-face.

This year she added the VARK Inventory to her classroom. She found that students were not at all surprised about their learning style score. However, they were surprised that she was interested in knowing what they were.

Lizz now tries to provide a range of teaching strategies to meet the diverse learning needs of her students. For the visual learners, she does demonstrations and flowcharting—many with animations. For the auditory learners, she lectures. For the reading/writing learners, she gives comprehensive, but incomplete lecture notes, so they may add details as they listen to lectures. For the kinesthetic learners, who comprise the vast majority of her students, she assigns hands-on classroom activities and programming assignments.

Although each of us may have a dominant learning style, we generally have one or two secondary learning styles. By providing a range of learning experiences, learning is reinforced through more than one channel. It also helps to enhance those styles that are less fully developed.

Whether you use the MBTI or the VARK in these ways, or you choose to use other ways to discover your students' learning needs, finding information about your students helps you to adapt your teaching to foster a more equitable learning environment for all students.

Beginning Resources on Personality Types and Learning Styles

David Keirsey. *Please Understand Me II: Temperament Character Intelligence.*
  Prometheus Books. 1998. ISBN 1885705026
Isabel Briggs Myers with Peter B. Myers. *Gifts Differing: Understanding
  Personality Type.* Consulting Psychology Press. 1995. ISBN 089106074X

Online Testing Sites

www.hobbitlore.com/personality/index

This is a free and fun site based on the Myers-Briggs/Keirsey Personality Tests. The results of this test reveal which of the characters from the *Lord of the Rings* the respondent is most like. Although unreliable, unlike some other parodies versions of the MBTI or Keirsey Scale, these test results do give a reasonable analysis of personality type.

www.humanmetrics.com

A version of the MBTI is available at the site free of charge. The site also provides an analysis of one's style based on the test results.

www.keirsey.com

For less than $10.00, the Keirsey Scale is available at this site. This site provides a more extensive explanation of the personality types and access to more information about personality testing.

www.mbtypeguide.com/type/index

This is another online site for taking the MBTI.

www.vark-learn.com This is the official site of the VARK Learning Inventory. The test and additional resources information are available at this site. There is no charge for downloading the VARK Inventory.

ESTABLISHING A SUPPORTIVE CLASSROOM CLIMATE FOR TEACHING AND LEARNING

COLLEGE AND UNIVERSITIES NATIONWIDE HAVE CODES OF CONDUCT for civil engagement, diversity statements, and/or policies and procedures for processing sexual harassment and discrimination complaints. In addition, specific responsibilities for faculty are delineated in institutional policy manuals. As just one example, the following two tenets of the Statement of Good Teaching Practices from Miami University, acknowledge the importance of creating a classroom climate that supports teaching and learning:

> Every instructor is responsible for treating students with courtesy and respect at all times. Courtesy and respect do not prohibit strong criticism directed at the student's academic errors and scholarly responsibilities.

> Every instructor is responsible for endeavoring to ensure that the learning environment is free from all forms of prejudice that negatively influence student learning, such as those based on age, ethnicity, gender, mental or physical impairment, race, religion, or sexual orientation.

In her book, *Creating Emotionally Safe Schools: A Guide for Educators and Parents*, Jane Bluestein (2001) expands on these two guidelines by suggesting a framework suggests for safe schools/classrooms which includes the following six freedoms:

- The freedom to *not* be good at a particular skill or subject and still be treated with dignity and respect
- The freedom from harassment or intimidation from peers or instructor
- The freedom to express one's own feelings and opinions without fear of recrimination from either peers or instructor
- The freedom to make choices and influence one's own learning, pursue personal interests and control various factors in the process of learning ... based on personal needs and preferences.
- The freedom from judgment, prejudice and discrimination based on academic, athletic, creative or social capabilities, learning-style preferences, temperament
- The freedom from judgment, prejudice and discrimination based on aspects of identity such as physical ability, race, religion, ethnicity, class, age, gender or sexual orientation

In both sets of statements, the expectations and desired outcomes are clear. In addition to providing a stimulating intellectual experience, instructors should manage the classroom dynamics so that all students have access to achieve the goals they set for themselves in a supportive and safe environment where they are acknowledged and accepted as they are.

For new instructors, this may seem a daunting task. When teaching a new course, it is difficult enough to keep up with the material and develop new handouts, assignments and tests. Add into the mix a student who is failing, a growing conflict between two students with diverse perspectives, or a student who constantly seems to challenge everything you say and the task may seem impossible.

Yet, it is a task of critical importance. In recent years, there has been increasing concern over incivility in the classroom. Disruptive behavior can range from students who are consistently late, inattentive or talkative in class to students who are openly hostile to the instructor or fellow students. Gonzales and Lopez (2001) suggest the following three steps to help instructors circumvent incivility in the classroom:

1. *Create behavioral standards*

   In communication, the process of letting others know your interpersonal limits is called boundary management. Fundamentally, this lets others know your particular views and limits about how you wish to manage your classroom. As a starting point, you would enumerate your specific classroom guidelines and expectations on your syllabus.

   As mentioned earlier, it is naïve to assume that all students know, let alone understand, the acceptable code of conduct you expect in *your* classroom. If they are accustomed to coming late or interrupting another student or the instructor to make a point in a class discussion in other classes, they will be likely to do the same in your class unless you are explicit in your expectations.

2. *Enforce consistent standards of behavior*

   Recently I attended a meeting of seven first- or second-year tenure-track faculty and several of their mentors. During that discussion, some of the newer faculty expressed the view that they were held hostage by student course evaluations. They feared that students would evaluate them harshly if the faculty were to confront behaviors they found inappropriate. Having read hundreds of classroom sets of course evaluations in my capacity as an administrator, it is much more likely that other students will evaluate you harshly if you allow a student to usurp control of the classroom. Bending over backwards to accommodate a disruptive student throws you off-balance and destabilizes the teaching and learning process. It is best to address any disruptive act as soon as it occurs and make a concerted effort to uphold any guidelines you set forth for your course.

3. *Examine your teaching style*

   In any two-way setting, to both parties are responsible for the success or failure of the communication. As the saying goes, "you cannot change the behavior of others, you can only change your own." By examining your teaching style you may discover that ineffective process dynamics are causing the problem. At the same time by finding ways to better adapt your subject matter to make it more accessible to the range of students in their classroom, you can create a more engaging classroom climate.

In the final sections of this chapter, I will elaborate on ways to enlist your students in creating and participating in collective ways to implement these three steps. The suggested approaches are meant to provide alternatives that will encompass your students' diverse learning needs as well as encourage mutual respect, shared responsibility for learning and mutual commitment to goals, effective communication and feedback, cooperation and willingness to negotiate conflict, and a sense of security in the classroom.

CREATING BEHAVIORAL STANDARDS: ESTABLISHING SHARED OBJECTIVES AND AGREED UPON NORMS

INSTEAD OF LOOKING AT A SAFE AND SUPPORTIVE CLIMATE as something for which you are solely responsible, you can empower your students to create it with you. Extending beyond your guidelines for classroom goals and behavior, there is a relatively simple technique from group-process consultation literature, to engage students in a process to establish shared classroom objectives and agreed upon norms (Reddy 1996).

Many faculty take the time to do ice-breaker exercises at the beginning of the semester. These activities give useful information about the student demographic make-up and individual goals. Climate setting goes a step further. It allows the class to determine their collective objectives and the ground rules that will serve as a foundation for their interactions with one another. Doing so leads to a collaborative environment where students work together to achieve shared goals as well as their own self-interests.

CLIMATE SETTING EXERCISE

1. Randomly divide the class into groups of three or four. Ask each subgroup to consider the following question, to capture their ideas on a flipchart or a piece of paper, and be prepared to report them to the rest of the class.

   - What needs to happen in this course this term to make the time and energy you spend worthwhile?

2. After the discussion seems to wane, approximately ten minutes, ask each group to take turns reporting out. You may write them down in full view of the class either on an overhead or a flipchart. If you wish you can have the students write themselves. (Professional facilitators

talk about the power of the pen. When you share the pen, power is dispersed.)

Some common responses to this question are:
A. To improve my abilities to …
B. To learn more about …
C. To be able to …
D. To get to know other students in the class
E. To gain a real world application of the course content
F. To get an A
G. To know that my views and opinions matter

3. When there are no new items to be added to the list, ask the entire class to synthesize a list of the four to six common objectives for the class. The key here is to make sure that everyone agrees with every item that remains on the lists. If even one person disagrees, the objectives are not shared.

4. Repeat steps 1 through 3, including reforming the subgroups, for the following question that will help to determine the class ground rules:

• How do we have to work together in order to achieve these outcomes?

Some common responses to this question are:
A. We will listen to understand the other person's view before we speak.
B. We will be an active participant in class and any groups we are in.
C. We will be prepared for every class.
D. We will ask others for their opinions.
E. We will be respectful to each other.

5. When the discussion is complete, post the objectives and ground rules in a prominent space in the classroom or on the course Web site. If that is not possible, distribute the objectives at the next class meeting for students to attach to their syllabus.

Both lists will provide general, shared guidelines for the remainder of the semester. The class can revisit the objectives as benchmarks for how well the course is progressing. Let's say that your students list "a real-world application of the course content" as one of the class objectives. Although you may think you are achieving this objective through the examples you use in class, four weeks into the term, a kinesthetic learner may raise the issue that they don't yet see an application. This allows for a discussion of kinesthetic ways of achieving the shared goals whether a field trip or a service learning opportunity. It may also empower the student to arrange a learning experience for the entire class that he sees as a real world application.

Ground rules generally provide the guidelines for maintaining civility and mutual respect in the classroom. They also establish normative behaviors that can serve as the basis for interventions in conflict situations. For example, assume one of your class' guidelines is: "We will listen to understand the other person's viewpoint before we speak ourselves." In a heated discussion between two students, where self-interest and being right begin to erode the supportive classroom climate, any member of the class can refer to this ground rule to bring their classmates back on track.

As you get more comfortable with this exercise, you can vary or expand the questions you pose depending on what it is you genuinely want to know from your students. For example, you might want to ask these additional questions:

- What are you personally willing to do in order to make this happen?
- What can I do to help you learn more effectively and/or participate in class more comfortably?

Another variation could be in the way you do the exercise. Students could first answer the questions individually on a three-by-five card and you could then open up the discussion to the entire class. Regardless of how many questions you ask or the process you use, this exercise establishes collective objectives and ground rules for the class providing a foundation for building a supportive classroom climate.

ENCOURAGING CONSISTENT STANDARDS OF BEHAVIOR: THE MEDIATED CLASSROOM

… In order to envision richer forms of community, students … need to learn listening, empathy, fairness, dialogue, conflict resolution, collaborative problem-solving— in the face of disagreement. —Carol Geary Schneider, President, AAC&U

CONFLICT IS INEVITABLE IN HUMAN INTERACTIONS. Depending on an individual's background, he or she may have very different metaphors for conflict based on previous life experience and particularly family of origin. Those metaphors could range from "conflict is war" to "conflict is understanding." Based on these deeply embedded metaphors, students and faculty alike may respond in a variety of unproductive ways when confronted with a classroom disagreement or dispute. Some individuals might avoid or acquiesce. Others might dominate by talking louder and more forcefully. In either instance, however, a dialogic, mutual understanding does not take place.

To get a better sense of the classroom conflict dynamics and the corresponding risks involved, it is useful to look at the three levels of conversation underlying disputes explained by Stone, Patton and Heen (1999) of the Harvard Negotiation Project. The first is the *What Happened Conversation*. At this level, the parties are arguing about who is right and who is wrong as well as the "truth" [as they see it] of the situation. In addition to the disparate views of the content or meaning of what happened, there is also a relational aspect. Disputants might be upset about what they believe to be the other person's intentions or motivations in saying or doing something with which they disagree or take offense. This type of conflict becomes a power struggle over proving one's own position. Educationally, this conversation represents an either/or orientation consistent with lower level, dualistic thinking.

The second level is *The Feeling Conversation* that for many is the most uncomfortable level of the three. Emotions are at the core of all conflicts. For a variety of reasons, most people have the tendency to stay out of the feeling conversation. They may fear losing face by expressing strong feelings or losing control or simply may not be able to identify and express what they are feeling. Or, their behavior may be governed by cultural mores about conflict. There is a tremendous irony in this phenomenon. Regardless of the reason, by avoiding the underlying feelings, there is little or no chance for mutual understanding or resolution. Students who are locked into this conversation may act out in inappropriate ways ranging from withdrawing to releasing tension through joking around in class to being openly defensive or hostile.

The third level is *The Identity Conversation*. This level raises questions about the implications of the conflict on the individual's self-image including what it says about the person as well as the impact it has his or her sense of self. From my experience with diversity training, when a discussion raises issues about an individual's core identity, there is a significant chance that it will become heated. Consider for example, a student with devout religious views confronted with a view opposing those teachings or a feminist hearing the instructor or a fellow student make what he perceives to be a sexist remark. In each instance, the identity conversation resonates deep within. And most likely, it will do so for all parties involved in the conversation.

As the instructor you play two important roles during the climate setting exercise explained in the last section. The first is as a model of effective communication for facilitating understanding. The second is as a partially removed observer who can help to guide the direction and nature of the discussion. These roles, which draw upon fundamental communication strategies for their success, are similar to those enacted by mediators in dispute resolution settings. Mediators are third parties who follow a delineated approach for understanding and acknowledging disparate perspectives. They operate as a neutral observer and do not impose a solution or come up with a definitive answer. Instead, they facilitate an equitable process for all parties.

In their book, *The Promise of Mediation: Responding to Conflict through Empowerment and Recognition*, Bush and Folger (1994) contend that conflict has the power to transform people and situations. Rather than approaching conflict resolution as a prescriptive process where problems are solved, they believe the process should encourage the parties to identify the issues for themselves in order to better understand the other's [and their own] perspective and to reach a truly mutual understanding as a result. The primary goal, then, is not the resolution. Rather, it is to strengthen each person's self-awareness and expand his/her willingness to acknowledge and be responsive to the other's frame of reference.

By applying this view to classroom interaction and adopting specific mediation communication strategies, you can create a mediated classroom. Rather than being an environment where conflict is avoided, remains unresolved, or where the instructor is solely responsible for maintaining order and civility, this approach can help to create an inclusive learning setting. The strategies for dealing with incivility or conflict in a mediated classroom are much less prescriptive and nonlinear than those used in dispute resolution. Nevertheless, they set the stage for effective communication allowing for multiple viewpoints to coexist leading to collaboration and dialogue rather than self-interest and argument. In addition, drawing on these approaches can help to build a community consciousness where all students can feel accepted for "who and where they are."

Talking About "Talking About"

In this approach, the parties—whether the instructor and a student, two students, or the entire class—discuss how they will engage in talking about the issue. It corresponds to the Introduction Phase of traditional mediation, where the process is explicitly laid out. In a mediated classroom, it is more open-ended, allowing the parties involved to determine the process for the conversation or discussion.

Talking About "Talking About" is exactly as the name implies. It is talking about how to talk about the potential or expressed conflict or act of incivility. It brings the transactional process to the forefront, allowing parties to create guidelines for how the conversation will ensue. The climate setting exercise in the previous section is an example of this approach.

Let's look at some other potential situations where this approach could be useful:

- A student is consistently late to class and disruptive when she finally gets there. You have tried to ignore it but today this behavior is on your last nerve.
- In a family studies class, you arrange for a panel on adoption including families representing cross-generational, homosexual, single parent, and intercultural adoption.
- You just assigned a group term project. Two students are at odds about the topic they would like to do.

Talking About "Talking About" encourages the parties to step back from the issue and plan how to deal with it in a constructive manner. In the situation with the late and disruptive student, you could ask the student to stay after class and then explain that you need to talk with her about her tardiness and would like to come up with a mutually convenient time for the conversation. In the second situation, the class can collectively determine a way to engage with the panelists in a respectful manner without tacitly agreeing with anything that they might individually find offensive. In the final situation, although your first inclination might be to try to resolve the conflict for the students, instead, you could encourage then to go back to their group to determine a collective way to talk about selecting a mutually acceptable topic for all members.

As in instructor, you can use this approach three ways. First, you can use and model it in the daily activities you plan for your classes as well as in your interactions with your students. Second, you can facilitate your students to use it with each other. Finally, proactively, you can embed Talking About "Talking About" in assignments. As part of the assignment for a group term project, for example, you could ask students to clearly delineate how they plan to work together to accomplish the project.

STORYTELLING

STORYTELLING GIVES THE SPEAKER a chance to share what he or she thinks and feels. It is that person's opportunity to have the floor *without interruption* and with the purpose of being heard and understood. In this approach the storyteller is given a "safe place" to express herself. No one, including the instructor, argues with her or questions her logic or facts. Without interruption, and with the attention of the listener(s), she then has the immediacy of those present to fully express her point of view. At the same time, by focusing on understanding and acknowledgment rather than agreement, the listener(s) can actually attempt to "hear her"—her individual and unique perspective as well as the background factors and life experiences which led to its creation.

Since storytelling is not just about what she thinks and feels, but, [as was said in the '60s] "where she is coming from," the following prompts can encourage the speaker to address all three levels of conversation underlying conflict:

1. From my point of view, this is how I see this problem ...
2. When I think about this situation, I feel ...
3. This issue is important to me because ...

As an instructor, you should not only encourage your students to storytell, you should consider doing it yourself. An experience I had as an undergraduate illustrates this point. Early in college, science was not a subject that interested me. My past experience with the sciences had been dry and clinical. So it became something I was required to take in order to graduate. Waiting until my junior year, I reluctantly signed up for a zoology class. The first day of that class, I was very closed-off and defensive. I resented taking the class and felt it had nothing to offer me.

I had the distinct good fortune to get Dr. Ingersoll as my professor. Throughout the course, he not only explained concepts, he told personal stories to illustrate those concepts. In one anecdote, Dr. Ingersoll told of having to incubate duck eggs to provide the live specimen for his research. One of the ducks, upon hatching, imprinted on him. Charley, as Dr. Ingersoll called him, followed him everywhere. When it came time for the research that required the death of the ducks, Charley suddenly disappeared. Somehow, it seems Charley was taken out into the woods far from the research site and left to revert to his natural instincts for survival. Admittedly, I have forgotten most of the specifics of what I learned in zoology as an undergraduate. But, to this day, I know what imprinting is.

Although this anecdote does not deal with a direct conflict between Dr. Ingersoll and me, by sharing his perspective, I overcame my own internal conflict about zoology and science in general. Through his stories, this man had such a dramatic effect on my learning and worldview I seriously investigated changing my major to zoology from English.

ACTIVE LISTENING

ACTIVE LISTENING IS AN INTERDEPENDENT communication activity with storytelling. While one person does the storytelling, the other(s) listen actively to what is being said. The goals of the listener(s) are to focus on understanding and to get a good sense of the storyteller's frame of reference. The listener does not have to agree with it, just work to truly comprehend it. Listeners are willing to do this in settings where they know that they will be afforded the same opportunity to express their point of view, whether in response to what is being said in the present or at a later date on another issue.

For kinesthetic learners, especially, active listening is one of those activities that need to be experienced to be understood. Every basic interpersonal communication text makes suggestions on the steps for active listening. However, knowing the steps and actually experiencing the process are two very different things. If you teach smaller classes, you might consider using the following simple ice-breaking exercise early in the semester to give your students the kinesthetic experience of listening for understanding and a model for doing it in your classroom.

Active Listening Ice Breaker

1. In advance of the class, determine five to seven questions about your students' views, life experiences, and/or identity dimensions. The questions should be relatively nonthreatening, but topics that they can respond to for at least two minutes.

Examples

- Discuss a time when your age affected how you were treated in either a positive or negative way.
- If you had an around-the-world airline ticket, what are the first three stops you would make? Why?
- If you could go to lunch with anyone who is alive today, who would you chose? Why?
- Discuss your high school experience or its equivalency.

2. The day of the exercise, ask your students to move the desks or chairs to form two, parallel rows facing each other. If there is an uneven number of students, one row will simply be longer than the other.

3. Next, tell the students they will be taking turns answering a series of questions you will pose to them. First, those in one row will have two minutes of uninterrupted time to answer the questions for the person facing them. Then, the second row will be given the same opportunity. The listeners may give nonverbal feedback, but are not allowed to speak or interrupt in any way. They should also focus on understanding what their partner is saying. A student seated in the extra chair is free to get up and listen in on the conversations.

   You serve as the timer and can flash the lights or say "stop" loudly at the end of each two-minute session. It will take a little while for the conversation to taper off to silence.

4. After both rows have answered the first question, ask the students in one of the rows to move down one chair. If there is a row with an extra chair, that is the row that should move seats.

5. You then repeat the process for any remaining questions you wish to ask. For this exercise to be effective, you should ask a minimum of four questions.

6. After you are finished, discuss listening with your students. Because there is a lot of extraneous conversation in the room during the exercise, it takes more energy for the students to listen to their partner. Students therefore, recognize that active listening takes energy. They also might observe that there are very few situations in their daily interactions where they are ever given the opportunity to speak without interruption. Many, in fact, comment that they found it difficult to fill the two-minute time slots. You may want students to discuss how this type of listening could apply in the classroom. Or you may prefer to explain

why this is the type of listening you would like to employ in your class, especially in classroom discussions or interpersonal conflicts.

RESPONDING

SOME PEOPLE BELIEVE THAT RESPONDING or giving feedback involves telling someone else exactly what they think about what was said. Although a form of feedback, it generally invokes the fast track to the *what happened conversation* and the accompanying defensiveness. On the other hand, no response is actually a response. It is generally perceived negatively and serves to invalidate rather than acknowledge the speaker. Paraphrasing and questioning are two potentially effective ways to give feedback and, in so doing, acknowledge the other person's perspective.

Paraphrasing is the act of repeating back what the speaker said in the listener's own words and with the desire to clarify understanding. It indicates that the listener is indeed listening with the intent to comprehend and in so doing acknowledge the importance of the speaker's perspective. When a listener paraphrases the underlying feelings in what is being said, it is called reflective paraphrasing. To encourage your students to use this form of feedback effectively, you might employ these two variations of listening structures suggested by Kagan and Kagan.

- **Paraphrase Passport**—In a discussion, a fellow classmate is to correctly paraphrase the idea or reflect a feeling of the classmate who previously spoke—before being allowed to contribute his own idea. Paraphrasing effectively grants him his passport to speak.
- **Response Gambits**—Here, the instructor may go one step further by using sentence prompts for students to designate specific responses, e.g., "One thing I understand about what you are saying is …" or "From what you said, I get the sense that you feel …"

Questioning can also be an effective means of providing feedback and gaining clarity. Sharon Ellison states, "We are using non-defensive communication when we ask questions … in an open, sincere way without trying to control how other people respond."[5] In a mediated classroom, the purpose of asking questions becomes a genuine desire to get more information and to understand accurately what the other person means, believes, and feels. Framing and posing questions about the three levels of conversation in a conflict situation give both the listener and the storyteller greater clarity. They may include:

1. Questions to get information about person's view
   - Can you give me an example?
   - Can you help me understand why…?
   - Could you tell me more about…?
2. Questions about the person's frame of reference on the topic/issue
   - From your experience, what motivates you to [see or feel]…?
   - Could you tell me about any previous experiences which contribute to you [seeing or feeling]…?
   - Is there something you think that I don't fully understand about your perspective?
3. Questions to check our assumptions
   - Are you [saying or feeling]…?
   - When you say…, does this mean…?
   - When you say…, do you feel…?
4. Questions to get at interests
   - What concerns you about…?
   - Specifically, how is … affecting you?
   - In what ways does … impact you personally?

FOUR COMPONENTS TO RESOLVING CONFLICTS EQUITABLY

IT IS IMPORTANT TO RECOGNIZE THAT not all classroom conflicts require resolution. In fact, in many instances, students learn more from attempting to reconcile the dissonance of disparate perspectives. However, in instances where resolution is desired or necessary, Fisher and Uri (1991) suggest following these four components of "principled negotiation:"

- Separate the people from the problem
  Here, the focus is on treating others respectfully and on dealing with the facts and nature of the problem, separately.
  Example   The class did not do as well as I had hoped on the exam.
  Contrast   Did any of you actually study for this test?

Example	Our group can't seem to come up with a topic that interests everyone.
Contrast	Everyone is so selfish. They want their topic to be the one we pick.

- Focus on shared interests, not separate positions

    The interests behind the positions are the underlying needs, fears, beliefs, and values that lead us to take that position in the first place. Although on the surface, two positions may seem incompatible, there may be underlying shared interests. Whether stating your interest in the conflict or encouraging students to do so, the focus should be on what the parties want most from the solution.

Example	I would like to find a way to help improve your performance in this course.
Contrast	I put a lot of time and energy in these lectures. If you don't start doing better than this, I am not curving the final grades.
Example	I want our group project to be something that is fun and educational.
Contrast	Look, you guys, my topic is better than his.

- Invent options for mutual gain

    Through collaboration, conflicting parties can come up with a better alternative that can meet their mutual goals.

Example	What are some ways we can come up with together to help you understand the material more effectively?
Contrast	I'll just set up a series of review sessions before the next exam. That should help.
Example	Why don't we brainstorm a list of possible topics and see if that helps us come up with one we can all be excited about?
Contrast	We are going to run out of time. Why don't we just try to combine Jim's and my topic somehow and just get this project done.

- Insist that the result be based on some objective criteria

The goal here is to use fairness and equity, not one person's will.

Example   If we changed the method of evaluation, we would be violating departmental standards for this course. We will need to look at other alternatives.

Contrast   That is not going to work. No one else in my department gives that type of exams.

Example   We said we wanted a topic that we all like, that would be interesting to the class, that would expand our knowledge in a specific area, and that we could present easily on Powerpoint. Looks like we finally found our topic!

Contrast   This topic would be fun to do and we all like it. Let's just do it. We'll have a good time.

In the mediated classroom the instructor facilitates and models constructive transactional process. Whether you use the strategies in this section individually or in combination, they can provide a basis for a teaching and learning climate where conflicts are negotiated through the transformative power of perspective sharing.

Examining Your Teaching Style: Using Inclusive Pedagogical Channels to Promote Learning and Cultural Understanding

We do not see things as they are, we see them as we are. —Anais Nin

As the American culture becomes more and more diverse, so do college classrooms. And as Gloria Ladson-Billings (2001, 14) points out "… today, notions of diversity are broader and more complex. Not only are students likely to be multiracial or multiethnic, but they are also likely to be diverse along linguistic, religious, ability, and economic lines…."

Traditionally American higher education has an individual versus collectivist orientation. Students are encouraged to be concerned about their own goals and to surpass others to reach the "top of the ladder." Competition is the name of the game. In contrast in high context or collectivist cultures such as Asian, Latino/Latina and to a lesser extent, African American, the group goals are more important, cooperation is emphasized, success is based on your contribution to the group, and personal relationships are very significant.

You may be wondering how you will be able to meet theses seemingly divergent student goals. The key to making your subject accessible to all students is to accept that diversity calls for diversifying. Cuseo suggests the following ways to meet the range of student needs in your classroom:

- Diversify your instructional methods
  1. Vary the channels through which you present information as my colleague, Lizz, did—orally, in print, through diagrams or pictures or with "hands-on" experiences.
  2. Diversify instructional approaches you use in class. Use a blend of those that are student-centered such as class discussion, role-playing, and group work and those that are teacher-centered like lectures and demonstrations.
  3. Balance independent learning and interdependent learning. These assignments can range from individually complete projects, papers, or speeches to collaborative learning, and group service learning projects.
- Diversify your methods of assessing and evaluating student learning giving students a variety of ways to demonstrate their learning
  1. Beyond the traditional paper assignments and tests, students could among other things, give oral presentations, participate in group term projects, write poetry or short stories, interview experts and report on their findings, do slide or PowerPoint presentations, write and produce videos, or do a poster session.
- Diversify the makeup of in- and out-of-class groups to increase student exposure to different viewpoints
  1. Allowing students to self-select in-class groups can potentially disenfranchise some students. For example, an African American woman selected next to last in a class where she is the only person of her race and one of only a few women may experience some awkwardness not unlike being picked last for a team on the playground. From your perspective, you are just making a random assignment. But, it is possible from her perspective, she is experiencing another example of exclusion and the deeply imbedded societal racism she has faced throughout her lifetime. Since it is difficult to ascertain the variance in student beliefs, values, and attitudes and to avoid making determinations based on appearance, you may wish

to use a variety of random selection methods such as counting off by numbers, alphabetically, or by the season or month of birthdays.

2. Another alternative would be to assign students to groups based on their MBTI or VARK Learning Inventory results. Depending on your learning goal, you may vary the makeup in different ways. For team semester-long term project, you may want to assign a balance between thinking and feeling preferences so that the team focuses on both the task (thinking orientation) and the group-process dimensions of their project.

3. Vary the makeup of groups throughout the term. To ensure that students are exposed to the broadest range of voices possible employ selection strategies assigning students to new groups that are significantly different in makeup from those in which they participated before.

4. Vary the makeup of groups within an individual class. You can designate one person from each group to move to another group during the course of an in-class project or group discussion. Doing so can change the group dynamics and/or provide fresh insights.

By diversifying the methods you use for encoding the class content and providing a range of channels for their dissemination, you will acquire as Shulman calls it, *pedagogical content knowledge,* or tried and true ways to make your subject accessible to students with different attributes and backgrounds (Shulman 1987).

Uri Treisman provides a notable example to illustrate the impact of diversifying pedagogical approaches on the teaching and learning process. In his work with the high failure rates of African American calculus students at the University of California at Berkeley, he found that students from diverse backgrounds were perceived at-risk and in need of remediation. Even though these students were academically exceptional in their high school programs, from traditional perspectives, their high failure rate was attributed to lack of educational background, motivation, and family support for education.

Through his research, Treisman found that African American and Latino/Latina students were isolated in their learning whereas his Asian students formed informal study groups that became learning communities where they could work together to enhance their knowledge and collectively clarify course expectations.

Treisman developed a workshop program that emphasized collaborative learning through the use of small groups focused on helping these students succeed rather than avoid failure. "These workshop sessions encouraged students to work individually and in collaboration with each other when they were stumped. In addition to the learning that took place, students gained a strong sense of community and made lasting friendships from the positive interdependence they experienced" (Gillman). Treisman's program was so successful, that it was adopted by other colleges and universities.

Conclusion

When I began my career at the university level twenty-seven years ago, there was virtually no discussion of teaching. It seemed there was an underlying assumption that teaching ability was inherent in the ability to gain access to advanced degrees. There were few, if any, discussions about pedagogical, classroom climate, or inclusive teaching methods. Those of us standing before our first college classroom were on our own to determine the best ways to disseminate the vast array of information we hoped to impart to the eager minds before us.

In contrast, today there is an extensive body of knowledge both on scholarly teaching and the scholarship of teaching. In addition, colleges and universities have teaching centers, offer seminars on teaching and learning and provide a range of faculty development opportunities. As a teaching assistant or a first-time college professor, you should not expect to have an immediate, comprehensive understanding of the teaching and learning process nor a mastery of the vast array of pedagogical approaches available to meet the diverse academic needs of your students. It is my hope that you will use the resources in this chapter as a starting place for developing a transactional process pedagogy—one that will maximize your students' academic and social potential as well as facilitate the evolution of your unique teaching style.

•

Martha C. Petrone is a senior instructor of communications, Miami University—Middletown.

1. Anecdote used with permission of Harriet F. Chaney, facilitator and consultant, Mountain States Employers Council, Denver, Colorado.

2. Vark-Learn.com

3. www.Vark-Learn.com

4. Case study used with permission of Elizabeth Howard, Assistant Professor, Department of Computer Information Technology, Miami University—Middletown Campus.

5. Information from Powerful Non-Defensive Communication. A seminar presented by Sharon Ellison, Owner, Ellison Communication. August 2001.

REFERENCES

Anderson, J. 1999. Faculty responsibility for promoting conflict-free classrooms. In *Promoting civility: A teaching challenge,* New Directions for Teaching and Learning, no. 77, ed. S. M. Richardson, 69–76. San Francisco: Jossey-Bass.

Berger, C. R. 1979. Beyond initial interaction: Uncertainty, understanding, and the development of interpersonal relationships. In *Language and Social Psychology,* eds. H. Giles and R. N. St. Clair, 122–44. Oxford: Basil Blackwell.

Bluestein, J. 2001. *Creating emotionally safe schools: A guide for educators and parents.* Deerfield Beach, FL: Health Communications.

Bush, R. A. and Folger, J. P. 1994. *The promise of mediation: Responding to conflict through empowerment and recognition.* San Francisco: Jossey-Bass.

Cuseo, J. 2001. Series of specific, research driven strategies for capitalizing on classroom diversity to enhance student learning distributed on Professional and Organization Development Network in Higher Education listserv. [cited 11 October 2001].

DeVito, J. 1998. *The interpersonal communication book.* New York: Longman Publishing.

Fisher, R. and Ury, W. 1991. *Getting to Yes: Negotiating agreement without giving in.* 2d ed. New York: Penguin Books.

Gillman, L. Teaching programs that work. *Focus: The Newsletter of the Mathematics Association of American* 10 (1): 7–10.

Gonzales, V. and Lopez, E. 2001. The age of incivility: Countering disruptive behavior in the classroom. *AAHE Bulletin* (April): 3–6.

Kagan, S. and Kagan, M. Timed-pair-share and showdown: Single co-op structures for divergent and convergent thinking. *Cooperative Learning and College Teaching* 7 (2): 2–5.

Keirsey, D. 1998. *Please understand me II: Temperament character intelligence.* Prometheus Books.

Ladson-Billings, G. 2001. *Crossing over to Canaan: The journey of new teachers in diverse classrooms.* San Francisco: Jossey-Bass.

Lowman, J. 1984. Chap. 2 and 4 in *Mastering the techniques of teaching.* San Francisco: Jossey-Bass.

Magolda, M. B. 1997. Facilitating meaningful dialogues. *About Campus* (November/December).

Miami University. The Miami University policy and information manual. Section 5.4. Available from http://www.muohio.edu/mupim/5_4.html.

Myer, I. B. with Myers, P. 1995. *Gifts differing: Understanding personality type.* Consulting Psychology Press.

Nilson, L. 1998. *Teaching at its best: A research-based resource for college instructors.* Boston: Anker Publishing.

Palmer, P. 1998. *The courage to teach.* San Francisco: Jossey-Bass.

Perry, W. 1985. Different worlds in the same classroom. *The Journal of the Harvard-Danforth Center: On Teaching and Learning* (May).

Reddy, W. B. 1996. *Group level team assessment.* San Diego: Pfeiffer and Jones.

Shulman, L. 1987. Knowledge and teaching foundations of the new reform. *Harvard Educational Review* 57:9-10.

Stone, D., Patton, B., and Heen, S. 1999. *Difficult conversations.* New York: Penguin Books.

Tiberius, R. G. and Billson, J. M. 1991. The social context of teaching and learning. In *College Teaching: From Theory to Practice,* New Directions for Teaching and Learning, no. 45, eds. R. J. Menges and M. D. Svinicki. San Francisco: Jossey-Bass.

Treisman, U. Studying students studying calculus: A look at the lives of minority mathematics students in college. *College Mathematics Journal* 23 (5): 362-72.

MORE
than a
THERMOMETER
Using Assessment
Effectively

Catherine Wehlburg

TEXAS CHRISTIAN UNIVERSITY

Assessment per se guarantees

nothing by way of improvement;

no more than a thermometer

cures a fever.

—Ted Marchese

◆

Assessment and evaluation in higher education has had a long past, but a short formal history. The questions that are asked in assessment are not new questions at all. The process of education has always asked questions regarding student learning, How much do students know? What can be done to help them learn more? What would we like for students to know? Instructors have asked many of these questions in learning situations for hundreds, if not thousands, of years. Even looking at student learning at the institutional level is not new. Hutchings and Marchese (1990) point out that in the nineteenth century students were required to demonstrate their knowledge in a public manner. "A candidate for the bachelor's, therefore, faced a final hurdle of the senior declamation ... often these examinations were conducted orally, by and before outsiders" (p. 27). Assessing student knowledge is not a new concept. Using that information to focus on how to improve student learning by modifying teaching is, however, a new twist to this old idea. Using assessment and evaluation data to improve teaching is only part of the more recent push in assessment. Another reason that assessment has had so much publicity lately is the need to prove to constituencies that higher education was worth the time, money, and effort (Hutchings and Marchese 1990).

Current use of assessment and the institutionalization of assessment practices have been somewhat successful.

> To date, campus assessment efforts have been most meaningful and
> effective when they have been conducted within the disciplines, using
> processes and procedures that articulate desired outcomes and measure
> them in light of the department's mission. The common assumptions
> and methodologies of the disciplines provide the context for such efforts
> to assess and improve practices. Moving beyond disciplinary frames of
> reference to examine higher-order learning outcomes that cut across
> courses and curricula—that assess educational effectiveness at the level
> of the whole institution—is much more complex. (Evenbeck and Kahn
> 2001, 27)

This institutionalization of assessment is difficult, but it is necessary to provide a better look at the broader picture of higher education. Often the push to institutionalize assessment programs comes from an external mandate (i.e., regional accreditation association). This is unfortunate since assessment should be done to improve student learning at the "grass roots" level, but "regardless of the impetus, by taking hold of the assessment process and making it work for your individual campus, you will be able to improve the quality of learning for current and future students" (Wehlburg 1999, 9).

Using Assessment to Improve Student Learning

Ralph Wolff and Olita Harris (1994) describe stages that an institution typically goes through when addressing the (usually) mandated need for assessment. These stages are loosely based on the work by Elizabeth Kubler-Ross on the stages of death and dying (a fact that seems to amuse most faculty members!).

- The first stage is typically *denial*. Often faculty (and administrators) have vague feelings of uneasiness in this first stage and a need to maintain "the way things have always been done." Faculty may choose to picture assessment as the next new higher educational fad that will soon pass.

- Once an institution has seen that assessment is something that will have to be "done," that institution hits the second stage, *resistance*. Here, individuals see assessment as a threat to their department, course, or college. As part of this stage, some efforts are made toward an assessment plan, but these efforts are usually made by a small committee and are not seen as important by the entire campus.
- The third stage, *understanding*, shows a campus making efforts to define the assessment plan specific to the needs of that campus. Normally, this is where a census is taken of existing efforts of data collection and ongoing assessments of student learning and student satisfaction.
- In the fourth stage, *campaign*, assessment principles and guidelines are further defined and the institution is well on its way to a working assessment plan.
- In *collaboration*, the fifth stage, the specific and long-range objectives are clearly defined and the assessment methods being used have a wide range of support as being meaningful.
- Finally, in *institutionalization*, assessment is seen as a permanent part of the cycle of the institution and refinement of the assessment process is occurring.

Assessment is important and assessment programs can be quite complex at the institutional, departmental, and individual course level. The concept of assessment, however, is simple and its goal is to improve student learning by changing or enhancing teaching. As Patricia Cross (1993) states, "the ultimate criterion of good teaching is effective learning" (p. 20). Teaching and learning are certainly part of the same coin. And, according to Angelo and Cross (1993), "teaching without learning is just talking" (p. 3). When assessment is added to the teaching part, decisionmaking about teaching becomes something that is based on data, rather than gut feelings. As Grant Wiggins (1992) states, "good teaching is inseparable from good assessing" (p. 33).

The focus of this chapter is on how teachers can use data from assessment to improve and enhance student learning—a goal that is important to all who teach. Assessment of student learning outcomes is not the same as grading a student's work. Assessment is used to guide the educator by showing her/him the overall picture of learning across the student population (e.g., the course, the graduating class, all who complete the general education program). This is a much different view than an instructor could get by looking at an individual student. And, more importantly, assessment is designed to gain information about the teaching or the program rather than getting information about how well a particular student is meeting the standards of the course.

Assessment is the systematic process of gathering and using data to make informed decisions about the quality of student learning which in term leads to informed adjustment of teaching methodologies, assignments, and even course sequencing. Huba and Freed (2000) add that "the [assessment] process culminates when assessment results are used to improve subsequent learning" (p. 8). When assessing student learning (or anything else, for that matter), it is important to follow the basic steps in order to make the assessment activity a useful one. These steps are:

1. Decide on the learning outcomes/objectives. These include the skills, abilities, values, or knowledge that students should have as a result of the course, class period, learning process.
2. Choose an assessment tool (a way to measure) for each objective. Make sure that the measurement is one that will accurately reflect the amount of student learning based on the stated objectives.
3. Create or design the learning activities that would lead to the expected learning outcomes. This is what John Biggs (1999) calls "alignment" of the assessment process and of the course activities.
4. Measure the student learning outcomes. This is where the assessment data is collected.
5. Use the assessment data to modify the learning activities with the hope of increase or enhancing student learning. This step, closing the feedback loop, is critical. Without this last step, the gathering of assessment data does nothing for enhancing or changing the teaching/program. The data simply collects dust in someone's office. "Unless the data generated by assessment returns to the educational process to improve program and student performance, they will die upon dissemination" (Mentkowski 1994, 253).

Assessment activities are useful only when they lead to a better understanding and an improvement of education. This "culture of assessment" can be developed when assessment activities lead to a review of curriculum and/or goals and objectives in order to enhance the educational outcomes of students. To put this into the context of an example, Professor Jordheim teaches an introductory psychology course to freshmen. Her overall goals for the course are for students to:

- Increase knowledge of the major theories of psychology.
- Learn appropriate references in APA (American Psychological Association) style.
- Read, understand, and communicate information contained in a professional research article.

So, Professor Jordheim must first put these into meaningful student learning outcomes. While there is no one *right* way of writing student learning outcomes, they do need to be based on measurable behaviors and written in such a way as to clearly communicate to students and others what is expected. This is more fully discussed in the next section.

Once Professor Jordheim has clearly articulated the outcomes, she must decide how they will be measured. This can be done in a variety of ways—much of the decisionmaking depends on the teacher and the subject matter. For example, a test (created by the teacher or nationally normed) may be a good way to measure knowledge of psychological theories. Writing samples submitted by the student and evaluated by the teacher or another observer would be a method for measuring APA style referencing. Perhaps a videotaped sample of a student explaining the results of a published study would be a way to assess understanding of research articles. There is no limit to the methodology used to measure the outcomes. It is important to note that while these methods for measuring student learning may also be used for grading the student, their use for assessment goes beyond the individual student.

Now that the objectives and the subsequent measurements of these objectives are in place, Professor Jordheim must choose teaching techniques that will complement the learning she wants students to be able to do. This may mean that for some class periods she will lecture, use small-group discussions, assign papers, or videotape student reports. The teaching techniques should dovetail with the learning goals in an intentional way.

Using the chosen assessment to measure the student's learning (collecting the data) is the next step. Unfortunately, many professionals jump into assessment with this step and do not carefully choose outcomes, assessment tools, or teaching methods. It is important to know what is being measured and why.

Professor Jordheim must then interpret the data and use this information to make meaningful and appropriate changes in her teaching methods so as to increase or enhance student learning. The beauty of assessment is that it can give the teacher the information necessary to make intentional changes in teaching style and in assignments rather than the "shot in the dark" that may or may not work.

Finally, Professor Jordheim must reevaluate her goals, measurements, and teaching methods to ensure that all are still appropriate and she must make changes when necessary. Assessment is always a work in progress!

Recently, the focus of assessment in higher education has been moving away from being *teacher-centered* and toward a more *student-centered* outlook. For example, teaching used to be an activity whose goal was to transmit knowledge to students. Now, education involves creating the opportunity for a student to create and synthesize information that will (in many cases) lead to life-long learning. In this model, teaching and assessment are intertwined (Barr and Tagg 1995; Huba and Freed 2000).

Questions to Think About

- How do I know when my students are learning?
- How often do I think about my students' learning?
- If I intentionally use assessment, how should that affect the planning process that I go through before the semester/course/class period?
- How was I taught—from a student-centered or teacher-centered viewpoint?

DEVELOPING MEANINGFUL GOALS THAT ARE MEASURABLE

ASSESSMENT IS BASED ON VALUES. PETER KNIGHT (1995) goes so far as to say that "assessment is a moral activity" (p. 13). Knight (1995) explains that what we value in higher education is shown clearly by what we choose to assess and how we assess it. When an educator chooses goals and outcomes to measure in an assessment plan, that she/he is publicly stating what is important and what is respected. These goals and outcomes are usually put into the format of an instructional objective.

Objectives are a clear statement of what the student should learn. Behavioral objectives are instructional objectives that are stated in terms of observable behaviors and cognitive objectives are instructional objectives stated in terms of higher-level thinking operations. When writing usable instructional objectives, the following elements should be included:

- **Content**—what do students need to know in order to show that they have met the minimum requirements of the objective?
- **Action**—how will students demonstrate their knowledge? Think about the behavior that students should be able to show as a result of a particular course or class activity.
- **Context**—under what conditions will students demonstrate their knowledge? This focuses on where and when a particular behavior might be expected to occur.
- **Performance Criteria**—what standards are used to evaluate a student's performance? What level of performance is appropriate? Some may want to see test scores over 80% while other behaviors require that students perform the behavior perfectly each time.

Writing and using clear objectives may take a little longer in the beginning, but the importance of high-quality objectives cannot be understated. Using learner-centered assessment means that students must have the right to see what is expected of them and what information or skills they will be responsible for showing. In addition, an instructor who is able to intentionally plan for learning will be far ahead in terms of being able to use any assessment data for the benefit of student learning. "Every act of assessment gives a message to students about what they should be learning and how they should go about it" (Boud 1995, 35).

Questions to Think About

- How have objectives been used successfully in my experience?
- Looking at one course that I teach or participate, what objectives can I write that would be appropriate and measurable?
- How are objectives helpful? Why are they not used by all instructors?

Formative vs. Summative Evaluation

Formative and summative evaluation are often used in terms of course evaluations or student perceptions of teaching. Formative evaluation refers to an evaluation or assessment that will "suggest future steps for teaching and learning" (Weber 1999, 26) whereas summative evaluation is used for a measurement of final outcomes. Lockee, Moore, and Burton (2002) discuss a wonderful culinary example used by Robert Stake in describing formative and summative evaluation: "when the chef tastes the soup, it's formative; when the diners (or a food critic) taste the soup, it's summative" (p. 21).

When used with end-of-the-semester course evaluations, summative evaluation can certainly lead to changes in teaching practices, but these will not take effect in the current course and, therefore, the students giving feedback would not be affected. Summative evaluation (in the form of teaching evaluations) is required by most institutions. Unfortunately, this may be the only way that an instructor is gaining information about students and their learning. Many of the questions asked on these forms focus on the students' perception of the teacher. This is important, but it is not the same as gaining information about how much students have learned. Additional assessment activities are essential to really improve student learning. Formative evaluation activities can help the instructor gain more useful information.

Formative evaluation is often used by instructors to determine how much information students have at a given point and whether or not to proceed further. Formative evaluation is also ideal because it can provide instructors with immediate feedback. There are several formative evaluation tools that can be easily used during the semester or individual class period (see "Classroom Assessment Techniques" later in chapter). Many instructors have used a formative evaluation of student perception of teaching. This enables the instructor to make changes in teaching methods prior to the end of the semester. These can take the same form as the actual course evaluation form or they can be much more simple, asking only one or two questions, What have you learned today? What is the most important point that was made today? What could be changed in this class to help you learn more?

Formative evaluation allows the instructor to check for small increases in learning in a very short time or small changes in student perceptions. Summative evaluation, on the other hand, tends to be more global. Formative evaluation is most often something that occurs on a regular basis while summative evaluation usually occurs once a semester.

Anyone who is teaching and is concerned about the quality of student learning should use both formative and summative evaluation and assessment techniques. Students benefit when an instructor uses both since they are allowed the opportunity to comment on and affect change in the current class. In addition, students may use the types of knowledge/skills that are part of a formative evaluation instrument to focus their study.

Questions to Think About

- Can the same instrument be used for both formative and summative evaluation? How?
- What information would be most helpful to have that would be formative in nature for an instructor?
- Why is formative evaluation used less often than summative evaluation?

Thinking about Multiple Measures

Any test question, interview item, or assessment prompt has one thing in common: it only samples a small moment of behavior. Depending on the size of the instrument, that sample may be very small and may be impacted by several variables (e.g., mood, amount of sleep, time of day, point in the semester). Even when large numbers of items are used, such as a long exam or a detailed survey, a sample of behavior data is all that is collected. Because of this, it is important to ensure that data collected comes from multiple measures. This would include different types of measures as well as measures from the same instrument taken at different times.

When several measures are used to collect assessment data, it becomes clearer that there are "patterns of convergence in data that can be used to make appropriate educational and programmatic changes" (Revak and Scheffel 2001). This can better ensure that decisions about teaching methods, delivery methods, sequencing of courses, and so forth are made wisely. As institutions begin to use assessment of student learning outcomes in a systematic way, the data begins to show patterns of evidence that, over time, will give a clearer picture of student learning and how the institution has responded. As individuals within an institution become more aware of and dependent on the assessment data for decisionmaking, a culture of assessment begins to develop. At this point, the stage of *institutionalization* has been achieved (Wolff and Harris 1994).

Questions to Think About

- Why is it important to base decisionmaking on more than one measurement?
- How can behavior best be sampled?
- What can I do to find multiple measures for each objective in my course?

Authentic Assessment Techniques

Authentic assessment techniques involve any type of assessment that is somehow different from traditional assessment tools (multiple choice tests, for example). In order to be considered authentic, an assessment technique should "mirror applications of the assessed ability in real-life, nonacademic settings" (Davies and Wavering 1999, 40). More and more educators are using alternative assessment tools within the classroom. There are several reasons why using these alternative tools are worthwhile.

In the first place, using an alternative assessment tool will promote student learning because these types of instruments will require students to be reflective and active in demonstrating knowledge or in responding to the assessment prompt. When an instructor asks a class to write down the most important thing learned in that day's class, students are required to think about the class period, reflect on the information, and relate that information to other information that they may already have. By requiring self-reflection and providing these opportunities at regular intervals, the instructor will both better understand what students know and will promote learning in the class (Davies and Wavering 1999).

Alternative assessment tools will also provide the student the opportunity to engage in higher-level thinking. "If the ability to engage in complex reasoning is a desired outcome of higher education, assessments should challenge students to problem solve, make connections, explore assumptions, elaborate, and apply nonalgorithmic thinking. Multiple-choice tests hold limited capacity to assess more complex thinking and do not assess interests, attitudes, growth, or connective reasoning" (Davies and Wavering 1999, 42). Students will be required to be able to analyze, synthesize, and evaluate complex problems and issues outside of higher education. It is essential that institutions assess their ability while they are still able to make modifications in the student's experiences.

Using alternative assessment tools will allow for learning-style differences. John Gardiner's (1983) work on multiple intelligences has demonstrated the need for a variety of assessment and evaluation formats. "Mass testing, as we know it, treats students as objects—as if their education and thought processes were similar and as if the reasons for their answers were irrelevant" (Wiggins 1989, 708).

Finally, alternative assessment normally requires instructors to give clear and specific objectives so that students can understand and provide what is requested. For example, imagine a student who is asked to complete a multiple-choice exam in order to show knowledge. This does not require much explanation and the student does not need to understand what is being asked of her/him. Now imagine that same student being asked to complete a portfolio. Now the student must know what the objectives are and must understand the process. Moving from a traditional assessment tool (multiple-choice test) to an authentic assessment tool (portfolio) requires that the student become actively involved in both understanding and completion of the assignment.

Types of Authentic Assessment Tools

There are three major categories of alternative assessment tools: Ongoing/reflexive assessments, course content assessments, and culminating/synthesis experience assessments (Davies and Waverly 1999). Each category will be briefly described.

Ongoing/reflexive assignments include activities such as reflective journal writing or daily exit cards (cards on which students write responses to prompts which are handed in as students exit class). Both of these activities can be interactive as the instructor can respond back to individuals or the entire class. This type of dialogue is one important way of gaining information about what students know and how they are meeting learning objectives. Course content assessments are designed to "examine skills or products integral to mastery of course content" (Davies and Wavering, 41). These include peer evaluations and group work, and group presentations. Culminating/synthesis experience assessments include exhibitions, poster presentations, and portfolios.

A portfolio is a "purposeful collection of student work that exhibits the student's efforts, progress, and/or achievements. The collection must include student participation in selecting contents, the criteria for selection, the criteria for judging merit, and evidence of student self-reflection" (Paulson,

Paulson, and Meyer 1991, 60). Portfolios have been used for centuries in areas such as art, photography, and writing. Using to assess student outcomes in other areas, however, is a relatively new concept. The benefits of this type of alternative assessment are that there are several artifacts (e.g., documents, papers, videotapes, slides) that can be gathered and which can be used to measure student learning. Portfolios are also personalized for the individual institution, department, or class that is using it as a measurement tool. This individualization also points to one of the difficulties of using a portfolio for assessment purposes. Without specific guidelines, portfolios can become a collection of "stuff" that is almost impossible to use in any meaningful way.

Before students are asked to supply artifacts for the portfolio, they must know exactly what the outcomes are that are being measured and what type of artifact should be used. Some institutions are quite specific about what should go into the portfolio. For example, at Stephens College (Columbia, Missouri) portfolios are used to measure general education outcomes. Students are given a handout that outlines the components of the portfolio. They then work with a faculty advisor to choose the artifacts. This process can lead to the student having a much better understanding of the purpose of general education and can give the institution some rich and detailed information about the student body's knowledge of general education.

In order for portfolios to be used effectively in assessment, the outcomes must be specifically stated (as in any assessment program). These objectives must translate into a usable rubric for understanding and assessing the portfolio. The rubric should be designed prior to the collection of information when possible.

Questions to Think About

- What is authentic assessment? What experiences do I have with this type of assessment?
- In developing an authentic assessment tool, what types of objectives are most useful? Does writing the objectives for an authentic assessment instrument different from writing objectives for other types of assessment instruments?
- How could I use ongoing/reflective assessments and course content assessments in a current course?

CLASSROOM ASSESSMENT TECHNIQUES (CATS)

CLASSROOM ASSESSMENT TECHNIQUES (CATS) ARE DESIGNED to allow the classroom instructor to find out in a relatively short time what students are learning and to use that information to make changes in the delivery method used or in the assignments required. According to Angelo and Cross (1993), a CAT has the following characteristics:

1. *It is learner-centered.* Classroom assessment should allow the instructor to focus on gathering information from observation and using that information to improve student learning, rather than on observing and improving the instructor's teaching.

2. *It is teacher-directed.* A CAT that is chosen by the instructor will be used by that instructor in a specific context. Therefore, the "individual teacher decides what to assess, how to assess, and how to respond to the information gained through the assessment" (Angelo and Cross 1993, 4). This information can be used only by the instructor and need not be shared with anyone else.

3. *It should be mutually beneficial to both students and instructor.* Angelo and Cross (1993) believe that "because it is focused on learning, Classroom Assessment requires the active participation of students. By cooperating in assessment, students reinforce their grasp of the course content and strengthen their own skills at self-assessment. Their motivation is increased when they realize that faculty are interested and invested in their success as learners" (pp. 4–5). An instructor can also improve teaching by asking these three questions: What are the essential skills and knowledge I am trying to teach? How can I find out whether students are learning them? How can I help students learn better? As teachers gather information from students answer these questions, they improve their teaching and better understand the learning process.

4. *It is formative in nature.* The purpose of using classroom assessment techniques is to improve student learning—not to grade student's work. It is extremely important to remember that assessment is not about comparing student work to understand who understands the material and who does not. Assessment should focus the instructor on finding out how to improve

activities so that all students (or at least most of the students) have a better learning experience

5. *It is context-specific.* Classroom assessments are designed to address the specific needs of a specific class. In addition, the personality, methodology, and time available will all have some impact on the CAT that is chosen and how much information is given. Angelo and Cross (1993) state that "what works well in one class will not necessary work in another" (p. 5).

6. *It should be ongoing.* Classroom assessment should be an ongoing process that informs the instructor of how the class is going on a regular basis. This "feedback loop" is essential in assessment. Instructors who use a variety of CATs over time and use that feedback to make appropriate changes will find that students begin to participate more actively in the assessment process and in the class. After the first assessment and implementation of feedback, the instructor can use the same (or different) assessment again to check on the efficacy of the new/revised activity. Thus continuing the feedback loop.

7. *It is rooted in good teaching practices.* Using a classroom assessment technique and, even better, a series of CATs, simply involves what good instructors are already doing. "Teachers ask questions, react to students' questions, monitor body language and facial expressions, read homework and tests, and so on. Classroom assessment provides a way to integrate assessment systematically and seamlessly into the traditional classroom teaching and learning process" (Angelo and Cross 1993, 6).

In order to use a CAT, it is best to start with one simple technique and then follow up on that feedback with another. In other words, start simple! Angelo and Cross (1993) suggest using these three steps in the process.

Step 1·**Planning**—Select one, and only one, of your classes in which to try out the classroom assessment. Decide on the class meeting and select a Classroom Assessment Technique. Choose a simple and quick one.

Step 2·**Implementing**—Make sure the students know what you are doing and that they clearly understand the procedure. Collect the (usually anonymous) responses and analyze them as soon as possible.

Step 3·**Responding**—Make sure that your students know what type of information you received and how you will use that information. This can be done in an informal way: "About half of you seemed confused by this point and another third by this point. Let's talk about these two points."

Below are some of the more well-known and often-used CATs. Angelo and Cross's (1993) book describe fifty techniques.

BACKGROUND KNOWLEDGE PROBE

Description: At the first class meeting, many college teachers ask students for general information on their level of preparation, often requesting that students list courses they have already taken in the relevant field. This technique is designed to collect much more specific, and more useful, feedback on students' prior learning. *Background Knowledge Probes* are short, simple questionnaires prepared by instructors for use at the beginning of a course, at the start of a new unit or lesson, or prior to introducing an important new topic. A given Background Knowledge Probe may require students to write short answers, to circle the correct response to multiple-choice questions, or both.

Step-by-Step Procedure

1. Before introducing an important new concept, subject, or topic in the course syllabus, consider what the students may already know about it. Recognizing that their knowledge may be partial, fragmentary, simplistic, or even incorrect, try to find at lease one point that most students are likely to know, and use that point to lead into others, less familiar points.

2. Prepare two or three open-ended questions, a handful of short-answer questions, or ten to twenty multiple-choice questions that will probe the students' existing knowledge of that concept, subject, or topic. These questions need to be carefully phrased, since a vocabulary that may not be familiar to the students can obscure your assessment of how well they know the facts or concepts.

3. Write your open-ended questions on the chalkboard, or hand out short questionnaires. Direct students to answer open-ended questions succinctly, in two or three sentences if possible. Make a point of

announcing that these Background Knowledge Probes are not tests or quizzes and will not be graded. Encourage students to give thoughtful answers that will help you make effective instructional decisions.

4. At the next class meeting, or as soon as possible, let students know the results, and tell them how that information will affect what you do as the teacher and how it should affect what they do as learners.

MINUTE PAPER

Description: No other technique has been used more often or by more college teachers than the *Minute Paper*. This technique—also known as the *One-Minute Paper* and the *Half-Sheet Response*—provides a quick and extremely simple way to collect written feedback on student learning. To use the Minute Paper, an instructor stops class two or three minutes early and asks students to respond briefly to some variation on the following two questions: What was the most important thing you learned during this class? and What important question remains unanswered? Students write their responses on index cards or half sheets of scrap paper and hand them in.

Step-by-Step Procedure

1. Decide first what you want to focus on and, as a consequence, when to administer the Minute Paper. If you want to focus on students' understanding of a lecture, the last few minutes of class may be the best time. If your focus is on a prior homework assignment, however, the first few minutes may be more appropriate.

2. Using the two basic questions from the Description above as starting points, write Minute Paper prompts that fit your course and students. Try out your Minute Paper on a colleague or teaching assistant before using it in class.

3. Plan to set aside five to ten minutes of your next class to use the technique, as well as time later to discuss the results.

4. Before class, write one or, at the most, two Minute Paper questions on the chalkboard or prepare an overhead transparency.

5. At a convenient time, hand out index cards or half sheets of scrap paper.

6. Unless there is a very good reason to know who wrote what, direct students to leave their names off the papers or cards.

7. Let the students know how much time they will have (two to five minutes per question is usually enough), what kinds of answers you want

(words, phrases, or short sentences), and when they can expect your feedback.

MUDDIEST POINT

Description: The *Muddiest Point* is a very simple technique to use. It is also remarkably efficient, since it provides a high information return for a very low investment of time and energy. The technique consists of asking students to jot down a quick response to one question, What was the muddiest point in ——? The focus of the Muddiest Point assessment might be a lecture, a discussion, a homework assignment, a play, or a film.

Step-by-Step Procedure

1. Determine what you want feedback on—the entire class session or one self-contained segment? A lecture, a discussion, a presentation?
2. If you are using the technique in class, reserve a few minutes at the end of the class session. Leave enough time to ask the question, to allow students to respond, and to collect their responses by the usual ending time.
3. Let students know beforehand how much time they will have to respond and what use you will make of their responses.
4. Pass out slips of paper or index cards for students to write on.
5. Collect the responses as or before students leave. Stationing yourself at the door and collecting "muddy points" as students file out is one way; leaving a "muddy point" collection box by the exit is another.
6. Respond to the students' feedback during the next class meeting or as soon as possible afterward.

Questions to Think About

- How often should I use a CAT? Under what circumstances should I use a CAT?
- How does CAT information help me as a teacher?
- In designing a prompt for a CAT, minute paper, for example, what type of information do I need?

WEB-ENHANCED ASSESSMENT TECHNIQUES

CATS THAT ARE USED WITH TECHNOLOGY, *TECHNO-CATS*, can be of specific use in certain cases. When determining whether to use a nontechnology based

CAT or a Techno-CAT, there are several questions which should be addressed. These include: What can technology add to the CAT? Does the addition of technology increase the efficiency of the CAT?

Web-enhanced assessment techniques do have some advantages. For example, they can provide more flexibility to the instructor and to the students. If the student can access the CAT on her/his own time rather than waiting for class time, the student may be able to better provide information which will be more meaningful and more accurate. In addition, when little class time can be used for a CAT, connecting with students outside of class via the Web can be a real benefit. Deciding whether or not to use a Web-based assessment technique can also be affected by the number of students in a course. Very large courses can use Web-enhanced assessment activities in order to easily tabulate feedback. This feedback can be more immediate to both the student and the instructor.

There are several varieties of Web-based assessment techniques. They can be categorized into the following categories:

Low Tech Assessment Techniques. Examples of this type would include using an overhead projector or even a PowerPoint slide to show a series of prompts or questions to the students. This can be used with almost any regular CAT.

Asynchronous Assessment Techniques. These assessment techniques rely on the Web, but information from the instructor to the student (e.g., prompts, questions) and data from the students are not simultaneous. For example, emails, threaded discussions, online surveys or questionnaires are all useful ways of incorporating technology into assessment.

Synchronous Assessment Techniques. Using synchronous assessment uses information that is sent and received at the same time. Virtual chats, Power-Point displays of group Muddiest Points, or computer based classrooms in which students can share information electronically are all examples of these techniques.

Questions to Think About

- How can I modify a regular CAT to become a Web-enhanced CAT?
- In what situations would I want to use a Web-based assessment technique? What situations would not work using a Web-based assessment?

Making Course Evaluations Work as Assessment Tools

Course evaluations or student perceptions of teaching can be used as assessment tools (in both formative and summative evaluations). Depending on the types of questions that are asked, the information can often be appropriately used for course, program, or institutional assessment. It is imperative, however, to remember that these types of assessments measure self-reported student perceptions and not objectively measured student-learning outcomes. Therefore, while these can certainly be used as part of a program of assessment, they should not be the only measure.

Using a standard course evaluation tool (usually given at the end of the semester) during the semester can help an instructor to see the perceptions of the students within the class. This can be very helpful as it gives the instructor the opportunity to make appropriate changes in teaching and to address problems as they arise (rather than waiting until the end of the semester). Many instructors have found that using a shorter and more targeted course evaluation several times during the semester is more helpful. These shorter evaluations might focus on just one aspect of the course (a specific assignment or an area of content). When using a new teaching methodology, it is very useful to use an evaluation during the semester. For example, if an instructor is teaching a Web-enhanced residential course, students may have difficulties in understanding the Web portion of the course. Finding that out early in the semester would clearly enhance the learning of the students and will improve the end-of-the-semester course evaluations for the instructor.

One type of formative evaluation tools is the Small Group Instructional Diagnostic (SGID) feedback technique (Coffman 1991). This type of evaluation measures students' perceptions of a course during the semester while there is still time to make appropriate modifications to teaching or other course elements. The process generally involves another individual (often a colleague or a consultant from the institutional teaching and learning center) coming into the classroom and spending thirty to forty-five minutes of class time with the students in the classroom. With the instructor absent, students are divided among several small groups (depending on class size) and asked to identify course features that encourage or hinder the learning process. Students are also asked to discuss possible suggestions for change. The colleague/consultant and the whole class then generate a list of issues and recommendations. Consensus is important at this stage because the issues brought to the instructor need to be ones that the entire class is concerned about and not just the response of one or two students who may have an ax to grind. The information from the class is then given to the instructor by the colleague/consultant. This information is often arranged in topics: "Things to continue doing," "Things to consider changing," "Student suggestions for improving learning."

The goals of the SGID feedback process are:

- To increase and enhance student learning
- To assure a confidential exchange between teachers and students on their perceptions of a course while the course is still occurring
- To support teaching as a communicative art

The SGID is only one method of collecting qualitative data about teaching. It is important to consider the many variables that can affect the outcome of any data, but especially qualitative data. Nyquist and Wulff (1988) contend that "data collected to assist instructors in improving their teaching effectiveness must meet certain criteria" (p. 61). These criteria include: the complexity of the classroom environments, the context, and the perspectives of the participants.

Questions to Think About

- What difficulties exist in using course evaluations for the purposes of assessment? How are course evaluation data usually used?
- How can data from course evaluations be used for assessment purposes?

INTEGRATING ASSESSMENT INTO CLASSROOM EXPERIENCE

WHILE MUCH OF THE WORK THAT AN INSTRUCTOR DOES in the classroom is seen as individual and private, all are components of a larger community activity—the process of education. When trying a new assessment tool, it is important to remember that each assessment is only a small measurement of an activity and that each instructor's part in education is all part of a bigger picture. This is shown in the following tale:

This is a story about a little wave, bobbing along on the ocean, having a grand old time. He's enjoying the wind and the fresh air-until he notices the other waves in front of him, crashing against the shore.

"This is terrible," the wave says. "Look what's gong to happen to me!"

Then along comes another wave. It sees the first wave, looking grim, and it says to him, "Why do you look so sad?"

The first wave says, "You don't understand! We're all going to crash! All of us waves are going to be nothing! Isn't it terrible?"

The second wave says, "No, you don't understand. You're not a wave, you're part of the ocean (Albom 1997, 179-80).

Assessment and evaluation tools are only as good as the meaning that the data give to the instructor and the extent to which that meaning is used to improve or enhance teaching. Even though assessment is often thought of as a means to provide accountability and show success, the real purpose of assessment is to improve student learning by giving the instructor the means to make effective changes in teaching. These are concepts that should be shared throughout a department or an institution just as the water is shared by the waves in the ocean.

By thinking about assessing student learning from the beginning and incorporating it into the regular cycle of the teaching process, instructors can become better teachers and students will learn more and will see learning as a worthwhile and important activity.

Questions to Think About

- How does assessment fit into teaching?
- In terms of planning, what role can assessment play?
- What uses should assessment data play in designing a new course or modifying an existing one?

•

Catherine Wehlburg is the director of the Center for Teaching and Learning, Texas Christian University.

REFERENCES

Albom, M. 1997. *Tuesdays with Morrie.* New York: Doubleday Publishers.

Angelo, T. A., and Cross, P. K. 1993. *Classroom assessment techniques.* 2d ed. San Francisco: Jossey-Bass

Barr, R. B., and Tagg, J. 1995. From teaching to learning: A new paradigm for undergraduate education. *Change* 17:13-25.

Biggs, J. 1999. Assessment: An integral part of the teaching system. *AAHE Bulletin* 51 (9): 10-2.

Boud, D. 1995. Assessment and learning: Contradictory or complementary? In *Assessment for learning in higher education,* ed. P. Knight, 35-48. London: Kogan Press.

Coffman, S. J. 1991. Improving your teaching through small group diagnosis. *College Teaching* 39 (2): 80-3.

Cross, P. 1993. Involving faculty in TQM. *AACC Journal* (February/March): 15-20.

Davies, M. A., and Wavering, M. 1999. Alternative assessment: New directions in teaching and learning. *Contemporary Education* 71:39-45.

Evenbeck, S., and Kahn, S. 2001. Enhancing learning assessment and accountability through communities of practice. *Change* 33:24-34.

Huba, M. E., and Freed, J. E. 2000. *Learner-centered assessment on college campuses: Shifting the focus from teaching to learning.* Needham Heights, MA: Allyn and Bacon Publishing Company.

Knight, P. 1995. *Assessment for learning in higher education.* London: Kogan Press.

Lockee, B., Moore, M., and Burton, J. 2002. Measuring success: Evaluation strategies for distance education. *Educause Quarterly* 25 (1): 20-6.

Mentkowski, M. 1994. Creating a context where institutional assessment yields educational improvement. In *Assessment and program evaluation,* eds. J. S. Stark and A. Thomas, 251-68. Needham Heights, MA: Simon and Schuster Higher Education Publishing Group.

Nyquist, J. D., and Wulff, D. H. 1988. Using qualitative methods to generate data for instructional development. In *Face to face: A sourcebook of individual consultation techniques for faculty/instructional developers,* ed. K. G. Lewis, 51-64. Stillwater, OK: New Forums Press.

Paulson, L. F., Paulson, P. R., and Meyer, C. 1991. What makes a portfolio a portfolio? *Educational Leadership* 48:60-3.

Revak, M. A., and Scheffel, D. L. 2001. A top ten list of assessment tools for academic courses and programs. In *A collection of papers on self-study and institutional improvement,* ed. Susan E. Van Kollenburg. Chicago: The Higher Learning Commission of the North Central Association of Colleges and Schools.

Weber, E. 1999. *Student assessment that works: A practical approach.* Needham Heights, MA: Allyn and Bacon Publishers.

Wehlburg, C. 1999. How to get the ball rolling: Beginning an assessment program on your campus. *AAHE Bulletin* 51 (9): 7-9.

Wiggins, G. 1989. A true test: Toward more authentic and equitable assessment. *Phi Delta Kappan* 70:703-13.

———. 1992. Creating tests worth taking. *Educational Leadership* 49:26-33.

Wolff, R., and Harris, O. 1994. Using assessment to develop a culture of evidence. In *Changing college classrooms: New teaching and learning strategies for an increasingly complex world*, eds. D. Halpern and Associates, 271-88. San Francisco: Jossey-Bass.

Teaching & Learning
IN COLLEGE

A RESOURCE FOR EDUCATORS

· FOURTH EDITION ·

THE EDITOR

Gary Wheeler is the Senior Associate Executive Director for Academic Affairs and Professor at Miami University's comprehensive regional campus in Middletown, Ohio. He received a B.F.A. (1973) from the University of Connecticut in Storrs, CT, and an M.F.A. (1976) from Arizona State University in Tempe, AZ, both in studio art and art history.

Gary S. Wheeler

Wheeler's main areas of interest in higher education have been in organizational development, technology integration with academic curricula, leadership for collaborative change, instructional improvement, assessment, and full- and part-time faculty development. He has conducted workshops on topics related to teaching and learning, cultural competence and diversity, part-time faculty, assessment, technology and leadership. He serves as a consultant-evaluator, c-e team chair, AQIP (Academic Quality Improvement Project) facilitator, and as a member of the Accreditation Review Council for the Higher Learning Commission (North Central Association). He also works closely as an associate with the TLT Group—the technology affiliate of the American Association for Higher Education, serving as a consultant and workshop leader.

His recent books include A Primer of Visual Design (New York: Prentice-Hall, 2001) and TypeSense, 2nd edition (New York: Prentice-Hall, 2000) both with Susan Wheeler. He also wrote a chapter, "Teaching and Learning with Technology," in A Handbook for Adjunct/Part-time Faculty and Teachers of Adults, 4th edition, Donald Greive, editor, (Elyria, OH: Info-Tec, 2001, pp. 97-118).

INDEX

A

Action Learning Project (Hong Kong), 25
action learning sets, 16
active learning, x, 7, 81, 119
Active Learning: Cooperation in the College Classroom (Johnson), 4
active listening, 150, 166
activity, Aristotelian theories of, 85
Affirmative Action, 42
Alumni Teaching Scholars Program (Miami-OH), 13
American Association for Higher Education (AAHE), 10
Anderson, James, 145
Angelo, T. A., 24, 189
Arizona State University, 41
Assessment: x, xiii, 5, 47, 49, 53, 56, 172, 177-186, 189; course content, 52, 187; culminating/synthesis, 187; culture of, 181; institutionalization of, 178-179, 185; peer, 30, 147-148; plans, 179, 182; student-centered, 182-183; teacher-centered, 182
Assessment to Promote Deep Learning (Suskie), 9
assessment tools: 52, 179-180, 185-187, 194; Background Knowledge Probe (CAT), 191; Classroom Assessment Techniques (CAT), 189-191; Minute Paper (CAT), 192; Muddiest Point (CAT), 193; Techno-CATS, 193; web-enhanced, 193-194
Associate Degree Colleges: 96-97, 99-101, 103-105, 107-109; community colleges, 99; economic development services, 100; junior college movement, 97; open door policy, 104; tribal colleges, 100; vocational training, 99, 112
Association of American Colleges and Universities (AACU), xii, 44

B

C

Conflict Mediation Program (UCLA), 42

conflict resolution: 6, 68, 150, 157-159, 163; classroom, xiii, 82; principled negotiation, 169; process dynamics, 158; process management, 146; questioning, 168; reflective practice, 151; Talking about "Talking About", 164; What Happened Conversation, 162

Coor, Pres. Lattie (Arizona St. Univ.), 41

Council of Graduate Schools, x

course design, 53, 55, 61, 63

course evaluation, 158, 184, 195

course objectives, 160. *See also instructional objectives*

Cox, Milton, xii, 28

critical thinking, 147

Cross, Patricia, x, 10, 24, 179, 189

curriculum, 41, 46, 48, 57, 62, 67, 75, 143, 181

curriculum design, 51-52, 60, 75

Cuseo, J., 172

D

demographics. *See faculty demographics and student demographics*

Design for Diversity (Wisconsin), 43

DeWaters, J. N., 79

Dewey, John, 8

Dialogues on Diversity Forums (Michigan), 42

distance education: 5, 7, 108, 117, 126, 135; asynchronous distance learning, 54, 126, 194; hybrid course delivery, 54; synchronous distance learning, 126, 194

diversity, 13, 21, 41, 44, 46, 145, 159, 162, 171-172

Diversity Action Council (PSU), 45

Diversity Council (UCLA), 42

Diversity Discussion Workbook (OSU/UNC/UWLS), 43

Diversity Opportunity Tool (Vanderbilt), 43

Diversity Web (Maryland), 44

Doctoral/Research Universities: 127-136; German learning model, 128; government funding of, 129; private industry, support of, 129

E

educentricism, 148

evaluation. *See course evaluation or student evaluation*

Evenback, S., 178

experiential learning cycle (Kolb), 16

F

Faculty: needs of, 11-12; rank, 12, 13, 21, 25, 105; salary, 107, 115-116, 118, 124, 132-134; responsibilities of, 108

faculty demographics, 12, 13, 95, 105-107, 110, 114, 115, 123-125, 131-134

faculty development, 13, 28, 31, 47-48, 109, 136, 151, 174

faculty learning communities, xii, 1-3, 10, 14-33, 79

faculty mentoring, 12, 21, 25, 136, 158

faculty research, 57, 124, 132-134

feedback, student. *See student feedback*

fees, instructional, 99

financial aid, 103, 115, 123, 131

Fuller, R., 80

G

Gabelnick, F., 21

Gamson, Z., 82

Gardiner, John, 187

Gillepsie, M. L., 72

Gonzales, V., 157

graduate programs, 46

graduate student assistants, 124-125, 126, 130, 136, 151

group work, 147

Guided Self-Inquiry Inventory, 149-151

Gumport, P. J., 129

H

Harper, William Rainey, 97
Harris, Olita, 178
Harvard Negotiation Project, 162
Harvard University, 128
Heeding New Voices: Academic Careers for a New Generation (Rice), 10, 14
How People Learn (Bransford), 2

I

ice-breaker exercises, 159, 166-168
institutional mission, 52, 92, 99-101, 111, 121, 123, 128
institutions, history of, 96-99, 109-111, 120-121, 127-128
institutions, types of, 92, 120
instructional design, *see course design*
instructional objectives, 4, 7, 160, 183. *See also course objectives*
Intergroup Relations Center (ASU), 41
Internet, 5-6, 65

J

Johns Hopkins University, 128
Joliet Junior College (IL), 97

K

Kahn, S. 178
Karpiak, I. E. 12, 14
Keirsey Scale 152
kinesthetic learners, 166
Knight, Peter, 182
Knowledge Net (AACC), 101
Kubler-Ross, Elizabeth, 178

L

Ladson-Billings, Gloria, 145, 171
learner-centered learning, *see student-centered*
learning activities, 180
Learning Communities: Creating Connections (Gabelnick), 9
learning domains, 143, 186
learning environment, *see classroom climate*
learning objectives, *see instructional objectives*
learning outcomes, xi, 9, 10, 24, 50, 52, 54, 69, 145, 157, 178-180, 185, 188
learning styles, 51, 56, 65-66, 68-69, 84, 108, 149-152, 155, 187
Lilly Post-Doctoral Teaching Fellow Program, 13
Lopez, E., 157

M

Master's Level Institutions, 120-121, 123-127; normal schools, 120; teachers
    colleges, 120
Meiklejohn, Alexander, 8
Mentkowski, M., 180
mentoring. *See faculty mentoring or student mentoring*
Morrill Acts of 1862 & 1890, 121
multiculturalism, *see diversity*
multiple intelligences, 187. *See also learning styles*
Myer-Briggs Type Indicator (MBTI), 152-153, 173

N

National Science Foundation, 95
Newman, F., 54
Nicomachean Ethics (Aristotle), 85
Nilson, Linda, 148

O

Ohio Board of Regents, 16
Ohio State University, 43

P

Palmer, Parker, 36, 61, 74, 83, 145, 148
Paloff, , R. M., 7
pedagogical approaches, *see teaching approaches*
peer learning, 56, 71
personality types, 153-154
phronesis, 85
poiesis, 85
portfolio, teaching, 63
portfolios, learning, 5
Portland State University (OR), 45
Pratt, K., 7
Praxis, 85
Preparing Future Faculty Initiative (AACU), xii
Professional and Organizational Development Network (POD), 3
proseminar, 8-9
Putnam, Robert, 3

Q

Quinlan, K.M., 16

R

reactive tinkerers, 70
reflective tinkerers, 70
Reinventing Undergraduate Education (Boyer Commission), 62
Richlin, Laurie, xiii
Rockefeller Foundation, 129

S

T

U

U.S. Department of Education, 95, 108, 136
U.S. Department of Education Fund for the Improvement of Post-Secondary
     Education, 16
University of Berlin, 127
University of California System, 130
University of California, Berkeley, 173
University of California, Los Angeles, 42
University of Chicago, 97
University of Maryland, College Park, 44
University of Michigan, 42
University of North Carolina, 43
University of Washington Law School, 43
University of Wisconsin State System, 43
University Professors at Mid-Life (Karpiak), 12

V

Vanderbilt University, 43
VARK Learning Styles Inventory, 152-153, 161, 173
von Humboldt, Wilhelm, 127

W

web site development, *see technology*
Wehlburg, Catherine, xiii
Wiggins, Grant, 179
Williamson, C.K. (Bud), 13
Wolff, Ralph, 178
World Wide Web (www) networks, *see technology*

Y

Yale University, 128